# Designing Inclusive Public Toilets

# Designing Inclusive Public Toilets

## Wee the People

Jo-Anne Bichard and Gail Ramster

BLOOMSBURY VISUAL ARTS
LONDON · NEW YORK · OXFORD · NEW DELHI · SYDNEY

BLOOMSBURY VISUAL ARTS
Bloomsbury Publishing Plc, 50 Bedford Square, London, WC1B 3DP, UK
Bloomsbury Publishing Inc, 1385 Broadway, New York, NY 10018, USA
Bloomsbury Publishing Ireland, 29 Earlsfort Terrace, Dublin 2, D02 AY28, Ireland

BLOOMSBURY, BLOOMSBURY VISUAL ARTS and the Diana logo are
trademarks of Bloomsbury Publishing Plc

First published in Great Britain 2025

Copyright © Jo-Anne Bichard and Gail Ramster, 2025

Jo-Anne Bichard and Gail Ramster have asserted their right under the Copyright,
Designs and Patents Act, 1988, to be identified as authors of this work.

For legal purposes the acknowledgements on pp. xix–xx constitute an
extension of this copyright page.

Cover design: Louise Dugdale
Cover image © PandaVector/iStock

All rights reserved. No part of this publication may be: i) reproduced or transmitted in any form, electronic or mechanical, including photocopying, recording or by means of any information storage or retrieval system without prior permission in writing from the publishers; or ii) used or reproduced in any way for the training, development or operation of artificial intelligence (AI) technologies, including generative AI technologies. The rights holders expressly reserve this publication from the text and data mining exception as per Article 4(3) of the Digital Single Market Directive (EU) 2019/790.

Bloomsbury Publishing Plc does not have any control over, or responsibility for, any third-party websites referred to or in this book. All internet addresses given in this book were correct at the time of going to press. The author and publisher regret any inconvenience caused if addresses have changed or sites have ceased to exist, but can accept no responsibility for any such changes.

A catalogue record for this book is available from the British Library.

A catalog record for this book is available from the Library of Congress.

ISBN:  HB:    978-1-3503-4604-8
       PB:    978-1-3503-4603-1
       ePDF:  978-1-3503-4606-2
       eBook: 978-1-3503-4605-5

Typeset by Integra Software Services Pvt. Ltd.
Printed and bound in India

For product safety related questions contact productsafety@bloomsbury.com.

To find out more about our authors and books visit www.bloomsbury.com
and sign up for our newsletters.

*Wee the People is dedicated to two wee people,
William and Emmeline*

# Contents

List of figures  x
Notes on the authors  xvi
Preface  xvii
Acknowledgements  xix

**1  Introduction**  1
It's just a public toilet, right?  1
About this book  2
The research  5

**2  Designing inclusive public toilets in the twentieth century**  15
Inclusive design research on public toilets  18
Popular perspectives of public toilets and their legacy  24
Other uses of the toilet  25
Public toilets today: How many are there?  32
The complexity of having a wee in public  35

**3  Inclusive design**  41
Architecture + Product + Service = Inclusive public toilets  42
Accessibility regulations and guidance  46
How to design inclusive public toilets  49

**4  Everybody goes**  57
The body's needs  57
The mind's needs  64
What if our needs are not met?  66

**5  The journey**  77
Where do we need toilets?  77
Finding toilets  87
Signs at the door  95

## 6  Crossing the threshold  107

The toilet's situation  107
Making an entrance  111
Is it open?  112
Turnstiles and stairs  114
Navigating the space  116
A sense of cleanliness  117
A sense of comfort  118
The toilet queue  119
Which cubicle?  121

## 7  Closing the door  133

Designing privacy  133
A comfortable size  139
Drips and slips  140
Doors and hinges  140
Locks  143
Toilets locked from the outside  150
Hooks and shelves  154

## 8  In the cubicle  163

The toilet  164
Wiping or washing  174
The flush  177
Sanitary and disposal bins  183
Grab rails  186
Alarms  188
Leaving the cubicle  190

## 9  Water and wellness  195

Washing hands  195
Drying hands  206
Sensing the space  213
Designing loo-topia  217

**10 Rethinking public toilet provision** 225

Who provides it? 225
Who pays for it? 230
Who cleans and maintains it? 239
Engaged: How to change things for the better 243

**11 Conclusion** 255

Glossary 259
Recommended reading 261
Bibliography 263
Index 279

# Figures

All figures are credited to the Public Toilets Research Unit Archive unless otherwise stated in their captions.

## Chapter 1

1.1   This way to the toilets  10

## Chapter 2

2.1   Victorian public toilets at Rothesay, Bute in Scotland  16
2.2   The UriLift  17
2.3   Penny-in-the-door locking system  18
2.4   Paddle gates to public toilet provision  18
2.5   'As far as I'm concerned it's neither public nor convenient'. Campaign poster for the Spastics Society c. 1979–1982, highlighting the inaccessibility of UK public toilet stock  23
2.6   Graffiti in a public toilet  29
2.7   A community toilet taken out of general use and now 'for customers only'  30
2.8   A sign reads 'Please use toilets provided' in an effort to tell people there are alternatives to public urination  31

## Chapter 4

4.1   Free menstrual products  62
4.2   Community notices in a café toilet aimed at locals, particularly families  65
4.3   Information poster in direct line of sight for anyone using the hand dryer  66

4.4    A publicly accessible standard toilet with a view near the South West Coast Path  69
4.5    Information poster reading 'Our public toilets remain closed', for residents and visitors to a seaside town  71

# Chapter 5

5.1    Publicly accessible toilets at a major train station  78
5.2    Well-signposted public toilets in a city park  79
5.3    Regional Thameslink train service overhead display  81
5.4    Sign informing passengers within a London Underground station that toilets are provided, in the ticket hall  82
5.5    Disabled parking bays outside a toilet block in a car park, Newborough Forest, Anglesey  84
5.6    Public toilets in Matlock, Derbyshire  84
5.7    Public toilets on the seafront promenade, Clacton-on-Sea, Essex  85
5.8    Public toilets within a town hall complex  86
5.9    The Toilet Map, centred on Glasgow  89
5.10   Destination sign at a car park listing the available facilities  91
5.11   Hastings local map of toilets  92
5.12   A temporary low-level directional sign  92
5.13   Fingerpost sign specifically for toilets  94
5.14   Map of community toilets  94
5.15   The Welsh national toilet logo  95
5.16   Women's toilet symbol, on the toilet roof at the London Stadium (formerly the Olympic Stadium)  96
5.17   Active symbol for wheelchair-user/accessible toilet  97
5.18   Grace's sign toilets at V&A Dundee  98
5.19   The Changing Places toilet sign  99
5.20   A toilet symbol for a standard facility  100
5.21   Ambulant toilet symbol depicted by showing grab rails  101
5.22   Clear opening hours at the entrance to a public toilet  102
5.23   Opening hours sign on the back of the toilet door  103
5.24   Sign listing alternative toilets at a department store  103

# Chapter 6

6.1 Hatagaya Public Toilet, Tokyo, Miles Pennington/UTokyo DLX Design Lab. Architectural Design: Kotaro Imai Laboratory and Kentaro Honma Laboratory from Institute of Industrial Science at The University of Tokyo  109
6.2 Public Toilets designed and gifted to the town of Kawakawa, New Zealand by Friendensreich Hundertwasser  110
6.3 Public toilet at a cycle park in Gävle, Sweden. Design and construction: Danfo  111
6.4 Glass panel in external door  112
6.5 Toilet entrance with privacy wall  113
6.6 Public toilets after dark, Kings Cross, London  114
6.7 Sainsbury's signage to show the way out of the toilets  117
6.8 A typical queue for the women's toilets, at a train station  119
6.9 Unisex wheelchair-accessible toilet with corner WC – plan view (Diagram 18 of Building Regulations: *Approved Document M* Vol. 2. 2015, 2020)  122
6.10 Changing Places facility  123
6.11 Ambulant single-sex toilet cubicle (not self-contained), plan view showing minimum dimensions (Diagram 5.1 of Building Regulations: *Approved Document T*, 2024)  124
6.12 Fully enclosed self-contained universal toilet, plan view showing minimum dimensions (Diagram 4.1 of Building Regulations: *Approved Document T*, 2024)  127

# Chapter 7

7.1 Fully enclosed cubicle  134
7.2 Partitioned cubicles  135
7.3 A partitioned cubicle with minimal gaps  135
7.4 Individual urinals with partitions  137
7.5 Trough urinal with partitions  138
7.6 An individual, lockable urinal on the left next to a gender-neutral public toilet  138
7.7 A row of cubicles with self-closing doors  141

7.8   Ambulant cubicle with outwards-opening door, indicated by a handle  143
7.9   A mechanical, inclusive lock where we can see the door cannot be opened  145
7.10  Colour-coded lighting showing from a distance if a toilet is available  145
7.11  Lock indicator with colour-coding and labels  146
7.12  Inclusive lock in accessible cubicle  147
7.13  Electronic lock on a train  150
7.14  Passcode lock in a restaurant  151
7.15  RADAR lock from the inside  153
7.16  Two hooks for coats and bags on the side wall  155
7.17  A child seat in a larger cubicle  156
7.18  A drop-down baby-changing table  157
7.19  An effective hook design  157
7.20  Shelf in standard cubicle, above the cistern  158
7.21  Bespoke baby-changing area with individual handwashing and surface space for belongings  159
7.22  Stoma-friendly standard cubicle  159
7.23  Warning about drug use in a café toilet  160
7.24  Hooks opposite urinals  161

# Chapter 8

8.1   Toilet sign with legs crossed  163
8.2   Stainless-steel toilet pan with small rimmed 'seat'  166
8.3   Resin composite toilet pan  166
8.4   Child-sized toilet next to standard toilet  169
8.5   Child-sized toilet seat on a standard toilet pan  169
8.6   Accessible toilet with a back rest, obstructed by the toilet lid  171
8.7   Combined air and water flush system that requires closing of toilet lid to work  172
8.8   A toilet lid that conceals the flush operation when open  173
8.9   Squat toilet in Japan  173
8.10  Large drum toilet paper dispenser in the accessible toilet  175
8.11  Single-sheet double toilet roll dispenser  176
8.12  A sensor flush in an accessible toilet  178
8.13  A sensor-flush sign  179

8.14  An accessible push-button flush  180
8.15  Paddle or spatula lever flush handle  181
8.16  Paddle flush installed on the correct side of the accessible toilet pan  182
8.17  Paddle flush installed on the wrong side of the accessible toilet pan  182
8.18  Sanitary bin blocking access to the flush  185
8.19  Sanitary bin factored into the layout of the cubicle at design stage  185
8.20  Grab rails in unisex accessible toilet with corner toilet  186
8.21  Grab rails in an ambulant toilet, in Sainsburys  187
8.22  Grab rail in ambulant cubicle with large sanitary bin  188
8.23  Alarm cord on the side closest to the toilet pan, between the grab rail and the basin  189
8.24  Euan's Guide card fitted to an alarm cord  190

# Chapter 9

9.1  Sign pointing to toilets and handwashing facilities during the Covid-19 pandemic. South Terminal, Gatwick Airport  196
9.2  Communal handwashing and drinking water outside gender-neutral toilets  198
9.3  Handwashing at a shopping centre  199
9.4  Lever-arm tap  201
9.5  Unintuitive sensor tap layout  202
9.6  Sensor tap instruction  203
9.7  A tap too short for the basin  204
9.8  Water and soap positioned at the same height  205
9.9  High-power dryers with splashback to protect paintwork  208
9.10  High-power dryer with drip tray  208
9.11  Sign to alert people to a concealed sensor-operated dryer  210
9.12  Child (three) about to be blown in the face by a hand dryer  211
9.13  Hand dryers at two heights, for different height people  212
9.14  Indoor greenhouse at London Victoria station  214
9.15  Natural light through high-level windows above the cubicles  215
9.16  Colour choices within a set of toilets  215
9.17  Decorative wallpaper in the cubicle  216
9.18  Graphical floor pattern, creating the optical illusion of changes in level  217

9.19  Drinking water tap at a publicly accessible toilet  218
9.20  Vanity unit with shelving and mirrors at a family resort  219
9.21  Seating area for bottle feeding at a department store  220
9.22  Wudu facility for ritual washing before prayer  221

# Chapter 10

10.1  Public toilet in a South Staffordshire village  226
10.2  Infant feeding area at a shopping centre  228
10.3  2theLoo publicly accessible toilet in a retail unit at Covent Garden, London  232
10.4  Payment via paddle gate that accepts coins and card payment  233
10.5  Donation box for Heart of Hathersage community-designed and built toilets  236
10.6  Standard toilets at Victoria Station, London  237
10.7  'How would you rate this restroom today?' survey. Legoland, Windsor  242
10.8  Early graphic for the Engaged model, showing a retail unit as both public toilet and bookshop  244
10.9  Award-winning public toilet with flower shop. Westbourne Grove, London  245
10.10 WCityStop.info, providing public toilets and council information from a repurposed retail unit. Wolverhampton  245
10.11 Concept design for an extension to a public toilet unit, as a coffee shop  248
10.12 Two shipping containers, where one is a toy library and the other is a public toilet, with public play space in between  248
10.13 Concept design for a new public amenity: part-public toilet, part welfare space for delivery drivers  250
10.14 Concept design for public toilet and co-working space, with public seating and planting  250

# Chapter 11

11.1  'This way to your new public toilets' promotional and directional sign, for Lloyd Street, Manchester  258

# Authors

**Jo-Anne Bichard** is Professor of Accessible Design at The Helen Hamlyn Centre for Design, Royal College of Art, UK. She is a design anthropologist whose award-winning research involves ethnographic methods. Her research themes focus on wellbeing and the built environment, of which public toilets are key for increased mobility. She has also explored themes of self harm in public space and new inclusive technologies towards justice in conflict-related sexual violence. Her partnership and collaborations with Gail Ramster include co-leadership of the Public Toilets Research Unit and co-director of Public Convenience Ltd.

**Gail Ramster** is a senior research associate in inclusive design at The Helen Hamlyn Centre for Design, Royal College of Art, UK. In her fifteen years as a researcher, she has focused on people-centred and co-design approaches with citizens and communities. As well as co-leading the Public Toilets Research Unit, she has explored service, information and urban design challenges, from people's hopes and fears for autonomous vehicles to developing digital tools for community engagement. She is a director of Public Convenience Ltd which runs the website The Toilet Map.

# Preface

*Designing Inclusive Public Toilets: Wee the People* is the work of Professor Jo-Anne Bichard and Gail Ramster. Part inclusive design guide, part manifesto, it is based on our research into inclusive and accessible public toilets, undertaken independently and together over the last twenty years. This has been enhanced by our genuine interest in public toilets. We talk about toilets constantly, and inevitably have our own anecdotes, which we recognize as only reflecting our limited experiences within the social circles we inhabit and how others perceive us. With this in mind, here is a little about who we are, how we live and how we came to be interested in public toilet design.

**Jo-Anne** is a white, autistic woman who grew up working class. She was born in Croydon and grew up in a village on the last stop of a London red bus route. An only child, and with both her parents working, childcare was shared with her maternal one-armed grandfather and her wheelchair-using grandmother. Her father was deaf, so Jo-Anne came to experience disability as a normal aspect of daily life. Diagnosed as epileptic at age eleven and leaving school at sixteen with barely any qualifications, Jo-Anne first trained as an auctioneer but then moved to London to follow her passion for vinyl records. She subsequently worked in record retail in London, San Francisco and Chicago.

In her thirties, Jo-Anne returned to the UK and to education. She completed an evening access course at Morley College, then a degree in Social Anthropology at Goldsmiths College and a Masters in Science Communication at Imperial College. Her MSc was undertaken whilst also working as a research assistant on a project looking at the impact of brain imaging technologies for medics and patients. Jo-Anne's undergraduate dissertation was an ethnographic study of women's use of space in a Turkish bath. This, and her experience working with vulnerable people, led to her first toilets project at University College London, where she also began her PhD in architectural studies on access to public toilets. Jo-Anne joined the Royal College of Art Helen Hamlyn Research Centre in 2006 and met Gail a few years later. Together they have continued to explore the good, the bad and the ugly in the design of public loos. Jo-Anne does not drive, so relies on public transport and public loos, more so post-menopause. She is an avid collector of whatever she is newly obsessed with.

**Gail** is a white, middle-class, non-disabled cis-woman. She grew up in rural England, in a South Staffordshire village outside Wolverhampton. She was influenced by her grandmother and mother who both had a keen eye for poor design in everyday objects, and how things could be made easier to use. She became more aware of designing for different ages and abilities when all her grandparents developed dementia. Gail moved to London for university where she has lived ever since, albeit with a few adventures in her early twenties studying and working in France, Spain and the USA. She studied mechanical engineering at Imperial College with a year at l'Ecole Centrale de Lyon, France, and, later, an MA at the Royal College of Art in Industrial Design Engineering. Here she developed her fascination with improving the design of the mundane and 'everyday' that centred on public toilets. Before returning to the RCA as a researcher, Gail worked in wayfinding design at signage design company Endpoint, designing the system for Aston University's main building, rumoured to be the biggest brick building in Europe, where she made great efforts to make sure her signs correctly directed people to the nearest loo.

Outside her research, her experiences of public toilets were mainly as a young woman with an enthusiasm for shopping, and an avid user of public transport, encompassing local buses, the London Underground and cross-country trains. In the last decade, her experience has expanded to that of a mother-of-two, helping her to understand the needs of babies, children and the adults who look after them. She has always loved walking in London and has now begun cycling too. Public toilets are the infrastructure that underpin her lifestyle.

# Acknowledgements

Our thanks go to Bloomsbury especially Louise Baird-Smith, Joseph Skingsley and Olivia Davies.

Thanks also to our anonymous reviewers for their constructive comments.

We are extremely grateful for the support and encouragement we have received from the Royal College of Art, especially Dr Emma Wakelin, our Pro-Vice Chancellor of Research; and at The Helen Hamlyn Centre for Design, in particular Dr Melanie Flory and Dr Katie Gaudion. We would also like to thank all our colleagues at UCL and the RCA, past and present, who have endured our never-ending conversations about toilets.

We are indebted to the RCA researchers who worked with us on many of the projects featured in this book: Catherine Greene, Elizabeth Raby, Imran Nazerali, Dr Rosanna Traina, Indira Knight and Madelaine Dowd.

Special thanks go to our collaborators on The Toilet Map, Neontribe, for making our 'can the map show this?' desires a reality for all, namely Harry Harold, Oliver Barnwell, Rupert Reddington and all the volunteer developers who keep the project going, committing so much time, energy and enthusiasm to help people to find toilets.

This book hopes to improve some aspects of public toilets. Many others work alongside us in other ways. Raymond Martin of the British Toilet Association for dedication to keeping public toilets relevant. John Griggs for ensuring the importance of toilet design in the British Standards. Gillian Kemp for her campaigns for better public toilets and toilets for truck drivers. Eleanor van den Heuvel for TACTful leadership and Vin Goodwin Access Auditor extraordinaire. Rupert Williams for his insightful and award-winning film *Bathroom Privileges* and our collaborators in the Toilet Manifesto for London Group: Margit Physant, John McGeachy and John Miles.

Internationally, we'd like to thank Dr Marni Sommer for her work on New York toilets; Annika Lundkvist, Marta Trakul and Wicktoria Mockallo for their work on Warszawa toilets; Nat Hosono, Atsushi Kato and the Japanese Toilet Association; and Jack Sim of the World Toilet Association.

Thanks are also due to Luke Turner, Professor Barbara Penner, Emerita Professor Clara Greed, Susan Cunningham, Michelle Barkley and Emerita Professor Julienne Hanson.

Our friends, with special thanks to Andrew Knight and Dr Jamie Gilham for proofreading and sharing their insightful comments and Paddy Howe who, on hearing of the book's outline, commented *'so it's "wee the people"'*.

Our families – our parents, the wee Ramsters, William and Emmeline and our husbands Ben and Steven for their support, endurance and patience *('how many urinals and cubicles were in the men's?')*. You know those questions won't stop with this book.

Lastly, this work would not exist without the hundreds of people who shared their experiences with us, our participants in toilet research ... thank you.

# 1  Introduction

## It's just a public toilet, right?

Well, yes and no.

Public toilets might seem uninteresting but are indispensable. They are a civilizing element of our built environment, but they are also taboo. We are biological beings who excrete but cultured beings who have collectively decided that only in this specific environment will we wee and poo (and vomit and manage menstruation and take a moment to withdraw from public life and get changed and …).

Public toilets are one of the most mundane aspects of our landscapes, in our cities, towns and countryside – it's 'just' a public toilet. Yet public toilets are essential for our movement around and between these cities, towns and countryside. If it's 'just' a public toilet, what's the big deal?

In the UK, we had a glimpse into life without public toilets during the Covid-19 lockdowns of 2020–2021,[1] when everything closed except essential businesses. Some of those businesses such as supermarkets we had come to rely on for toilet provision as well. During lockdown we could still buy our essentials (remember the shortage of toilet paper?) but if we needed the loo during this rare excursion from our homes, it was tough luck. Yet many people during their daily exercise or shopping trip have to plan around their continence. Yes, they can 'go' before they leave home but for some on medication or who have a medical condition, they may need to use the toilet again before they start the journey home, and there was nowhere for them to do so. By the summer of 2020, when things had relaxed a bit and the sun was shining, people were able to socially distance outside. But hang on, what about the loos? Local authorities had been hesitant up to this point to open toilets. Businesses, like the coffee shop round the corner that you might sometimes pop into, could sell you a takeaway cappuccino – but no, you couldn't use the loo.

What resulted is that we sort of lost our social toilet training. People weed in bottles and pooed in flowerbeds. What were they supposed to do? We were outside. We were spending quality socially distanced time with family and friends who we had not seen in months. We were not going home just because there were no loos. Find a bush instead! We discuss more on the fall-out of the pandemic in Chapter 4, but what it did is give us a glimpse of life without this civic amenity.

The public toilet is a place where nature meets culture. With this meeting of body with a design artefact comes a number of cultural considerations. Toilets come with politics, rights of access, social rules and etiquette, hygiene concerns and a bad reputation. These issues push design beyond merely meeting the functional needs of the body. It is more than just a public toilet, it is 'a highly contested site. It shelters a very intimate activity that takes place in public space in proximity to complete strangers'.[2]

## About this book

***Designing Inclusive Public Toilets: Wee the People*** has been written as a design guide based on our research into toilets in the United Kingdom. There is a rumour, perhaps an urban myth, that when someone joins an architectural practice, the first job they are given is to design toilets. It has come to be seen as a joke, a place where everyone starts – at the bottom. We suggest that this design task actually represents the space that most people will visit – you are guaranteed that more people will see the toilets you have designed then the top floor boardroom – and those people will come away with either a pleasant or unpleasant experience. We urge you to make it pleasant, make it memorable even. People do remember good toilets, and they tell their friends and family; some even blog about them. They also remember the bad ones, equally sharing the experience. This book is for these architects and designers who might be commissioned or assigned to design a 'temple of convenience'.[3] You never know, it might win 'Loo of the Year'![4]

***Designing Inclusive Public Toilets: Wee the People*** is also for those charged with commissioning the design, from the local authority, the supermarket or department store manager to the owner of a small business and the manager of a community, event or faith space. If you decide to upgrade your toilet provision, what aspects have you considered? Poor toilet design is not only bad for society, it is bad for business. Someone might love to come back to your restaurant, community group or town-by-the-sea, but cannot if the toilets are akin to 'an assault course'.[5] We hope this book will give you an insight into what to ask of your designers and architects so that you can be sure your toilets are as inclusive as possible to meet the needs of your customers, visitors and wider community.

***Designing Inclusive Public Toilets: Wee the People*** is also a manifesto for members of the public. If your local public toilet is threatened with closure, what can you do about it? Local newspapers love stories about public toilets. They are also one of the key 'doorstep' issues for local politicians and councillors, alongside problems like bins and dog mess. Many older people cannot leave their homes as often as they like, or sometimes at all, due to a lack of public toilets and similar experiences are recounted by many disabled people and their families. First-hand accounts can really help to explain how critical toilets are to the communities that surround them, and how they can be improved rather than taken away.

***Designing Inclusive Public Toilets: Wee the People*** is for policymakers and politicians both at a local and national level. Often hampered by budget cuts, we hope this work will contribute to the evidence you need to make decisions in favour of keeping toilets open and building new ones, to help make your constituency, town centres, local attractions and public buildings more inclusive for all.

***Designing Inclusive Public Toilets: Wee the People*** draws from our inclusive design research in which each project developed its own methods to involve people in the process. Once we leave our homes and the safety and sanctity of our own domestic bathrooms we are in the hands of the designers, architects and planners for our bodily needs. This book gives a foundation for architects and designers on the issues, experiences and expectations of participants we have worked with. How you as designers, architects, planners and built environment decision makers involve people in your own inclusive design process is up to you, but we know you will find it rewarding and informative.

***Designing Inclusive Public Toilets: Wee the People*** is written in everyday language. Where possible we have avoided 'defecation' and 'urination' for 'wee' and 'poo', and we use toilet interchangeably with loo. We use puns – it is about public toilets after all, and most people find the subject raises a smile if not outright funny – and this is how the public tends to communicate toilets when we talk about them at work and with family and friends. We do not languish on the issues of why we as UK citizens find humour in toilets as a legacy of our Victorian forbearers' avoidance of the 'unmentionable'. Instead, we use this humour to break down the embarrassment many people feel talking about public toilets to highlight just how important they are.

Here is an example of a typical conversation we will have on a weekly basis:

Q: So, what do you do?
A: I'm a design researcher, I specialize in inclusive design.
Q: Oh, what's that?
A: Well, it's where we involve people in research to hopefully design things that are more accessible for everyone.
Q: Like what?
A: Well … my specialist subject is public toilets.
Q: [Nervous laughter] [Pause] I remember a toilet I once used …

Once we get past the awkwardness of the subject, we find *everyone* has a toilet story. And of course, should we win awards for our work, we are always 'flushed with pride'.

**Designing Inclusive Public Toilets: Wee the People** is a story of two halves. In the first half of the book (Chapters 2–4), we set the scene. In Chapter 2, we will present the modern legacy of our public toilet network, focusing on two design researchers who set the bar for designing inclusive public toilets. We will also consider other uses of public toilets that often result in an approach to design that created more barriers to access.

In Chapter 3, we give an overview of inclusive design and how for the public toilet this spans different design disciplines, which cover the external environment, the architectural interior, the products that furnish that interior and the service that ensures it all runs smoothly – each part has an important role to play and the failure of one can result in a failure of the provision and a bad experience for the user.

Chapter 4 considers who needs the public toilet. Everyone, right? But a large percentage of the population needs it more than others and much of the current stock is not meeting their needs. What happens if there are no toilets?

We then begin our second half where we will take you on a journey: in Chapter 5 we leave the house and our familiar toilet to make our way to work, visit friends and relatives, shop, have a day out. Where do we expect to find toilets? Maybe we are disabled, maybe we are on medication that increases the need to wee, maybe we are with young children or are older ourselves. Most likely we have more than one need. Before we leave the house, we want to know our needs will be met. How do we find information about public toilet provision, both at home and out in the world? Here we discuss online information, wayfinding and destination signs, thinking about what people need to know, when we need to know it and how best to communicate this in words and symbols.

Once found, the journey continues inside the loo. In Chapter 6 we discuss potential design barriers when making the journey from outside the toilet to the cubicle itself, as well as the types of cubicles: there are many to choose from, but which design will best meet our needs (and will it be open, clean and free from a queue)?

In Chapter 7 we take a look at privacy through the walls, doors and locks that create the notion of a private space within a setting that is anything but. By Chapter 8, we are finally ready to use the toilet: what are the design decisions that may affect our ability to and experience of using the loo? In Chapter 9 we are done and go to wash our hands. The design of this ritual is both an important element of public hygiene and a restorative process for our body and minds. Can the public toilet go further than the removal of germs, and be a place to refresh our bodies and minds when away from the public stage? Can we design loo-topia?

Having covered the details of the public's needs and how they influence the inclusive design of public toilets, in Chapter 10 we think about the service providers and the decision makers, and the challenges they face regarding provision. We suggest some alternative ways in which public toilets can be designed into our natural and urban environment. Our conclusion suggests new directions in which designers, decision makers, politicians and communities can take things, to go beyond the issues raised in this book.

# The research

**Designing Inclusive Public Toilets: Wee the People** is based on the last two decades of our individual and joint research. Initially we worked independently: Jo-Anne as a design anthropologist researcher on the VivaCity project at the Bartlett, University College London; Gail as a student on the Royal College of Art's Industrial Design Engineering MA, where as well as writing her thesis on the design of women's public toilets, she won a City of Westminster innovation competition with Sat-Lav, an SMS-based system to find your nearest loo.[6] Since 2009 we have worked at the Helen Hamlyn Centre for Design (formally the Helen Hamlyn Research Centre), the longest-running research centre at the Royal College of Art, on inclusive design research.

**Designing Inclusive Public Toilets: Wee the People** draws from the following six public toilet research projects that we have worked on.

## VivaCity 2020: Urban Sustainability for the Twenty-four Hour City

The Inclusive Design of Public Toilets in City Centres (2003–2006) was one project within a research consortium called VivaCity 2020 (2003–2008).[7] Funded by the Engineering and Physical Sciences Research Council (EPSRC), the focus of this £2.75 million research consortium was to explore the essentials of Designing Sustainable Cities.[8] The work involved five universities[9] and considered a number of key issues from urban design decision-making: crime, housing, mixed use, the senses and the city, and of course public toilet provision, especially for disabled people. The public toilets project (or 'away from home' toilets as we called them then) was led by Professor Julienne Hanson (co-creator of Space Syntax[10] for spatial analysis), Professor Clara Greed (author of *Inclusive Urban Design: Public Toilets* (2003))[11] and Jo-Anne as Research Fellow. The research focused on the incoming Part 3 of the Disability Discrimination Act – Access to goods and services – which had a deadline for implementation of 2004. It is one of the UK's largest empirical research projects on the subject of toilets: 550 people of all ages and abilities shared their experiences of using public toilets via surveys, interviews or focus groups.[12] The research identified fifty design features of the **accessible toilet** and created an audit tool to assess how the implementation of the design was going in the lead up to the 2004 deadline of the Disability Discrimination Act. They found that of 101 accessible toilets audited not one had met the guidance laid out in the British Standards BS8300[13] or the Building Regulations Part M.[14] This research was also the first to reveal issues with toilet design for neurodiverse populations especially the use of blue lights and the noise of hand dryers.[15] It developed the newsletter *The Toilet Paper*[16] for participants to be updated on the research progress. Jo-Anne undertook a secondary analysis of the qualitative data captured in the project by re-examining 166 interviews and focus group transcripts for her PhD, *Extending architectural affordance: the case of the publicly accessible toilet*.[17]

## TACT3: Tackling ageing continence through theory, tools and technology

Gail and Jo-Anne joined forces at the Royal College of Art to work in the TACT3 (2008–2012) research consortium which included six universities, led by Brunel University.[18] Funded by a unique collaboration of all UK research funding councils under The New Dynamics of Ageing programme, TACT3 was awarded £1,278,470 to explore the issue of continence management and concerns for older people. Jo-Anne led the work package 'Challenging Environmental Barriers to Continence', which explored how our ageing population managed their daily continence concerns outside the home. Compared to the VivaCity 2020 study, this focused more on the **standard toilet cubicle** within **publicly accessible toilets**. Following feedback from the older persons advisory group that this was a problem that impacted all ages, Gail and fellow research associate Catherine Greene conducted telephone interviews with 101 adults of all age brackets, including parents of newborns to those aged over ninety, to understand their experiences of needing, finding and using toilets when away from home. This work extended the inclusive design consultation beyond users to include interviews with twenty professionals with experience of providing toilets, from shopping centre architects to train station managers. Following analysis of the research data, Gail and Catherine developed concept designs around the key issues. One issue for both the public and providers was finding and sharing accurate information about where toilets were and what was available. In response to this we developed The Great British Public Toilet Map[19] (see Chapter 5).

## Robust Accessible Toilets (RATs)

In 2010 Gail consulted with Hertfordshire Constabulary and the British Toilet Association on their *Publicly Available Toilets: Problem Reduction Guide (2010)*.[20] Following this consultation, we developed Robust Accessible Toilets (RATs), a six-month project funded by the Economic and Social Research Council to explore how elements of Design Out Crime may not be compatible with inclusive and accessible design in public toilets. We also captured community responses to toilets that had been closed or were threatened with closure. RATs used a secondary analysis of data collected on the TACT3 project alongside its own research to produce its key output, *Publicly Accessible Toilets: An Inclusive Design Guide*.[21]

# GREAT BRITISH PUBLIC TOILET MAP

## The Great British Public Toilet Map

The Great British Public Toilet Map, rebranded in 2024 as The Toilet Map, was initially an output of TACT3, built as a website focused on a pilot area of London to campaign for councils to publish more open data about their public toilets.[22] In 2013, Gail secured funding from the Nominet Trust (now Social Tech Fund) to redesign The Great British Public Toilet Map as a national website. The project collected data through Freedom of Information requests and built a crowdsourcing interface for public contributions, shifting its focus from being a user and campaigner of open data to an open data creator and provider. Subsequent funding from Open Data Institute in 2016 helped the project to create a public toilet 'explorer' webpage[23] to support the analysis and improvements of toilet location data.

# TINKLE
## Toilets Innovation and New Knowledge Exchange

### Publicly Accessible Toilets after COVID-19 and TINKLE

During the pandemic, Jo-Anne and Gail secured funding from the Royal College of Art to undertake desk-based research on how to design inclusive public toilets for pandemic and post-pandemic environments, based on academic, media and government outputs. Research associate Imran Nazerali came onto the team to carry out this research and develop concept designs, published in *Publicly Accessible Toilets after COVID-19,* an update to our previous inclusive design guidance.[24] Jo-Anne and Gail also sat on the British Standards committee for *Guidance on safe working during the COVID-19 pandemic,*[25] contributing to guidance on workplace toilet provision. In 2020, Gail and Jo-Anne set up the Toilets Innovation and New Knowledge Exchange (TINKLE),[26] a web-based resource for designers, architects and researchers in public toilet design.

## Engaged: A toilet on every high street

Our most recent project, 'Engaged: A toilet on every high street'[27] (2021–2023), was funded through the Mayor of London's Designing London's Recovery[28] programme and a second award from the Royal College of Art. Engaged investigated whether empty retail space could be reused as part-public toilet, part-business to meet Londoners' needs for inclusive high street toilets, as well as playing a role in high street regeneration and post-pandemic public health infrastructure. The RCA Engaged team included design researchers Madelaine Dowd, Indira Knight and Dr Rosanna Traina, and worked in partnership with PiM. studio Architects,[29] an architectural practice in East London.

We interviewed eight experts from urban design, government, retail and commerce from across the country. Together with a literature review of government policy and urban design guidance relating to toilets, this revealed the extent of the national need for public toilets on high streets, the barriers and opportunities for improvement, and expert responses to our Engaged proposal. We then focused on London by running a workshop with regeneration officers from thirteen London borough councils to better understand the feasibility and opportunity for Engaged at regional level. Finally, we ran hyperlocal activities in one borough, Hackney, which included a walking tour, pop-up activities at a market and an online co-design workshop to identify specific gaps in provision and how Engaged could fulfil these to benefit local people. Based on these insights, PiM. studio Architects developed a series of designs for both temporary and permanent public toilet structures. The research was supported by a qualitative survey run by the Greater London Authority's TalkLondon[30] platform about the access Londoners had to public toilets in their local high streets and town centres, which received 2,689 responses.

***Designing Inclusive Public Toilets: Wee the People*** shares in their own words some of the experiences from the hundreds of people who have been so kind to participate in these research projects. Those we have interviewed about their experiences of needing, finding and using public toilets are the driving force behind our desire for more inclusive toilet design.

We also share perspectives from professional stakeholders with whom we have spoken: civil servants, council officers, politicians and councillors, police and community support officers, transport providers, retailers and café operators, toilet manufacturers and providers, developers (of both land and software), cleaners and maintenance workers, and toilet attendants.

We have built working relationships with charities representing people whose needs are not always met, community groups running toilets, and local people and campaign groups fighting to keep, improve or open new facilities. The insights from these groups are also embedded in this book.

***Designing Inclusive Public Toilets: Wee the People*** seeks to give you the reader a glimpse into the complexity of taking a wee in public. If we add caring responsibilities, bladder and/or bowel urgency and disability into the mix, we hope you can see how a natural act can be fraught with considerations, worries and stress. It really does not have to be this way. An inclusive design approach can ensure that as many people as possible can access the toilet. We strongly encourage readers not to just take our word for it but to use this book as a starting point for your own inclusive design journey. How might you improve upon this?

**Figure 1.1** This way to the toilets.

# Notes

1. J. Bichard and G. Ramster, 'A mighty inconvenience: How Covid-19 tested a nation's continence', *Built Environment* 47(3) (2021): 402–16, https://doi.org/10.2148/benv.47.3.402.
2. J. Bichard and J. Hanson, 'Inclusive design of "away from home" toilets', in R. Cooper, G. Evans and C. Boyko (eds), *Designing Sustainable Cities* (Chichester: Wiley-Blackwell, 2009), 87.
3. L. Lambton, *Temples of Convenience & Chambers of Delight* (Stroud: Tempus Publishing Ltd, 2007).
4. Loo of the Year Awards. Available online: https://www.loo.co.uk/ (accessed 2 January 2024).
5. J. Bichard, *Extending architectural affordance: The case of the publicly accessible toilet*, PhD thesis, Bartlett School of Graduate Studies, University College London (2015): 363. Available online: https://discovery.ucl.ac.uk/id/eprint/1467131/ (accessed 2 January 2024).
6. Department of Communities and Local Government (2008) *Improving Public Access to Toilets: Guidance on Community Toilet Schemes and SatLav*. Available online: https://webarchive.nationalarchives.gov.uk/ukgwa/20120920031420mp_/http://www.communities.gov.uk/documents/localgovernment/pdf/1064520.pdf (accessed 2 January 2024).
7. VivaCity 2020. 'Urban sustainability for the twenty-four hour city'. Available online: http://www.vivacity2020.co.uk/ (accessed 27 January 2024).
8. R. Cooper, G. G. Evans and C. Boyko (eds), *Designing Sustainable Cities* (Chichester: Wiley-Blackwell, 2009).
9. Lancaster University, University of Salford, University College London, London Metropolitan University and University of Sheffield.
10. B. Hillier and J. Hanson, *The Social Logic of Space* (Cambridge: Cambridge University Press, 1989).
11. C. Greed, *Inclusive Urban Design: Public Toilets* (Oxford: Architectural Press/Elsevier, 2003).
12. Bichard and Hanson, 'Inclusive design of "away from home" toilets'.
13. British Standards Institute, *BS8300-2 Design of an accessible and inclusive built environment* (London: British Standards Institution, 2018).

14  Building Regulations, *Approved Document M: Access to and use of buildings. Vol. 2: Buildings other than dwellings* (2015) (amended 2020) [pdf]. Available online: https://assets.publishing.service.gov.uk/media/60b0ea89d3bf7f43560e324a/Approved_Document_M_vol_2.pdf (accessed 21 December 2023).

15  J. Hanson, J. Bichard and C. Greed, *The Accessible Toilet Design Resource* (London: University College London, 2007) [pdf]. Available online: https://discovery.ucl.ac.uk/id/eprint/4847/1/4847.pdf (accessed 2 January 2024).

16  VivaCity Publications, *The Toilet Paper Newsletters*. Available online: http://www.vivacity2020.co.uk/publications/index.html (accessed 2 January 2024).

17  Bichard, *Extending Architectural Affordance*.

18  Brunel University, University of Sheffield, University of Manchester, University of the West of England, Bristol Urological Institute and the Royal College of Art.

19  *The Toilet Map*. Available online: https://www.toiletmap.org.uk (accessed 2 January 2024).

20  British Toilet Association and Hertfordshire Constabulary (2014), *Publicly Available Toilets. Problem Reduction Guide* [pdf]. Available online: http://www.btaloos.co.uk/wp-content/uploads/2014/01/PubliclyAvailableToiletsProblemReductionGuide.pdf (accessed 2 January 2024).

21  G. Knight and J. Bichard, *Publicly Accessible Toilets: An Inclusive Design Guide* (London: Royal College of Art Helen Hamlyn Centre for Design, 2011) [pdf]. Available online: https://rca-media2.rca.ac.uk/documents/Publicly-accessible-toilets-2.pdf (accessed 28 May 2024).

22  J. Bichard and G. Knight, 'Improving public services through open data: Public toilets', *Proceedings of the Institution of Civil Engineers – Municipal Engineer*, 165 (3) (2012): 157–65, https://doi.org/10.1680/muen.12.00017.

23  *The Toilet Map: Toilet Explorer*. Available online: https://www.toiletmap.org.uk/explorer (accessed 2 January 2024).

24  I. Nazerali, G. Ramster and J. Bichard, *Publicly Accessible Toilets after COVID-19* (London: Royal College of Art Helen Hamlyn Centre for Design, 2021) [pdf]. Available online: https://rca-media2.rca.ac.uk/documents/PAT_COVID19.pdf (accessed 2 January 2024).

25  British Standards Institute (2020), *Guidance on safe working during the COVID-19 pandemic* [pdf]. Available online: https://www.bsigroup.com/en-AU/topics/novel-coronavirus-covid-19/covid-19-guidelines/ (accessed 2 January 2022).

26  Toilets Innovation and New Knowledge Exchange (TINKLE). Available online: https://tinkle.rca.ac.uk (accessed 2 January 2024).

27  G. Ramster, J. Bichard, M. Dowd, I. Knight and R. Traina. 'Engaged: A toilet on every high street'. Available online: https://www.rca.ac.uk/research-innovation/research-centres/helen-hamlyn-centre/engaged-a-toilet-on-every-high-street/ (accessed 2 January 2022).

28  Greater London Authority (2023), 'Designing London's recovery'. Available online: https://www.london.gov.uk/programmes-strategies/business-and-economy/support-your-business/challenge-ldn/past-challenges/designing-londons-recovery (accessed 2 January 2022).
29  PiM.studio Architects. Available online: https://www.pim.studio (accessed 15 October 2024).
30  Greater London Authority (2024), 'Talk London'. Available online: https://www.london.gov.uk/talk-london/ (accessed 2 January 2024).

# 2  Designing inclusive public toilets in the twentieth century

In this chapter there is a little background to share on the recent history of public toilet provision and the varied inclusive designs that have supported it. This will give a picture of some of the legacies of the UK's public toilets that we have dragged into the twenty-first century.

In her landmark work 'A world of unmentionable suffering: Women's public conveniences in Victorian London' on the design history of a Victorian public toilet in Camden in North London, Barbara Penner stated that '… a lavatory is not simply a technological response to a physical need but a cultural product shaped by complex and often competing discourses on the body, sexuality, morality and hygiene'.[1]

The legacies of such shaping still echo in our built environment today. In many UK towns and cities, the Victorian public convenience still exists. Some are now celebrated as prime examples of a time and place where attention to detail in the design of facilities took prominence. The Rothesay public toilet in Scotland (Figure 2.1) is currently the Isle of Bute's second most popular attraction on Trip Advisor due to its historical design, whilst Hull has two grade II listed Victorian public conveniences. However, in reference to Penner's quote it is noticeable that many of the Victorian provisions still in use have stunning architectural and design features only in the men's provision.

The UK's modern public toilet in our built environment begins with the 1848 Public Health Act. This introduced a range of processes to improve sanitation, drainage and sewage. The Great Exhibition of 1851 in London's Hyde Park showcased 'halting stations'. Designed by sanitary engineer George Jennings, the toilet facilities for men and women were initially met with scepticism but were used by over 800,000 visitors for the cost of a penny, giving Jennings a profit of nearly £2,500. The penny fee for use would become a cultural euphemism for using the toilet and not mentioning the act, to 'spend a penny'.

By 1855 Jennings had convinced the City of London of the benefits of public toilets and the first subterranean provision was opened. Sites for public toilets

**Figure 2.1** Victorian public toilets at Rothesay, Bute in Scotland. Credit: Allan Wright/Alamy Stock Photo.

were often placed underground replacing existing urinals and close to the existing sewer infrastructure. These early facilities took up minimal space at street level but also served to hide the 'unmentionable' from polite Victorian society. The placing of toilets out of sight and only accessible by flights of stairs set in motion design exclusions that continue to this day.

Many of these facilities were for men only and it would take another forty years to provide public loos for women. During this period urinals were also found around London and reflected a time when male engineers, architects and decision makers determined city design. The needs of women were not discussed or considered. This effectively lay the foundations of the Victorian city as an abled and gendered space. In a perceived 'innovation', this Victorian approach to toilet design and provision would repeat itself at the turn of the millennium with the introduction in many UK cities of temporary urinals distributed around 'hot spots' especially at weekends. Some cities would install a more permanent solution with the 'UriLift' (Figure 2.2), a urinal that remained underground during the day only to emerge at night to meet the needs of men.

The next watermark was the Public Health Act 1936, which gave local authorities the right to provide public toilets on or under the highway.[2] Local authorities were permitted to build public toilets if they saw fit, but there was no enforced requirement to do so. This discretionary provision exists to this day with

**Figure 2.2** The UriLift.

the UK now a 'postcode lottery' of public loos based on boundaries and local authority budgets.

The 1936 change also came with a gendered perspective as those local authorities who built toilets could charge fees for cubicles but not for urinals, resulting in men being able to wee for free whilst women had to pay. This remained the law until 2008 when the Public Health Act[3] would be amended under the Sex Discrimination Act,[4] removing the urinal exemption and resulting in everyone either having to pay or being given free access.

Collecting fees for toilet use was often achieved by the penny-in-door locking system (Figure 2.3) and later the introduction of turnstiles. However, in 1963 The Public Lavatories (Turnstiles) Act[5] banned the use of turnstiles, requiring them to be removed from public toilets due to safety concerns and that they were an access barrier for 'disabled people, people with luggage or pushchairs, pregnant women etc'.[6] This made many public toilets free to use. The Act did not apply in Northern Ireland, and only applies to council-managed toilets, meaning those that were privately managed, such as provision in train stations, could still feature turnstiles. Only recently have Network Rail removed turnstiles from their twenty managed stations, as part of a major redesign to a more people-centred toilet provision.[7]

**Figure 2.3** Penny-in-the-door locking system.

**Figure 2.4** Paddle gates to public toilet provision.

The 2012 London Local Authorities Act[8] established an exemption for London borough councils to the Public Lavatories (Turnstiles) Act. The justification was that councils, in particular the City of Westminster, did not wish to reintroduce turnstiles, but did want to use paddle gates (Figure 2.4), similar to those found at train station ticket barriers, to take payment. The House of Lords argued that these would be considered a form of a turnstile, so the 1963 Public Lavatories (Turnstiles) Act was superseded in London.[9]

## Inclusive design research on public toilets

The removal of turnstiles in the 1960s saw some functional changes to the design of the UK's public toilet stock with progress to making them more accessible. However, in the United States, research that began at the end of the 1950s would go on to become 'a classic of user-centred design research'.[10]

### 'The Bathroom' by Alexander Kira

The first comprehensive study on the use of and attitudes to the bathroom that directly involved users was undertaken at Cornell University's Centre for Housing and Environmental Studies in the United States and published in 1966. *The Bathroom* by Alexander Kira[11] presented a user-centred holistic account of the domestic toilet, shower and bath that considered social and cultural perspectives as well as psychological and physical experiences. Beginning with a survey of one thousand households, the work would also include key ergonomic studies of how people actually used the fittings and fixtures of the bathroom including during urination and defecation.

Whilst this ground-breaking research focused mainly on the needs of people in their domestic bathroom (and would also include ecological concerns on water saving), in the revised edition of *The Bathroom* in 1976, Kira makes astute observations towards the experiences and expectations in the use of public bathrooms including the needs of ageing and disabled people.

Acknowledging that the design responses to the body's needs have varied between cultures and historical periods, these needs still have to be met. This biological fact would frame the progression of public toilet provision as directly related to the history of urbanization, public health and its relation to sanitation. Kira describes a public toilet as one that 'is provided in the interest of public convenience, sanitation and health in a communal location by, or on behalf of a communal agency for use by anyone with need. Needs in this situation may arise from one or two circumstances. First being away from one's own facilities – being "caught short".[12] Second, not having facilities of one's own.'[13]

Direct connections were made between the twentieth-century's development of public toilets and the development of public transport. The resulting decline of public toilet provision in the United States was recognized as due to the car-driven culture of the suburbs and the decline in pedestrianization resulting not only in closures but fewer public toilets being built. A shift in preferences from public to private provision highlighted that the poor maintenance of 'municipal' (public) facilities increased the preference and use of business-based (private) provision.

Contemplating the wider social and psychological aspects of public toilets, Kira found the general negative attitudes extended to a wider aesthetic of acceptable and unacceptable design.

Considering the notion of 'publicness', several factors define a user's experience of the public toilet including:

- The degree of others from oneself
- The extent of usage
- The level of cleanliness and maintenance

The key psychological barrier was 'stranger danger', and that the stranger was microbe-based.[14] This also intensified the complexity of our own feelings towards body waste and the process of elimination and generates the temporary sense of ownership or 'my' space when using the public toilet cubicle. But this sense of ownership can be disrupted on seeing the previous user's waste. These 'territory privacy violations' are realized 'because of general social taboos against discussing, watching or acknowledging elimination functions' which lead users to 'mutually screen and ignore each other'.[15]

Kira felt the provision of toilets also projected an 'image of the host': the provider of the facilities. Here, users as members of the public are guests and their experience of provision can leave them with a lasting impression that is extended to the provider. This includes perceptions of hygiene and maintenance of the business or area. Public toilets with large footfalls that are not adequately cleaned and maintained will be shunned. In contrast, facilities with exceptional provision are talked about, recommended and even visited just to see and/or use the toilets. In 1976, Kira recalled the Four Seasons restaurant in Manhattan as an example of highly valued toilet provision. A similar 'word of mouth' recommendation continues today with numerous blog posts[16] recommending unusual toilet provision, albeit predominately customer-only.[17] Yet the attention to detail in the interior design highlights that some businesses recognize their toilet provision can also be a factor in generating business. Not all businesses place emphasis or value on their toilet provision as 'restrooms are seen as non-productive in terms of space utilisation and investment'.[18] Research has yet to establish just how much poor toilet provision may deter customers or visitors.

Considering the planning and design for public facilities, there is not one kind of public toilet. Kira identified forms of provision based on degrees of 'publicness', attributing facilities as being:

- highly public
- virtually private
- sequential
- simultaneous use
- carefully controlled access
- providing highly visible management

Yet, despite having different degrees of publicness all toilet provision shares common problems of location, identification, maintenance, supervision and vandalism.[19] *Designing Inclusive Public Toilets: Wee the People* extends this list of common problems to note that access to the facility and the design of the provision itself should also be considered.

Kira also notes that key contextual issues framed public toilet design such as:

- users will often be in a hurry (due to being en route somewhere)
- they will have more items of clothing (especially in winter with coats, hats and gloves)
- they will most likely be carrying bags and/or luggage

After bearing in mind the needs of non-disabled (although not explicitly stated) men and women, in 1976 Kira's research extended to the design requirements of disabled and older people. He also added an innovative perspective by considering social and psychological aspects of disability, although the work would not include the same ergonomic considerations. However, the work did acknowledge that the community which he referred to is vast and highly diverse in composition, culture, degree of impairment, age and ability. It was not assumed all disabled and older people would have difficulties with toilet use but recognized that a high proportion were likely to.

Within the physical design considerations, and encompassing the wide variation in the degree of impairment involved, attention should be paid to:

- visual and auditory impairment
- sensory and tactile loss
- loss of equilibrium and balance
- impairment of judgement and reflexive responses to stimuli
- circulatory impairment
- loss of manipulative ability
- loss of locomotion ability

Although physical bodily changes may not be associated with any particular disease or condition, there must be accommodation within the built environment to support all ageing populations to ensure that they can 'continue to function with a degree of normality and independence'[20] and with assistance if required.

Recognizing that toileting and personal hygiene can be strenuous, and the facilities hazardous even for young non-disabled people, personal body needs and functions remain the same. Where going to the loo was previously easy, bodily changes can make this both physically and personally difficult.[21]

Psychologically, Kira recognized that social attitudes towards the ability to toilet and manage continence can result in the loss of self-esteem. Linking attitudes to toilet-training, the child is praised for successful toileting, whilst the adult is resented for loss of continence due to its continued degeneration of a condition, the body and the self. A loss of personal privacy contravenes deeply embedded values, generating discomfort and embarrassment by crossing the line of privacy *for* others and privacy *from* others.[22] These psychological factors have to be considered in toilet design in conjunction with the physical barriers that prevent everyone toileting with dignity, comfort and ease.

Kira concludes *The Bathroom* with a call for a more inclusive design approach, by stating that:

> the ultimate irony is that most of the 'special' requirements necessary for aged and disabled persons are really not that special. Basically, they represent careful attention to human needs and in many cases would be equally suitable and useful for the normal population. What is perhaps really 'special' is that in the case of aged and disabled persons, we cannot permit ourselves the casual adaptation to an unresponsive environment that we normally tolerate.[23]

## Designing for the Disabled *by Selwyn Goldsmith*

Whilst Kira's research was being undertaken in the United States, in the UK architect Selwyn Goldsmith was conducting his own research on access to the built environment for disabled people including the issues with public toilet provision.

Goldsmith, a disabled architect, had a ground-breaking influence on architectural design in the UK. His research, publications and design recommendations would set the template for inclusive and accessible design and brought increased mobility and independence to millions of disabled people, especially through the provision of more accessible toilets.

In 1961, a survey of London's toilets revealed that 60 per cent of provision still occupied the Victorian footprint of underground facilities. These were difficult if not impossible for many people to use due to limited mobility, wheelchair use (Figure 2.5) or care of young children still using prams. These restrictions were noted by Goldsmith and would become the foundation for his book *Designing for the Disabled* (1963)[24] first published in 1963 (revised in 1967 and 1976). The 1976 (third) edition would be supplemented by interviews with 284 wheelchair users in which access to public toilets especially in public buildings emerged as the major concern, and, as Penner (2013) notes, produced 'the nearest equivalent to Kira's work on bathroom use for people with disabilities'.[25]

Reflecting on the US floorplate of accessible cubicles included in the gendered provision, Goldsmith recognized that many carers of disabled users, especially wheelchair users, would be partners of a different gender, for which it is taboo to

**Figure 2.5** 'As far as I'm concerned it's neither public nor convenient'. Campaign poster for the Spastics Society c. 1979–1982, highlighting the inaccessibility of UK public toilet stock. Credit: Scope.

enter the user's gender-specific toilet. To counter this, Goldsmith recommended a separate unisex cubicle which would go on to be recommended in the British Standards BS5810 Unisex Accessible Toilet (now updated in BS8300 Design of an accessible and inclusive built environment).[26] The separate accessible cubicle has gone on to be an icon of access and is embedded in the legal requirements of the Building Regulations Part M.[27]

On reflection, Goldsmith admitted that 'the idea that [the unisex accessible toilet] could be right for every disabled person was always absurd',[28] and it can be argued that the design still has ramifications today. The legacy of such separate design and provision can be considered, for some inclusive design theorists, to continue a special needs approach as opposed to being truly inclusive. It has also resulted in standard toilet provision remaining inaccessible and causing pressures on the single accessible toilet. Users who benefit from the accessibility of the unisex accessible toilet include those who require the fixtures and fittings of the cubicle but whose disabilities are invisible and those accompanying children should they need to keep pushchairs or their children in the cubicle with them.[29]

Goldsmith's work has played a major role in creating wider access for disabled people in the built environment, especially through increased awareness of accessible toilet facilities. Whilst a large percentage of provision offers unisex accessible cubicles in addition to standard facilities, many small businesses and chains include one or two unisex/gender neutral accessible cubicles as their standard toilet provision, reflecting a more inclusive environment shared by all.

## Popular perspectives of public toilets and their legacy

In the September 2023 issue of the *New Socialist*,[30] Hannah Boast began her essay 'Public Toilets and Public Luxury' with a quote from V. I. Lenin: 'When we are victorious on a world scale, I think we shall use gold for the purpose of building public lavatories in the streets of some of the largest cities of the world.'[31] Boast summed up this quote by saying 'If this remark showed [Lenin's] disdain for gold, it inadvertently described the importance of public toilets to any socialist project.'

Generally, public toilets are not seen as 'nice' places. In the VivaCity study a survey[32] was undertaken asking 211 participants (87 men, 124 women): 'Do you use public toilets?' In answer, 63 per cent of men and 69 per cent of women responded 'no'. When asked if they preferred 'private provision' such as toilets in cafés, department stores, etc., 82 per cent answered 'yes' (79 per cent men, 83 per cent women). Yet when asked if there should be more 'public toilets', over 80 per cent also responded 'yes' (90 per cent men, 80 per cent women).[33] This illustrates the kind of love/hate relationship we currently have with our public toilets. We would prefer not to use them due to their bad reputation, but also value them as community assets.

The Royal Society for Public Health's (RSPH) 2019 report *Taking the P\*\*\**[34] in a survey of 2089 adults found that the perceived dirtiness of public loos was the main reason people avoided using them, followed by bad smells (see Chapter 9) and the lack of toilet paper (see Chapter 8). Women reported the highest concerns for these categories. Concerns on safety were cited by less than a fifth of respondents.

Once upon a time, public toilets were the example of civic infrastructure and even 'the barometer of civilisation'.[35] When did these facilities have their reputation flipped? There is no clear answer to this because of several mitigating factors that contribute to our perspective of public toilets as spaces where dirty things happen. Stead (2009) suggests that our perceptions are shaped by our language or more precisely the euphemisms we use for going to the loo.

> Euphemisms serve to avoid direct reference to, and therefore potentially embarrassing or shameful confrontation with, certain culturally determined taboo objects and activities. Such taboos vary but can include 'sex; death; excretion; bodily functions; religious matters and politics'.[36]

This list of taboos can all be found in the public toilet,[37] and it may be that the need to avoid direct reference to something that is akin to breathing (we all do it and we all have to do it) reflects a deeper relationship we have with our bodies. Poo after all is a 'biomarker for human health' that will include cells, mucus, fats, proteins and the stuff we couldn't digest.[38] Poo, through faecal transplants, is now being used to combat C. Diff (*Clostridium difficile*),[39] a particularly serious infection that can occur after taking antibiotics. Despite this lifesaving matter, the Health Services Advisory Committee[40] classifies human waste as 'offensive'. Perhaps this top-down perspective seeps into our wider perceptions of public toilets as offensive, dirty and disgusting places and ultimately unloved and uncared for. Would these perceptions be shifted if we saw them as key aspects of our public health infrastructure? What if they became strategic points for faecal transplant testing? It sounds far-fetched but as we begin to develop more knowledge of our gut's biome, could a strategic programme include building more public toilets as public health one-stop shops?

## Other uses of the toilet

Colin Cockfield, a former police architectural liaison officer, once told us that the three issues facing toilets are 'sex, drugs and rocking the bowl'. In many ways it seems strange that such activities happen in a place with an association of being dirty. Yet these activities often result in the closure of public toilets.

Kira (1976) noted that the reputation of public toilets is tainted by its 'off bounds' character, making provision 'more attractive for a variety of increasingly anti-social and criminal activities'.[41] He asserted that this reputation has in many ways been 'institutionalised' resulting in public loos being considered a 'safe place' for non-toileting activities such as sexual encounters, illegal substance use and vandalism. Kira considered the 'helplessness and immobility' of a person using the loo, especially those who will be partially undressed, presented opportunities for 'those who take advantage of users at this moment'.[42] Such helplessness and immobility will be intensified if a user is also disabled or older.

## Sex ...

Having sex in public toilets has been one of the facility's historical legacies and in many ways comes from design; the historical intention to hide the unmentionable in part resulted in the Victorian subterranean loos. For facilities above ground there was an element of camouflaging. Many resembled cottages, lending the term to the activity of men seeking sex with other men in public toilets: 'cottaging'. Under section 71 of the Sexual Offences Act 2003[43] both heterosexual and homosexual sexual activity in public toilets is against the law (although it is noted that the law uses 'he' in its direction).

The RSPH survey noted that more women than men were concerned with safety in public toilets (both under 20 per cent). Public loos are also reported to be 'spaces of male fear'.[44] The Office of National Statistics (ONS)[45] data on sexual assault reported that 15 per cent of women and 43 per cent of men between ages of 16-59, had, since the age of 16, experienced assault by a stranger, with 5 per cent of women and 10 per cent of men reporting that assaults took place in a park or other public open place. There are no ONS figures for attacks in public toilets specifically. Gender-based violence is a global problem and for many 'home is the most dangerous place'.[46] Fear of violence in public is especially acute for women, with public toilets becoming central in debates on women-only spaces as spaces of safety, yet there is no data to support this.

A more recent phenomenon with the rise of mobile phone and camera technology is voyeurism by taking photos of other users whilst in the toilet, both at the urinal or in the cubicle. This can be designed out by reducing opportunities for this either under or over the door or cubicle wall, and ensuring that privacy screens are in place between users at urinals.

As going to the loo is a private act that requires a private space, such space also gives opportunities for other private activities. We cannot and should not compromise the privacy of public loos; for many people more privacy is desired and should be designed in. Can sex be designed out of public loos in other ways? A number of tweaks to aspects of the design have taken place, for example many on-street and park public toilets do not include mirrors or instead have very distorted stainless-steel plates, especially in the men's provision. This is to deter eye contact in mirrors as the initial set-up for further sexual encounters.[47] This denies men the opportunity to check themselves, check their hair or check their tie (if they wear one). Deterring a minority through such target-hardening design approaches affects everyone. Sex in public toilets is against the law for everyone and presents a challenge for design to design out negative behaviour but not by creating an environment that is unwelcoming and inaccessible to the majority of legitimate users.

## Drugs …

People who inject drugs will sometimes do so in public. A ten-year study in Sydney, Australia concluded in 2003 and found that 47 per cent of people who inject drugs do so on the street and 39 per cent do so in public toilets.[48] Why are public loos used for this? Research suggests an element of immediacy to inject drugs and avoid getting sick from withdrawal, with the privacy of the toilet cubicle required due to the stigma of being a drug user.[49]

At the end of 2023 the ONS reported 4,907 drug poisoning deaths in England and Wales in 2022,[50] with 3217 identified as drug misuse. This number has been rising since 1993 when records began. The charity Crisis report that mental health and addiction problems are one of the root causes of homelessness.[51] The last 'snapshot of rough sleeping', published in February 2023, estimated that on a single night in autumn 2022, 3,069 people slept rough due to not having a home, a rise of 74 per cent since 2010.[52] The ONS reported that 259 homeless people died from drug poisoning in 2021.[53]

What these grim statistics reveal is that for people who are rough sleeping and who are also people who inject drugs, the public toilet may be the only place they have to manage their addiction. There is no public data of overdoses or deaths in public loos from drug use in the UK, but the British Toilet Association report there is increasing evidence of facilities being used for drug use.[54]

An initial design intervention introduced 'blue' ultraviolet lights into public toilets. Described as 'symbolic violence' by Parkin and Coomber (2010), blue lights prevent people who inject drugs from seeing veins in their arms so as not to use the public loo for drug use. The lights may not deter injecting but result in riskier injecting behaviour leading to overdose.[55] Hanson et al. (2007)[56] found that many disabled and older people found the blue light environment extremely off-putting:

> I have a problem with those blue lights. I have a syndrome where my eyes react to light and where my pupils don't change from dark to bright light rapidly. I'm not visually impaired but I do find blue lights very disorientating. It would be difficult to transfer and feel comfortable.
>
> **WHEELCHAIR USER**

I went into a toilet with blue lights. It made me feel dizzy and disorientated. It was the disabled toilet, and I couldn't see if the floor was wet.

**OLDER PERSON**

People with visual impairments reported that blue lights made it difficult for them to navigate their way around the toilet. People with stomas reported that the blue light made it difficult to assess if they had cleaned their stoma adequately when changing ostomy bags, and carers of neurodiverse children reported that the blue lights created such an alien environment that it scared them and resulted in refusals to use the loo. Anecdotally, police architectural officers reported that the blue light was also found to have created an erotic environment increasing incentives for sex in public loos.

Recognizing that local authority public toilets are for everyone requires designers to think inclusively and even consider accommodating some of the non-toileting activities that may take place there. Where the toilet is located may have a specific remit on this. Toilets in town centres or areas identified with drug use should consider the installation of sharps bin to deter littering of IV needles. The *Publicly Available Toilets Problem Reduction Guide* (2010)[57] gives an overall perspective for key issues designers of public toilets to be aware of and recommends the installation of sharps chutes embedded into the wall for outside service and collection. This avoids needles being dangerously disposed of in sanitary bins or with general rubbish.

## … and rocking the bowl (vandalism)

The biggest issue facing council-maintained public toilet provision, especially due to the costs involved in repair and the inconvenience of closure, is vandalism: the deliberate destruction of public loos. We have been collecting news reports on public loos for many years and have noticed a distinct rise in reports of vandalism in the last few years.

Vandalism of a public loo can take many forms. Ceramicware such as toilet pans and basins can be smashed. Large rolls of toilet paper and paper towels can be stuffed down the toilet blocking it. Taps can be broken or left on, causing flooding. Doors and toilet seats and lids and toilet paper dispensers can be ripped off their fittings. Paper towels can become fuel for fires. Graffiti can be written, drawn or painted on walls, sometimes extreme and offensive (Figure 2.6). There is a lack of data concerning which types of provision are subjected to vandalism (the men's, women's or disabled toilets) and if vandalism of one type of provision results in all provision being closed. Vandalism of toilets is more frequent but not limited to council-maintained facilities. When toilets are targeted, this can

**Figure 2.6** Graffiti in a public toilet.

be used as a justification for restricting access, whether through payment systems, by only unlocking toilets on request, or by restricting access to certain groups (Figure 2.7).

Design to counter vandalism has often and understandably responded to a crime reduction and defensive brief. Interventions have included removing toilet seats (so they cannot be damaged), push-operated taps to reduce flooding or stainless-steel all-enclosed handwashing units to remove opportunities to damage handbasins. As with other design-out-crime ideas, this also designs out legitimate use, whether it is someone unable to reach the handwashing unit or without the strength to push the tap (see Chapter 9). People with cognitive disabilities may find handwashing units difficult to use due to their lack of familiar visible objects such as a soap dispenser, tap handles and a hand dryer. Ensuring standard toilet provision is both robust and accessible is essential for more inclusive toilet provision.

Accepting that public loos are spaces that everyone of all genders, social status and abilities has a right of access presents interesting challenges for designers. To favour a solution focused primarily on crime reduction and the behaviour of a minority risks making public toilets inaccessible to a majority.[58]

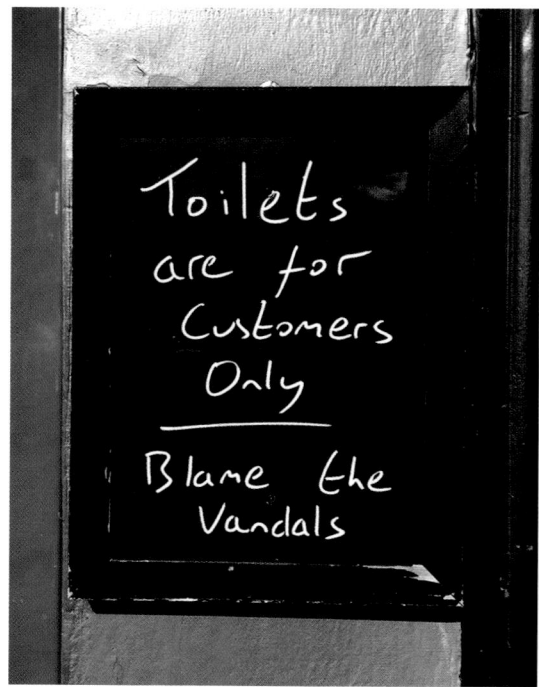

**Figure 2.7** A community toilet taken out of general use and now 'for customers only'. Credit: Paul Burgess.

## What if there are no public toilets?

Street urination (and defecation) is a specific problem for local authorities but nearly half of local authorities and police forces had no by-laws prohibiting public urination, and those that did rarely enforced them,[59] with recorded instances of public urination offences halving from 2010 to 2018. There appears to be a lack of oversight regarding upholding the law on street excretion and with the lack of public loos especially in the evening, many people are left with no option but to urinate and/or defecate in public. Once this behaviour is established it is difficult to break and can seemingly legitimize a place to pee (Figure 2.8).

The RSPH (2019)[60] described how concerns about street urination prompted the building of the first public toilets in the 1880s and their 2019 survey reported that 16 per cent of total respondents often used a back alley or bush to urinate due to a lack of toilet provision (41 per cent of men and 71 per cent of women reported they never did this).[61]

**Figure 2.8** A sign reads 'Please use toilets provided' in an effort to tell people there are alternatives to public urination.

Street urination and defecation also known as 'wild toileting'[62] puts pressures on already-limited street cleaning budgets and is particularly unpleasant for street cleaners. It is estimated that the combined cost of street cleaning in the UK is £694 million which is equivalent to £12.33 per head,[63] effectively costing us quite a lot more than spending a penny.

# Public toilets today: How many are there?

The UK's public toilets are frequently reported as being in decline, sometimes as a result of the behaviours we have just overviewed. What is less clear is how extensive this is and anyone who wants to find out how many toilets there are will find it is a difficult task. The UK government has not collected data on the number of public toilets since 2000,[64] and the information is now spread across hundreds of local authorities. When counting toilets, what do we define as a public toilet, and is it only public toilets that we are interested in or is the category of **publicly accessible toilets** more relevant? The idea of an absolute number of toilets becomes almost meaningless. However, if a definition for a count is established and stays consistent, we can look at the change in those toilet figures to see if there are more or fewer than there were in the past. This is still a statistic that is very easy to get wrong. Here are a few things to look out for.

- Check what each data source is categorizing as a public toilet.
- Check what region the dataset covers: just one constituent country (e.g. England); England and Wales, Great Britain or the UK.
- Check that the same data source has been used across the time period of the closures, so we are comparing like for like.
- Check the language used. If a toilet has dropped off a dataset, has it actually closed or is it no longer included in the authority's statistics? For example, someone else may now be managing it.

Where can we find the data? There are a few sources of data available to the public:

- Valuation Office Agency (VOA)
- Freedom of Information Requests
- Ordnance Survey
- The Toilet Map
- Welsh Government data

## *Valuation Office Agency (VOA) data*

Covers England and Wales

This data includes public toilets eligible for business rates. It is only for properties ('hereditaments') that are wholly or mainly public toilets.[65] Toilets are still included even if the council applies an exemption; this changes the rateable value to zero, though this is an important point to check as the Non-Domestic Rating (Public Lavatories) Act 2021 will mean that exemptions now apply to far more facilities than previous years.

This data is often cited by MPs in parliamentary debate, from which we have access to secondary sources of VOA data for the following years: 2000 (6,087 toilets);[66] 2002 (5,882 toilets); 2003 (5,701 toilets); 2004 (5,539 toilets);[67] 2008 (5,084 toilets);[68] 2014 (4,627 toilets); 2016 (4,383 toilets) and 2021 (3,990 toilets).[69] Based on these figures from the VOA, we can say that 2,097 public toilets have stopped being active, rateable public conveniences between 2000 and 2021 in England and Wales, which is a reduction of 34 per cent.

## Freedom of Information Requests

Covers United Kingdom

In 2018, BBC News[70] investigated the change in council-run public toilets across the UK between 2010 and 2018 by submitting Freedom of Information requests to all responsible local authorities for figures for the two dates. They recognized that a reduction in the figure did not necessarily mean toilets had closed and instead reported 673 toilets, or 13 per cent, that were no longer maintained by the council. They also identified thirty-seven councils that no longer maintained any public toilets.

Of the fifty councils that reported the biggest reductions, most said this translated to some (if not all) closures. However, the story has another side. Cornwall Council, for example, transferred ownership of over 200 of their 247 toilets to smaller authorities, with just 16 toilets closing. This approach showed how the story of what is happening to our public toilets is very localized and council-specific, and completely hidden by national statistics.

## Ordnance Survey

Covers Great Britain

Ordnance Survey holds data on the location of public toilets across Great Britain rather than the UK, so excluding Northern Ireland. Public Toilets feature within their Points of Interest dataset, which included 8,919 public toilets in 2023. No more detail is public on how these toilets are defined or where the data is sourced from. This dataset is also available within the PointX product,[71] a commercial product produced by Ordnance Survey and Landmark Solutions.

A 2022 BBC News article used Ordnance Survey's Points of Interest dataset to show changes on the high street over the Covid-19 pandemic, between 2020 and 2022.[72] This showed a 2.3 per cent decrease in public toilets across the UK. It can also search by postcode, which would return the percentage change in public toilets for the relevant local council. Absolute numbers of facilities are not given.

## *The Toilet Map*

Covers the United Kingdom

The Toilet Map (formerly known as The Great British Public Toilet Map),[73] created as an output of our research in collaboration with design and development company Neontribe, has collected toilet data since 2014. This includes location data and meta data (information on the facilities provided, opening hours, etc.), and includes publicly accessible toilets.

The original 2014 dataset was from three sources. The first was open data from individual councils, National Rail Enquiries, and the Open Street Map project. Next, we added data from Freedom of Information requests sent to all relevant councils. These two sources produced a dataset of over 9,000 toilets. We then added a crowdsourcing interface, meaning the public can add, edit and remove data. This has grown the dataset to over 15,000 toilets in 2024.[74] The increase in toilet data does not correlate to an increase in toilets, just an increase in the volume of data the project holds. The dataset has been reused by other apps and websites under a Creative Commons Attribution licence.

## *Welsh government data*

Covers Wales

The Welsh government provide a collated dataset and map of over 1,000 publicly accessible toilets in Wales, as identified by each Welsh council as part of their toilet strategy.[75] This assesses the provision of all publicly accessible toilets (as defined in the guidance) within the council area. The datasets are compiled on wales.gov.uk and made available through the Welsh Toilet Map.[76] It can be reused by local authorities under the Public Sector Geospatial Agreement. It includes additional information such as the type of facilities provided and the opening hours.

# The complexity of having a wee in public

Since public toilets first appeared on the streets of London in the 1850s, they have caused controversy, initially through only being accessible to men, then by only being accessible to non-disabled people. The drive to increase access to public loos has led to a more people-centred inclusive design approach, led by Kira in the United States and Goldsmith in the UK. We suggest that despite some of Kira's historical legacies for inclusive design carrying through to improvements in provision, they have not been thought through. This can be seen in the 'casual adaptation' of multiple cubicle design where cubicle walls and doors are not fully enclosed. In these designs functional elements such as cleaning access and anti-crime measures have taken precedence over the need for privacy and a sense of one's own space which, albeit attending to a natural function, requires privacy when using the toilet in public.

As spaces where the unmentionable happens, public toilets have become tarnished with a bad reputation. As the most private spaces in public they are magnets for wider private activities, consolidating their notoriety. However, these activities will not move on without wider social initiatives. Scotland has become the first country in the UK to open Drug Consumption Facilities,[77] recognizing that people who inject drugs need privacy as well as attempting to move the activity out of the public toilet and into a specialist facility where help and support can be reached. However undesirable non-toileting activities are, people, especially those who are sleeping rough, should not be denied access to toilet provision.

The complexity of having a wee in public is further complicated by knowing where we can go 'to go'. We still do not have an accurate total for the number of public toilets in the UK. Yet public loos are essential to support us in our daily activities outside the home. The Welsh government has led the way by making toilet strategies a requirement for local authorities, part of their framing of toilet provision as central to public health, and after the Covid-19 pandemic, the English, Scottish and Northern Ireland governments should follow suit. Now well into the twenty-first century, we would argue that it is time to challenge such notoriety, rethink how provision can be offered and make changes through inclusive design.

# Notes

**1** B. Penner, 'A world of unmentionable suffering:@ Women's public conveniences in Victorian London', *Journal of Design History* 14(1) (2001): 35–52.

2. *Public Health Act 1936 c.49 Part II Public sanitary conveniences*. Available online: https://www.legislation.gov.uk/ukpga/Geo5and1Edw8/26/49/part/II/crossheading/public-sanitary-conveniences/enacted (accessed 17 January 2024).

3. *Public Health Act 1936 s. 87(3)(c) (revised)*. Available online: https://www.legislation.gov.uk/ukpga/Geo5and1Edw8/26/49/part/II/crossheading/public-sanitary-conveniences (accessed 11 January 2024).

4. Department of Communities and Local Government (2008), *Improving Public Access to Better Quality Toilets: A Strategic Guide* [pdf]. Available online: https://webarchive.nationalarchives.gov.uk/ukgwa/20120920031546mp_/http://www.communities.gov.uk/documents/localgovernment/pdf/713772.pdf (accessed 30 January 2024).

5. *Public Lavatories (Turnstiles) Act 1963 c.32*. Available online: https://www.legislation.gov.uk/ukpga/1963/32 (accessed 29 January 2024).

6. Department of Communities and Local Government, *Improving Public Access to Better Quality Toilets: A Strategic Guide*, 44.

7. Network Rail (2020), *Design Manual NR/GN/CIV/200/04: Public Toilets in Managed Stations* [pdf]. Available online: https://www.networkrail.co.uk/wp-content/uploads/2021/06/NR_GN_CIV_200_04-Public-Toilets.pdf (accessed 24 November 2023).

8. *London Local Authorities Act 2012 Part 3 Section 6*. Available online: https://www.legislation.gov.uk/ukla/2012/2/section/6/enacted (accessed 24 November 2023).

9. Hansard, London Local Authorities Bill (13 October 2010) H.L. 516 col. 376. Available online: https://hansard.parliament.uk/commons/2010-10-13/debates/10101328000003/ LondonLocalAuthoritiesBill(Lords)(ByOrder) (accessed 11 January 2024).

10. B. Penner, 'Designed-in safety', *Places Journal* October 2013, https://doi.org/10.22269/131015.

11. A. Kira, *The Bathroom: Criteria for Design* (New York: Ithaca, 1976 [1966]).

12. The phrase 'caught short' implies that we should be planning better, or to have 'gone before we left'. In many ways it chastises the public as if we are children or should have returned to our own homes by now even though some will need toilets a lot or unexpectedly. In many ways 'caught short' can be seen as subtle victim-blaming.

13. Kira, *The Bathroom*, 194.

14. Kira, *The Bathroom*.

15. Kira, *The Bathroom,* 202.

16. I. Watkins, 'London's most beautiful (and bizarre) toilets', *Design My Night*, 29 January 2024. Available online: https://www.designmynight.com/london/blog/london-beautiful-bizarre-toilets-instagram (accessed 31 January 2024).

17. 'Lady's guide to the 9 best loos in London', *A Lady in London* (no date). Available online: https://www.aladyinlondon.com/2016/01/best-loos-london.html (accessed 21 December 2023).
18. Kira, *The Bathroom*, 212.
19. Ibid., 216.
20. Ibid., 241.
21. Kira, *The Bathroom*.
22. Ibid.
23. Kira, *The Bathroom*, 255.
24. S. Goldsmith, *Designing for the Disabled: The New Paradigm* (London: RIBA Publications, 1976 [1967] [1963]. Reprinted London: Routledge 1997.)
25. B. Penner, *Bathroom* (London: Reaktion Books, 2013).
26. British Standards Institute. *BS8300-2 Design of an accessible and inclusive built environment*.
27. Building Regulations, *Approved Document M: Access to and use of buildings. Vol. 2: Buildings other than dwellings*.
28. Goldsmith, *Designing for the Disabled*.
29. J. Bichard, J. Hanson and C. Greed, 'Who put the P in policy? The reality of guidelines and legislation in the design of the accessible toilet', *Proceedings of INCLUDE 2007* conference (Royal College of Art, London, 2007). Available online: https://discovery.ucl.ac.uk/id/eprint/2999/ (accessed 18 January 2024).
30. H. Boast, 'Public toilets and public luxury', *New Socialist*, 30 September 2023. Available online: https://newsocialist.org.uk/public-toilets-and-public-luxury/ (accessed 24 November 2023).
31. V. I. Lenin ([1921] 1965), in Boast, 'Public toilets and public luxury', 109–16.
32. The survey was undertaken in Westminster and Clerkenwell in London and the city centres of Manchester and Sheffield. In total 211 people responded (87 men, 124 women). They did not identify themselves as disabled and were aged from sixteen to over sixty-five.
33. Bichard and Hanson, 'Inclusive design of "away from home" toilets'.
34. Royal Society for Public Health (2019), *Taking the P\*\*\*: The Decline of the Great British Public Toilet* [pdf]. Available online: https://www.rsph.org.uk/static/uploaded/459f4802-ae43-40b8-b5a006f6ead373e6.pdf (accessed 7 January 2024).
35. R. Stanwell-Smith (2019), in *Taking the P\*\*\*. The Decline of the Great British Public Toilet*. Royal Society for Public Health [pdf]. Available online: https://www.rsph.org.uk/static/uploaded/459f4802-ae43-40b8-b5a006f6ead373e6.pdf (accessed 7 January 2024).
36. R. Wardhaugh (2002), cited in N. Stead, 'Avoidance: On some euphemisms for the "smallest room"', in O. Gershenson and B. Penner (eds), *Ladies and Gents Public Toilets and Gender* (Philadelphia: Temple University Press, 2009), 126.

37  There are a number of deaths reported in public toilets most commonly from drug overdose but also from retreating to the space when feeling unwell.
38  T. Newman, 'The 7 wonders of poop', *Medical News Today*, 1 February 2019. Available online: https://www.medicalnewstoday.com/articles/324254 (accessed 7 January 2024).
39  NHS, 'Clostridium difficile (C. diff) infection', 8 February 2022. Available online: https://www.nhs.uk/conditions/c-difficile/ (accessed 7 January 2024).
40  Waste Industry Safety and Health Forum (2015), *Managing Offensive/Hygiene Waste Safely. Formal Guidance Document* [pdf]. Available online: https://www.wishforum.org.uk/wp-content/uploads/2019/06/WASTE-22-.pdf (accessed 28 December 2023).
41  Kira, *The Bathroom*, 207.
42  Kira, *The Bathroom*.
43  *Sexual Offences Act 2003: Sexual activity in a public lavatory*. Available online: https://www.legislation.gov.uk/ukpga/2003/42/section/71 (accessed 8 January 2024).
44  S. E. H. Moore and S. Breeze, 'Spaces of male fear: The sexual politics of being watched', *The British Journal of Criminology* 52 (6) (2012): 1172–91, https://doi.org/10.1093/bjc/azs033.
45  Office of National Statistics, *Nature of Sexual Assault by Rape or Penetration, England and Wales: Year Ending March 2020*, 18 March 2021. Available online: https://www.ons.gov.uk/peoplepopulationandcommunity/crimeandjustice/articles/natureofsexualassaultbyrapeorpenetrationenglandandwales/yearendingmarch2020 (accessed 8 January 2024).
46  M. Dawson, 'Home is the most dangerous place for women, but private and public violence are connected', *The Conversation*, 24 November 2021. Available online: https://theconversation.com/home-is-the-most-dangerous-place-for-women-but-private-and-public-violence-are-connected-171348 (accessed 9 January 2024).
47  Glass mirrors are also often not fitted in men's public toilets to deter them being smashed and used as weapons.
48  MSIC Evaluation Committee, *Final report on the evaluation of the Sydney medically supervised injecting centre* (Sydney, 2003), cited in *Safer Drug Consumption Facilities – Evidence Paper* (Scottish Government, October 2021) [pdf]. Available online: https://www.gov.scot/binaries/content/documents/govscot/publications/research-and-analysis/2021/10/safer-drug-consumption-facilites-evidence-paper/documents/safer-drug-consumption-facilities-evidence-paper/safer-drug-consumption-facilities-evidence-paper/govscot:document/safer-drug-consumption-facilities-evidence-paper.pdf (accessed 8 January 2024).

49  A. Crabtree, G. Mercer, R. R. Horan, S. S. Grant, T. T. Tan and J. A. Buxton, 'A qualitative study of the perceived effects of blue lights in washrooms on people who use injection drugs', *Harm Reduction Journal* 10(22) (2013). Available online: https://harmreductionjournal.biomedcentral.com/articles/10.1186/1477-7517-10-22 (accessed 8 January 2024).

50  Office for National Statistics, 'Deaths related to drug poisoning in England and Wales: 2022 registrations', released 19 December 2023. Available online: https://www.ons.gov.uk/peoplepopulationandcommunity/birthsdeathsandmarriages/deaths/bulletins/deathsrelatedtodrugpoisoninginenglandandwales/2022registrations (accessed 8 January 2024).

51  Crisis, 'Everybody in: How to end homelessness in Great Britain'. Available online: https://www.crisis.org.uk/media/239951/everybody_in_how_to_end_homelessness_in_great_britain_2018.pdf (accessed 30 October2024).

52  Department of Levelling Up, Housing and Communities, 'Rough sleeping snapshot in England: Autumn 2022', 28 February 2023. Available online: https://www.gov.uk/government/statistics/rough-sleeping-snapshot-in-england-autumn-2022 (accessed 8 January 2024).

53  Office for National Statistics, 'Deaths of homeless people in England and Wales: 2021 registrations', released 23 November 2022. Available online: https://www.ons.gov.uk/peoplepopulationandcommunity/birthsdeathsandmarriages/deaths/bulletins/deathsofhomelesspeopleinenglandandwales/2021registrations (accessed 8 January 2024).

54  British Toilet Association, 'Activities'. Available online: http://www.btaloos.co.uk/?page_id=305 (8 January 2024).

55  S. Parkin and R. Coomber, 'Fluorescent blue lights, injecting drug use and related health risk in public conveniences: Findings from a qualitative study of micro-injecting environments', *Health and Place* 16 (2010): 629–37. Available online: https://ora.ox.ac.uk/objects/uuid:d9f9b17b-b4a4-47e1-a6b5-890e57235c90/download_file?file_format=application%2Fpdf&safe_filename=Parkin%2BBlue%2BLights%2BHealth%2BPlace%2B2010.pdf&type_of_work=Journal+article (accessed 8 January 2024).

56  Hanson, Bichard and Greed, *The Accessible Toilet Design Resource*.

57  British Toilet Association and Hertfordshire Constabulary, *Publicly Available Toilets Problem Reduction Guide*.

58  Knight and Bichard, *Publicly Accessible Toilets: An Inclusive Design Guide*.

59  L. Jones and R. Schraer, 'Reality check: Public toilets mapped', BBC News, 15 August 2018. Available online: https://www.bbc.co.uk/news/uk-45009337 (accessed 7 January 2024).

60  Royal Society for Public Health, *Taking the P\*\*\**:

61  Ibid., 10.

62. E. Saner, 'The war against wild toileting: Is there any way to stop people weeing – and worse – in the street?' *The Guardian*, 5 April 2023. Available online: https://www.theguardian.com/society/2023/apr/05/the-war-against-wild-toileting-stop-weeing-street-urinating (accessed 7 January 2024).

63. A. Gouk, 'The true cost of litter and fly tipping in England', *In Your Area*, 27 August 2020. Available online: https://www.inyourarea.co.uk/news/the-true-cost-of-litter-and-fly-tipping-in-england (accessed 7 January 2024).

64. Department of Communities and Local Government, *Improving Public Access to Toilets: A Strategic Guide*.

65. *Non-Domestic Rating (Public Lavatories) Act 2021*. Available online: https://www.legislation.gov.uk/ukpga/2021/13/contents (accessed 9 January 2024).

66. Hansard, *Written Answers to Questions (8 Jun 2005)*. H.C. Vol. 434, Part 83, col. 563W. Available online: https://publications.parliament.uk/pa/cm200506/cmhansrd/vo050608/text/50608w03.htm#50608w03.html_wqn0; *Hansard (Non-Domestic Rating (Public Lavatories) Bill*. H.L. Vol. 811, col. 432. (2021). Available online: https://hansard.parliament.uk/lords/2021-03-17/debates/90B02AA3-684B-4374-A2D1-22520CBFE582/Non-DomesticRating(PublicLavatories)Bill# (both accessed 15 October 2024).

67. Hansard, *Written Answers to Questions*.

68. Hansard, *Written Answers (13 Mar 2008)*. H.C. Vol. 473, Part 66, col. 584W. Accessed online: http://www.publications.parliament.uk/pa/cm200708/cmhansrd/cm080313/text/80313w0012.htm (accessed 15 October 2024).

69. Hansard, *Non-Domestic Rating (Public Lavatories) Bill*.

70. Jones and Schraer, 'Reality check: Public toilets mapped'.

71. *PointX*. Available online: https://www.pointx.co.uk/suppliers (accessed 6 December 2023).

72. M. Easton and Data Journalism Team, 'Postcode checker: How has your high street changed since 2020?' BBC News, 6 December 2022. Available online: https://www.bbc.co.uk/news/uk-63799670 (accessed 6 December 2023).

73. The Toilet Map.

74. The Toilet Map, 'Toilet explorer'.

75. Welsh Government (2018), *The Provision of Toilets in Wales. Statuary Guidance* [pdf]. Available online: https://www.gov.wales/sites/default/files/publications/2022-02/the-provision-of-toilets-in-wales-local-toilets-strategies.pdf (accessed 30 October 2024).

76. DataMapWales (2019), 'National Toilet Map'. Available online: https://datamap.gov.wales/layers/geonode:national_toilet_map (accessed 30 October 2024).

77. J. Cook, 'UK's first consumption room for illegal drugs given go-ahead', *BBC News*, 27 September 2023. Available online: https://www.bbc.co.uk/news/uk-scotland-66929385 (accessed 9 January 2024).

# 3  Inclusive design

Designing inclusive public toilets means involving people in the design process. This will give designers and architects awareness of how people see, use and even work around a design. But who are the 'people'? As we described in Chapter 2, initial inclusive design perspectives considered the needs of older and disabled people, but that this focus should not result in 'special' designs. Roger Coleman, one of the key initiators of inclusive design noted that 'considering the life-course as a whole, disability and ageing can be recognised as normal rather than exceptional experiences'.[1]

A recent example of how the considerations of inclusive design continues to expand is through guidance on designing for neurodiverse people, such as the British Standards design guide *PAS 6463: Design for the Mind – Neurodiversity and the Built Environment – Guide*,[2] which we discuss later in this chapter. Our design research on public toilets continually tries to extend who we include, to try to include 'everyone', as everyone will need to use the toilet. Leading inclusive design adviser Julie Fleck points out that 'impairment is normal, part of the human condition, something we all experience to a greater or lesser extent throughout our lives. Designs that ignore difference and diversity are ignoring ourselves, excluding the majority and denying the obvious'.[3]

One thing to bear in mind when designing an inclusive public toilet is that not everyone will make their choice based on their social designation. Many people who are disabled use the standard toilet provision. Many older people who do not consider themselves disabled prefer the accessible cubicle. Parents and guardians of young children have different approaches as to whether they use the toilet of their gender or their child's (which in turn may depend on whether it is them or their child who needs the toilet), or whether they use the accessible toilet instead. People also have different ideas around when a child can, or should, use a toilet unaccompanied rather than use a toilet not for their gender. This transition point for all users can also go back and forth, depending on the context of the toilet in question.

In this quote, where a person describes their difficulty with the standard provision, it could be because there was no accessible alternative or it could be their preference, or that they don't consider themselves disabled.

The clearance of the door is so close to the actual toilet that I find it quite difficult … I think anyone would even if they didn't have crutches, they have to kind of manoeuvre themselves around the door when there is no gap … you literally open the door and it's like the door is practically touching the toilet so it's a tight squeeze.
**USER WITH WALKING AIDS**

Many inclusive designers involve users in the development of a building, a product or a service, but for public toilets we suggest this engagement should be extended to those who own and service facilities. Each contributor to the design research, whether user, owner, manager or cleaner, will have expert knowledge and experience which can help ensure that a public toilet is accessible. This will help to deliver provision that meets the public need and expectations of a clean and functional environment.

# Architecture + Product + Service = Inclusive public toilets

The inclusive design of public toilets is not the responsibility of a single design discipline but should bring together three broad and distinct areas of design, that of architecture, product and service design. An inclusive environment needs to be furnished by inclusive products, which can be accessed for use and maintenance, as the products will play an essential role in delivering an inclusive service. Poor service of the toilet can be as detrimental as the lack of space or the inaccessible products that furnish it, and in some cases, even more so. People do not like to use a dirty toilet and in general there has been a heightened sense of hygiene since the pandemic. A dirty toilet with no toilet paper reminds the user that no one is taking care of the facility or the provision, and by extension, that the users are not cared for either. In publicly accessible toilets within the business sector, this can reflect onto the business itself.

The public toilet provides a key example of how getting things right can provide a positive experience that can encourage return visits to a place or business. Getting just one of the three areas wrong can make the simple act of visiting a public toilet akin to a 'nightmare'.[4]

Participants in our research shared a number of experiences with us which highlight when the design has not been fully considered from an architectural, product or service perspective.

> Some accessible toilets are not in very accessible places, there's stiff swing doors, narrow passageways with sharp turns. It's ok for me as I can walk but it must be very difficult for people in wheelchairs.
>
> **USER WITH CHRONIC HEALTH CONDITION**

> Even though some businesses are complying with the law, it has not been thought out clearly … whilst the toilet is ok, it's down a narrow passageway that was blocked by equipment.
>
> **USER WITH CHRONIC HEALTH CONDITION**

Here, two facets of design have been overlooked, namely the design of the route to the toilet cubicle, and then the servicing of that route to ensure it is accessible. The latter example, in which the route is blocked by cleaning equipment, often comes up in a similar guise when the accessible cubicle itself is used as a storeroom. A simple solution, especially given that toilets need to be cleaned, would be to include storage space for equipment and servicing materials (toilet paper, soap, paper towels, etc.) within the design.

In the following sections, we give a few introductory examples of architectural, product and service design where public toilets may, or may not, be considered inclusive.

## *Architecture*

All toilets need to be on accessible routes, not only for wheelchair users but for older people, those using walking aids, parents and carers with children in pushchairs, or people with shopping or luggage. If doors are required on the route, perhaps this is not the best place to situate the provision? We discuss where we need toilets, how to find them, and how to site, access and size the building and the cubicles in Chapters 5, 6 and 7.

Accessible toilet design also needs to consider how the choice and variety of wheelchairs has progressed. There are no standard dimensions for wheelchairs, as they will be best suited to the person using them. Sizes vary, particularly between manual and electric wheelchairs. Some wheelchairs will be larger than the dimensions that the accessible toilet allow for.

> The biggest problem is with the power chair. Some you can't turn around to shut the door … might be able to get in head on and use the loo but can't close the door. Sometimes I can twist round and close the door but then often I can't open it again.
>
> **WHEELCHAIR USER**

It is key for inclusive designers to remember that users do not present as singular personas and may have multiple needs. This is often overlooked when thinking about the design of the standard provision. As the standard toilets are generally not designed to be accessible to wheelchair users, they can inadvertently design out other people too, who would benefit from accessible routes or a bit more space. This highlights design that has not taken an inclusive approach.

> I got stuck in the loo when I was pregnant. It had one of those big loo roll holders and it blocked the exit. I was trying to get out between the edge of the door and the loo roll holder, and I became wedged, so I had to go back in again and come out a different way, but I couldn't get out that way either. I thought 'this is ridiculous, I've got to be able to get out' eventually I squeezed out, but I had to squeeze my bump.
>
> **PREGNANT USER**

Many existing standard toilet cubicles do not have enough space between the swing of the door and the toilet pan. The space is often further restricted by a toilet paper dispenser that is too large. To ensure a toilet cubicle has enough space to turn in front of the toilet (known as the 'column of clearance'), guidance should be followed and even exceeded. This would make toilets more comfortable during pregnancy. On average there are over 800,000 pregnancies a year in England and Wales[5] and pregnancy often means having to use the toilet more frequently, especially in the later stages. Post-pregnancy, parents will now have additional considerations, from changing their baby to just managing their own toileting whilst caring for a baby and often other children.

The ambulant cubicle is an increasingly common feature of standard provision.[6] This is usually placed at the end of a row of cubicles with an outwards-opening door, grab rails for support and a larger cubicle dimension. In many ways the inclusion of this cubicle presents one less environmental obstacle for people to negotiate but will also come with its own user pressures (see Chapter 6).

It is currently estimated that 64 per cent of the British population are overweight and predicted to become larger by 2040.[7] This increase in body size will make the current standard toilet difficult to access and could put pressure on the accessible toilet, as more people find standard provision uncomfortable to use. Previous guidance directed the column of clearance to be 450 mm. The 2024 Approved Document T of the Building Regulations[8] has increased the column of clearance to 465 mm so buildings from 2024 onwards should offer larger standard provision.

I try to use the disabled toilet because it makes it easier for me. I'm six foot three and weigh twenty-six stone so the cubicle has to be a realistic size, let's be fair, I can't get in a normal cubicle.
**OLDER USER**

## *Product*

If a product is going in an environment where everyone will use it, the product needs to be accessible to as many people as possible. We discuss in detail the products found in publicly accessible toilets in Chapters, 7, 8 and 9. In general, most of the products found in the accessible cubicle will have been chosen for their access considerations: lever flushes and taps; hand dryers at a reasonable height for a wheelchair user and with a reduced noise level for neurodiverse users; accessible toilet paper, paper towel and soap dispensers; hooks for coats and bags and at different heights. Some cubicles may even include a shelf or flat surface for users with colostomy and urostomy bags.

The accessible products are out there, and many tend not to be specialized or more expensive. Yet they are rarely included within the standard provision. As Coleman and Fleck state at the beginning of this chapter, ageing and impairment are the normal conditions of life. These may be temporary (a broken arm), situational (carrying a baby) or permanent (arthritis), which limits movement and comfort. Many people find certain door locks, flushes, taps, toilet paper, paper towel and soap dispensers in the standard toilet difficult to use. This may result in them using, and increasing pressure on, the accessible toilet provision. They may not require the extra space, but because the products designed and then chosen for the standard provision have not considered inclusion, people find the accessible loo more comfortable to use. Choosing inclusive products for the standard provision will create a more inclusive toilet experience.

The choosing and placing of products within standard toilets also needs access consideration. Will children be using the facility? There are very few settings where we can say with certainty, no. We are beginning to see more basins and hand drying products placed at child height, but other products that support their use of the loo have not been included. Maybe the lock should not only be physically accessible and visually legible but also at a height that a child can use.

## *Service*

A key challenge for designers of public toilet fixtures and fittings is to ensure the design is accessible to users but also accessible to those who will be cleaning, refilling and maintaining the product. Do the access considerations for the user make filling the soap dispenser difficult for the cleaner? If so, the dispenser might remain unfilled and restrict access to the user from a service perspective. This is why extending user consultation in the inclusive design process to those who service the environment is also crucial. Cleaners use the soap dispenser, the toilet roll holder and the paper towel dispenser but in a different way, so it is essential to ensure one user's access is not to the detriment of another's.

> Soap is really important. I have to wash my hands. I will not go to the toilet if there is no soap, or I can't use the dispenser.
> **DISABLED USER**

Keeping toilets serviced and clean is essential and talking to people who undertake these roles to understand how the toilet is cleaned and how certain aspects of design may be making this difficult is just as important as accessibility to the users. The ease and ability to clean to a high standard is key. This is especially important for toilets with high footfall which may need efficient cleaning a number of times a day. Understanding where the bottlenecks are in the cleaning and servicing process and making design decisions that consider these equally to access will ensure a better, more inclusive standard of provision.

Service design is something we consider throughout Chapters 5 to 9, from the point at which we first look for a toilet, to our ability to enter, use and leave it for the next person. This user journey has many touchpoints along the way. We also consider the pressures on service providers, looking at different models of provision, in Chapter 10.

## Accessibility regulations and guidance

Fleck has astutely noted that 'we have a toolbox full of legislation, technical standards, guidance documents and years of experience, but we don't use these tools effectively or learn from experience'.[9] Hence much of the public toilet stock we find in our built environment remain inaccessible to many users.

In England and Wales, guidance on designing toilets that are accessible to the public is governed by the Building Regulations *Approved Documents M: Access to and Use of Buildings. Volume 2: Buildings other than Dwellings*, also referred to as 'Part M'.[10] This regulation specifically directs the design of accessible, ambulant and Changing Places toilets. More recently, new guidance has been issued in the Building Regulations *Approved Document T: Toilet Accommodation* (or 'Part T').[11]

This has provided direction on standard and ambulant provision. The Building Regulations are legal structures and promote an inclusive design perspective.

Whilst not a legal requirement in the design and fitting of public toilets, UK design tends to follow the guidance of the British Standards BS6465: Sanitary Installations: code of practice parts 1–4[12] for standard provision and BS8300: Part 2: Design of an accessible built environment – code of practice[13] for accessible, ambulant and Changing Places provision. These are generally considered guides for good practice and recommend a minimum level of design that can be achieved and expanded on. By meeting the guidance as laid out in the British Standards, designers will usually have met the requirements of Building Regulations across the UK. However, this is often not followed, let alone exceeded. There is separate Health and Safety Executive guidance for toilets in workplaces.

## Design for the mind – Neurodiversity and the Built Environment

The inclusive design of public toilets has predominately focused on the physical barriers for older people, disabled people and those with related chronic health conditions (irritable bowel syndrome, ulcerative colitis, Crohn's disease, incontinence, etc.). In 2022, the British Standards Institute launched *PAS 6463: Design for the Mind – Neurodiversity and the Built Environment – Guide*,[14] aimed at considering how design might meet the physical and mental wellbeing of people who are neurodiverse, to include autism, attention deficit hyperactivity disorder, dyslexia, dyspraxia; or have neurodegenerative conditions such as dementias and Parkinson's. Considering neurodiversity and neurodegenerative conditions in design focuses attention to sensory and information processing differences between the neurotypical and the neurodiverse. The public toilet can be considered an extreme element of our built environment that can trigger a number of senses, so it is important that sensory experiences are also considered in the inclusive design of toilets to meet the needs of the neurodiverse.

PAS 6463 identifies 'numerous elements of the built environment that have the potential to contribute to sensory overload or "sensory shutdown", including:

a) sounds of various types, including intermittent or continuous, from loud to very quiet and particularly when unexpected;
b) visual 'noise' which may be caused by light, glare, shadows, colours, patterns, movement, proximity, technology or clutter;
c) Spatial and layout considerations; and
d) Unwanted or extreme sensory feedback through smell, touch, taste or temperature.'[15]

The development of PAS 6463 is an example of how the considerations of inclusive design continue to grow to include wider needs and experiences.

## Getting things up to standard

Progress in UK legislation has made the public toilet one of the most regulated public spaces for design in the built environment. Yet the minimum recommendations in best practice often result in cut corners and a misunderstanding of how the design of the space, fixtures and fittings need to be joined up. Many people find toilet provision just does not work for them and how they use the toilet.

Current provision is a patchwork of toilet designs. New buildings will (should) be completely accessible with the regulations and guidance followed in the toilet provision and the route to reach them. However, older buildings may have toilets that are far from fully accessible, with varying layouts that have been interpreted from guidance as the minimum that is required. This can make using the toilet challenging for many people. A favourite and perhaps lifelong visited place or business may now be off the agenda as health conditions and age make the toilet provision unusable. Many older buildings have public toilets that added accessible features many years ago but have not been updated to meet the needs of different wheelchair sizes or other aspects reflecting the diversity of users.

Access to goods and services for disabled people is enshrined in the Equality Act (2010)[16] but walk down many local high streets and you will see a lack of level access, narrow doorways, poorly laid out shops and restaurants and very little accessible toilet provision. Who is responsible for this lack of wider access? Is it the shop keeper or the landlord? What if every local high street had a fully accessible public toilet that not only met residents needs but also the needs of visitors? A community public toilet would mean a toilet is available for those who cannot use the toilet at their favourite place.

Other alternatives might be to encourage small businesses that have two standard separate-gender cubicles to refurbish them into one accessible cubicle. I asked this of a friend who is currently moving businesses, letting her know I was happy to advise if she wanted any ideas on how to make the toilets accessible. She responded that she could not do that because of her lease. How might landlords be encouraged and enticed to make their properties more accessible? It is currently estimated that four out of ten disabled people cannot access their high street.[17] Many high streets contain older building stock that is privately owned. Legislation for access and inclusive design recommendations as found in the Building Regulations mainly applies to new builds. This restricts many people from accessing older areas of their towns and cities, effectively carolling them into 'new' areas and restricting their access to wider goods and services. How much of this might be reversed if older and historical areas had just one fully accessible public toilet?

## How to design inclusive public toilets

It can be tempting for designers to design for their imagined typical user, and view any person, ability or circumstance outside this as something to think about at the end of the process, or perhaps never. For a more inclusive world, designers (and society) require a shift in mindset, to see inclusive design not as an add-on but as a fundamental part of the brief. Anything else is designing to exclude.

### *Where do we begin?*

Inclusive design is often achieved through people-centred approaches. This is where designers and researchers engage with people to learn about their lived experience: their needs, realities, challenges and possibilities. By understanding the reality of people's lives, recognizing them as experts of their own situation and working in partnership with them, designers can create more inclusive solutions. This is particularly important for people who are excluded by current designs.

This is the research phase of the design process, where we learn about the experiences of existing and potential users of our facility. This helps us to understand what is lacking with the current facility (if there is one), and to correctly define what the brief is that we are responding to. Perhaps the problem with the current toilet is not the internal fixtures and fittings but that the route to the toilets is too convoluted for the direction people are coming from, or the toilets are not open when demand is at its highest. Toilets are a part of our infrastructure and, as such, need to fit within and be supported by the wider landscape. The greatest toilet design will still fall short if the road outside is dangerous, or the signage is missing, or the bus stop is too far, or there is nowhere to park.

Talking to existing users is a good place to start, to understand who they are, how and when they use the facility, what changes they would make and what they wish to keep the same. However, we are not aiming to design for those who are already accommodated by the current toilet situation. Talking to others locally who do not use the toilets is critical, to find out if and why they are being excluded by design. Just because we do not currently see people with a certain need using the facilities does not mean that they do not exist, or that they would not wish to use it had they not been excluded. One of the first things we learn when carrying out inclusive design research is that it challenges our own assumptions. We think we know what people's experiences are and what is and is not relevant. When we begin to engage, particularly on a subject as private as toilets, we quickly realize we do not. It is one of the most rewarding moments in the design process.

Speaking with local groups and representatives across ability, age, culture, ethnicity, religion and gender can give us further insights. There may be local requirements such as a toilet to support the night-time economy, or a facility for bus or delivery drivers. These needs could also be met if known about and understood, in addition to those of the wider public. It is a difficult challenge to include everyone. Depending on the setting for the facility, we might prioritize some groups. For example, we would expect a family attraction to have more than adequate space for baby-changing, child-height toilets and basins and space for pushchairs, particularly compared with a bar or casino. However, people do not have a single identity. To use the example of a 'family', we must not only design for 'family' needs. Families include disabled people. Families are mostly made up of different genders. Families represent different cultures, they have different cognitive needs, they have different sensory sensitivities and are managing different medical conditions. Not recognizing people's complex and layered identities will also lead to exclusion within the group we are trying to include through design.

Some inclusive designs are put at risk due to other challenges to the service, such as designing for environmental sustainability, hygiene, financial constraints or resilience. Some changes made during the Covid-19 pandemic made toilets less usable, for example, taping off every other basin, increased use of strong chemicals or closing toilets entirely. Design ideas to reduce criminal activity in toilets, such as the use of ultraviolet lights (see Chapter 2), make for unpleasant and sometimes distressing environments for all users. It is an inclusive design challenge to design 'out' some behaviours without also excluding legitimate users.

If we seek to understand the system within which public toilets exist – who pays for what, what threatens them with damage or closure, how they are misused or abused, and what the law permits – we can work within this system to provide an inclusive facility, with support ready should things go wrong. Include wider stakeholders in your engagement such as other council departments, police and community safety, local support services and charities. This can avoid mistakes being made early on, such as situating toilets where there is poor lighting or no eyes-on-the-street, and have mechanisms such as staff training in place to understand public behaviour, assist people in the facility and offer support where possible.

Occasionally, more systemic change is seen that leads to a step-change in public toilet design. The Public Lavatories (Turnstiles) Act 1967,[18] Part III of the Disability Discrimination Act 1995,[19] the Public Health Act (Wales) 2017[20] and the Non-Domestic Rating (Public Lavatories) Act 2021[21] were all significant developments in how our public toilets in the UK are designed, affecting both the physical space and the provision of the service.

Once we understand people's needs and experiences, and how these interact with the wider parameters within the built environment, we are equipped to decide the brief for the toilet design. Keeping those we have engaged involved as designs develop, through user panels or advisory groups, will help to make sure our ideas truly meet the needs that they raised, and that we have not focused so much on one need that we have forgotten another. We could also bring people together to find collective solutions, facilitated by the designer. Encouraging people to think about what would work for others as well as themselves helps them to consider what is a preference rather than a need, particularly when there are conflicting requirements. Through this we can begin to prioritize, for when choices have to be made.

## *Is best practice best?*

Whilst we would always encourage first-hand research, particularly of the unique local audiences who are dependent on the facility or currently excluded, there is also a lot of best practice guidance about inclusive public toilet design. The layout designs within the Building Regulations and British Standards were created in response to someone's needs and have been settled upon after a lot of input and debate from experts and different user groups.

The reasons for these, such as why a basin should be at a certain height and not 20 cm higher or lower, or why a tap should be on the side nearest to the toilet and not the other, or why a full-length mirror is needed, is not always given. This lack of connection between people's needs and the design requirements can lead designers and installers to overlook certain details, or to make what seem like minor adaptations for their context without realizing this leaves the toilet unusable.

The lack of awareness around existing best practice for inclusive toilet design is one thing we have always sought to address, by sharing user quotes and explanations for designs alongside suggestions in our research.[22] It is an approach that we continue in this book. We can also think about what more could be done to make toilets inclusive beyond the current best practice, to meet needs that have so far been overlooked.

## Can one design fit all?

Perhaps the most satisfying aspect of inclusive design is when one design meets the needs of many people and their circumstances. By highlighting the abuse some people experience in **separate-gender toilets**, particularly from others in the facility who have misread or are ignorant of their gender, there has been more emphasis on **gender neutral cubicles** of a standard size as the main toilet provision. The concept of a gender-neutral toilet is not new. The wheelchair-user accessible toilet is termed 'unisex' in the Building Regulations, and small businesses like cafés may have one toilet for everyone, as do trains, coaches and aeroplanes. However, the focus on gender inclusion has resulted in more gender-neutral toilets within toilet provision where more than one toilet is provided. This design has benefits beyond removing the risk of gender-based abuse.[23] Shared facilities mean women need not queue whilst the men's toilet is half empty (or that men get a taste of the experience women have had for decades, but still the wait will be less – see Chapter 6). Those who need assistance from someone of another gender, or who cannot leave a dependant unattended can stay together. Floor-to-ceiling walls give further privacy for those who need it. If a basin is included within the cubicle, this further increases the number of needs that are met. By providing alternative gender-neutral facilities, we will reduce demand on the accessible toilet. This is just one example of how a toilet design can meet multiple needs, of which there are many in this book.

We could keep extending the quality of this toilet further, and make each cubicle a larger size, even equivalent to a toilet design that accommodates wheelchair users. Train services and on-street automatic public toilets have largely taken this approach, where every toilet is large enough to meet the dimensions of a toilet accessible to wheelchair users. In other settings, needs can start to conflict, and an increase of size may lead to a decrease in the overall number of toilets provided.

Some people's needs are even more specific. The Changing Places toilets are an example of this. This design includes a hoist and changing bench, for adults with profound and multiple disabilities (see Chapter 6). Whilst this could also be used as wider provision, the equipment is very expensive, and needs to be kept in working order for those who rely on it. For this reason, they are often locked until someone requests access. There are also elements of the design that make it incompatible with wider use: the Changing Places toilet pan is not against one wall so that there is space either side for carers, whilst the accessible toilet for wheelchair users always has the toilet pan in a corner, to allow one grab rail to be securely wall-mounted so the user can transfer themselves. Just providing one of these two layouts would not meet both user group requirements.

Rather than pursuing one design that absolutely everyone can access, inclusive design can mean providing different designs, to give everyone equity of provision within the context of use. The aim is not to give everyone the same toilet, but to give everyone equivalent opportunities to access public space and public life, by providing appropriate toilet infrastructure. One size will not fit all.

## Designing the future

The realization that we cannot design one thing for everyone allows us to ask an alternative if uncomfortable question. Who will we knowingly exclude? With a thorough understanding of the needs of all potential users, we will have to prioritize some over others. Real-world constraints such as budget or space have an influence, as well as the anticipated audience. These choices will limit not only how inclusive our toilets are but the access to the built environment around it. Investing in toilets is investing in a more inclusive world. Is there a source of support, which could increase the budget, or the space permitted? Could we attract new audiences by offering facilities that others do not? Can we meet the basic needs for safety, comfort and dignity that may be essential before someone can use the facility, but then push ourselves further, to also design the best experience?

Inclusive designers can also design for the future. What future challenges do we need to consider? Might there be negative consequences from the solutions we have tried to implement? The standard use of flush toilets in the UK is not energy efficient, placing huge demands on the water supply. The supply and cost of water and energy mean we will need more sustainable, carbon-neutral facilities. Could we produce energy through waste? How might the design of other objects change over time? Minimum dimensions for wheelchairs and mobility scooters change, as does the number of people using them. Reusable sanitary towels and menstrual cups, rarely mentioned a decade ago, are now a frequent consideration when discussing the benefits of basins in cubicles. Campaigns for invisible disabilities has increased awareness of those using stoma bags, which in turn has helped raise the need for disposal bins in men's cubicles.

What might the next thing be for designers to respond to or lead on, within inclusive public toilets? Our basic physical needs do not change, but how we manage them, and how inclusive our environments are to support us does change, as our society becomes more aware, more understanding and better.

In the next chapter, we begin to think more deeply about what people's needs are, and how it affects us when our needs are not met.

# Notes

1. R. Coleman, 'The case for inclusive design – an overview', *Proceedings of the12 Triennial Congress, The International Ergonomics Association and The Human Factors Association of Canada, Toronto* (1994), 1. Available online: https://www.yumpu.com/en/document/view/47045819/the-case-for-inclusive-design-a-an-design-for-all#google_vignette (accessed 20 January 2024).
2. British Standards Institute (2022), *PAS 6463: Design for the mind – Neurodiversity and the Built Environment – guide* [pdf]. Available online: https://www.bsigroup.com/en-GB/insights-and-media/insights/brochures/pas-6463-design-for-the-mind-neurodiversity-and-the-built-environment/ (accessed 27 June 2024).
3. J. Fleck, *Are You an Inclusive Designer?* (London: RIBA Publishing, 2019), 15.
4. The term 'nightmare' was used by many participants to describe features such as sizes of cubicles, door locks, toilet paper dispensers and toilet paper stock.
5. Office for National Statistics, 'Conceptions in England and Wales: 2021', released 30 March 2023. Available online: https://www.ons.gov.uk/peoplepopulationandcommunity/birthsdeathsandmarriages/conceptionandfertilityrates/bulletins/conceptionstatistics/2021 (accessed 20 January 2024).
6. Building Regulations, *Approved Document T: Toilet Accommodation* (2024) [pdf]. Available online: https://assets.publishing.service.gov.uk/media/664329a0ae748c43d3793a28/ADT_2024.pdf (accessed 3 June 2024).
7. A. Gregory, 'More than 42m adults "will be overweight by 2040"', *The Guardian*, 19 May 2022. Available online: https://www.theguardian.com/society/2022/may/19/more-than-42m-uk-adults-will-be-overweight-by-2040 (accessed 20 January 2024).
8. Building Regulations, *Approved Document T: Toilet Accommodation*.
9. Fleck, *Are You an Inclusive Designer?* 18.
10. Building Regulations, *Approved Document M: Access to and use of buildings. Vol. 2: Buildings other than dwellings*.
11. Building Regulations, *Approved Document T: Toilet Accommodation*.
12. British Standards Institute, BS6465 Sanitary installations:

    *Part 1 Sanitary installations. Code of practice for scale of provision, selection and installation of sanitary appliances* (London: British Standards Institution, 2006 +A1 2009).

    *Part 2 Sanitary installations. Code of practice for space requirements for sanitary appliances* (London: British Standards Institution, 2017).

    *Part 3 Sanitary installations. Code of practice for the selection, installation and maintenance of sanitary and associated appliances* (London: British Standards Institution, 2020).

*Part 4 Sanitary installations. Code of practice for the provision of public toilets* (London: British Standards Institution, 2010).

13  British Standards Institute, *BS8300-2 Design of an accessible and inclusive built environment*.
14  British Standards Institute, *PAS 6463: Design for the mind – Neurodiversity and the Built Environment – guide*.
15  British Standards Institute, *PAS 6463: Design for the mind – Neurodiversity and the Built Environment – guide* vii–viii.
16  *Equality Act 2010* (London: HMSO, 2010) Available online: https://www.legislation.gov.uk/ukpga/2010/15/contents (accessed 20 June 2024).
17  E. Elmsworthy, 'High street shops are inaccessible to nearly half of disabled people', *The Mirror*, 3 December 2018. Available online: https://www.mirror.co.uk/news/uk-news/high-street-shops-inaccessible-nearly-13682141 (accessed 2 May 2024).
18  Department of Communities and Local Government, *Improving Public Access to Toilets: A Strategic Guide*.
19  *Disability Discrimination Act 1995 Part III*. Available online: https://www.legislation.gov.uk/ukpga/1995/50/part/III (accessed 21 December 2023).
20  *Public Health (Wales) Act 2017 Part 8* [online]. Available online: https://www.legislation.gov.uk/anaw/2017/2/part/8/enacted (accessed 18 January 2024).
21  *Non-Domestic Rating (Public Lavatories) Act*.
22  Knight and Bichard, *Publicly Accessible Toilets. An Inclusive Design Guide*. Nazerali, Ramster and Bichard, *Publicly Accessible Toilets after COVID-19*.
23  G. Ramster, C. C. Greed and J. Bichard, 'How inclusion can exclude: The case of public toilet provision for women', *Built Environment* 44(1) (2018): 91–115.

# 4  Everybody goes

Our reasons for visiting public toilets relate to the needs of our bodies and our minds. These reasons match why we need toilets in our home, plus a few more. Our needs can be constant throughout our lives or change depending on our health, who we are with, the time of day or the reason we are out.

In this chapter, we look at the needs of people with continence conditions, the changing methods of managing menstruation and other bodily needs like feeling unwell or unclean. Then we discuss the mind's needs. Toilets can be a place to rest, hide or withdraw to as one of the only private spaces in public life.

Why do we need public toilets? We look at how toilets benefit society by increasing choice. By having public toilets, we can increase access to community groups, public transport, physical activity and types of employment. As we saw during the pandemic, by not having toilets, our lives become severely restricted.

Understanding these varied and personal needs for public toilets, the value toilets can add to our lives, and how toilet access affects people and society is the foundation of public toilet design.

## The body's needs

Public toilets meet many of our body's physical needs, in particular the expulsion of what it no longer needs. It does this through urination, defecation, menstruation and vomiting.

How we use toilets for these basic bodily needs is something that we keep hidden from others. We mostly use toilets alone and out of sight. We might discuss the queue, the handwashing area or décor of a loo, but not what goes on in the cubicle. We rarely see it on TV or recounted in literature for its intended purpose, though it sometimes features as a space of personal refuge. We know our own behaviour and habits, learnt from our families when we are first toilet trained. After that we are on our own unless a change in our bodies means that we must learn new behaviour around expelling waste. Age, ability, menstrual cycle, pregnancy and medical conditions all influence our use of toilets and shape our experiences of them.

That it is such a rarely discussed subject makes the design of public toilets more challenging. The taboo around how we use toilets for basic bodily functions makes it is easy to assume everyone uses a toilet in the same way, yet people have significant differences which affect how often they go the loo, the length of time they are there and how someone tends to their toileting needs.

Inclusive public toilet design must consider the needs of all, and to do so, we must understand the needs of people who rely on toilets most and whose experiences we hear least about.

## *Urination (having a wee)*

Urination is the main use of a public toilet. In some ways it is how we measure how good a toilet is, from the ones that we like ('I might as well "go", just in case') to those that repulse us ('I'll wait, even though I'm desperate').

Urinary incontinence can be a permanent condition or something that we experience temporarily. Reduced urinary continence or incontinence affects millions of people of all ages and in all stages of life from the very young to those in old age. It can be a symptom of a medical condition or a side effect of medication. It can be from changes in physiology such as hormonal changes, or from muscle weakness or damage.

Some people find that they need to go quickly (*urgency* or *urge incontinence*) or that they need to go too often (*frequency incontinence*). How often is too often? The normal frequency of urination varies from person to person, from three to seven times a day for a healthy adult,[1] though some may go more frequently if it is normal for them and they are happy with this.

Both frequency and urge incontinence can also lead to the feeling of needing to go only to find the bladder is empty. For some people this is due to medication such as if they are prescribed diuretics, or 'water tablets', which make people wee more. This may be the purpose of the medication, for example if the kidneys are not working properly, but diuretics are often prescribed for high blood pressure with the side effect of more frequent trips to the toilet.[2] Some people do not take their medication to avoid the reoccurring need to use the loo.

> They make you go a bit often. So, when I come out for the day, I don't take mine. Tempting providence.
>
> **OLDER PERSON PRESCRIBED DIURETICS**

*Stress incontinence* is the leaking of urine due to muscle weakness, such as when sneezing or during exercise. This affects up to 9 million people in the UK[3] most of whom are women who might develop stress incontinence through weakened muscles and additional pressure during pregnancy, muscle damage during childbirth or muscle weakness due to hormonal changes at a particular point in the menstrual cycle or more consistently after menopause.

*Overflow incontinence* is the leaking of urine due to the bladder not emptying fully or not sending signals that you need to wee. Prostate cancer treatment can also reduce urinary continence, though this is normally temporary[4] where patients may find they leak urine after weeing or retain urine and need a catheter.

If we do leak urine, whether a little or a lot, a good public toilet network helps. Whilst accidents happen frequently for young children and are a natural part of toilet training, as we get older it is embarrassing, even shameful. Quick access to a public toilet allows people to address the physical soiling and to rebuild their dignity when away from home.

> I have episodes of incontinence so I think it would help to be able to clean up by the side of the loo rather than having to go out into the communal washing area. A standard loo with grab rails and a sink would suit my needs.
> **OLDER PERSON**

> There's nowhere else to wash, especially if you've started your period or if the kids have an accident.
> **PARENT**

These and other types and incidents of incontinence influence the design of public toilets at multiple scales. At an infrastructure level, we need access to more toilets, need the information to find them and need to access them quickly. At a product design level, within the cubicle we need more space along with access to water, a shelf, a mirror and a basin to manage continence products and equipment or clean and change after incidents of incontinence.

## *Defecation (having a poo)*

People need public toilets to defecate. Whilst some people may not be comfortable pooing in a public toilet, others are not willing or able to wait, and there is no reason why they should. As with urination, some people need to poo more frequently, urgently, experience leaks or have less control over when they poo or how long they can hold it. 'Holding' can also cause urinary incontinence.

There are different reasons for bowel incontinence. One is *irritable bowel syndrome (IBS)*, which causes frequent 'flare-ups', with symptoms such as diarrhoea, constipation, flatulence and an urgent need to poo. A fifth of the adult population in the UK is thought to have IBS and though symptoms come and go, it will often be a lifelong condition.[5]

Irritable bowel diseases, which are different from but sometimes cause conditions like IBS, include *Crohn's disease* and *ulcerative colitis*. Here, parts of the bowel become periodically inflamed. This causes symptoms such as diarrhoea, stomach cramps and sometimes a feeling of needing to poo only to find that you do not.[6]

Changes to bowel movements or bowel incontinence can happen due to changes in diet. It can happen when the muscles or nerves in the area have been damaged, for example from childbirth, an accident or surgery. Some people experience long-term faecal conditions (constipation or diarrhoea) or may be on medication that affects their bowel movements like antibiotics or laxatives.[7]

> I'm not brave enough to explain that I can't wait as long and I don't think that people would really put up with it either … they'll be like, 'Well you can queue like everyone else' but at the same time, well, some people can't wait that long unfortunately.

**ADULT WITH BOWEL CONTINENCE CONDITION**

People with reduced bowel continence may use continence pads or pants which need to be changed as soon as possible after soiling. Foam plugs can be used to stop leaking. People may have a stoma created, where a new passageway is made through surgery so that urine or faeces do not pass out through someone's bottom but instead through a new opening on their abdomen. The main procedures resulting in a stoma are a colostomy, an ileostomy (these are both for faeces) and a urostomy (to pass urine). Urine or faeces will pass through the stoma into a stoma bag that is worn over it. People with a stoma cannot control when they pass wee or poo; it leaves the body into the bag when it is ready. This bag needs to be emptied or changed, depending on the type and how long it has been in use: bags can be 'closed', intended to be used once and thrown away as soon as they are full; or drainable, which need to be emptied into a toilet throughout the day[8] and the outlet cleaned.

These methods change how people dispose of their poo but not their need for a toilet. They also need access to a sanitary bin, a clean, flat surface (shelf), a mirror at least from the waist up (wheelchair-accessible toilets should already have full-length mirrors) and a basin. These need to be within the toilet cubicle. A changing table or a similar size flat surface is needed for babies and toddlers and is sometimes available for older children and adults through a Changing Places toilet.

Whether we can poo naturally or with the help of bowel continence products, it is likely to involve smells or sounds that we would be embarrassed to share with others. A reliable public toilet that provides comfort, privacy and dignity is important for people to feel confident when managing defecation, a completely natural but highly personal act.

## Menstruation

Menstruation is not a minor issue when thinking about public toilet design. Around half the population will menstruate for around thirty-five years of their life. They will experience a median of about 450 menstrual cycles and spend the equivalent of eleven years on their period.[9]

Needing to manage a period is a reason in itself for visiting a public toilet or another thing to check if we already need the loo. We might be looking for the onset of a period, need to check underwear for leaks, or to adjust, change, empty or remove menstrual products. Depending on the product, the point in the period and the person, we might need to visit the toilet from every two or three hours to once a day (or more, to see how things are going or adjust for comfort).

> If I'm out for more than a couple of hours when on my period I absolutely need to find somewhere. The worst is always a long train journey when the toilets are out of order.
> **FEEDBACK SENT TO THE TOILET MAP**

For the best part of a century, we have relied on disposable sanitary pads and tampons to collect period blood (Figure 4.1). We have managed with no more adjustments made to the public toilet than a sanitary bin in the cubicle and no changes in the infrastructure. In the last decade, a significant shift has happened in period products. Driven by environmental sustainability, the use of menstrual cups and washable period pants has dramatically increased in popularity.

Period pants, initially the product of specialist companies, are now produced by both high street retailers like M&S and Primark and sanitary product manufacturers like Bodyform.[10] They can also be used by anyone with urinary incontinence or to absorb sweat during sport, hot weather and hot flushes. However, period pants are not so easy to change in a public toilet, not least for anyone wearing trousers. Reusable sanitary pads are also used by some, which fit inside regular underwear and can be changed in a toilet then taken home to be washed.

**Figure 4.1** Free menstrual products. These were within gender-neutral toilet cubicles at a training centre.

Menstrual cups are having a bigger impact on the design of an inclusive public toilet. A menstrual cup, like a tampon, fits inside the vagina. Unlike a tampon which absorbs blood, the cup collects it and needs to be removed and emptied into the toilet before being cleaned and put back in.

This makes things interesting. Now we need to be able to remove, clean and reinsert the cup all whilst still sitting (or hovering – see Chapter 8) on the loo. We also want to wash the blood off our fingers before touching anything, like our own clothes, the lock and the toilet flush.

This can be done with toilet paper or a bottle of water held over the toilet bowl, but these are examples of how people make their own adaptations and compromises to be able to use their product of choice when out and about. A much better design is to have a cubicle that includes a basin. This is not an unusual request; it is already a standard feature of the accessible toilet. However, it is less acceptable for non-disabled people to use the accessible toilet for period management. This makes the need for a basin within the standard cubicle more mainstream.

What else could make a toilet more menstruation-friendly? Sanitary bins are needed by all genders for menstrual and continence products to be thrown away discretely into a container with a close-fitting lid.

A hook or shelf within reach of the toilet is also needed to get out or set down clean sanitary products and pack away any that have been removed for washing once home. The hook on the back of the door is too far away, the floor is too dirty, and balancing bags and other items on our laps whilst changing sanitary products is not inclusive or by any means possible for many.

## Other physical needs

Whilst the need to wee, poo and see to our periods are the main reasons we visit a public toilet, there are other needs related to our bodies where the public toilet is our best option. We might feel nauseous or have been sick and need to clean ourselves. When my three-year-old threw up all over herself and me, we were lucky to be next to a train station where the toilets were free and as it happens, quite beautiful, with brass taps and diffused lighting (though the shared trough basin was unfortunate when I realized the sick was floating past others to the drain). Had it happened at any other point in our journey we would have been left vomit-strewn, causing others to retch, and miles from home.

We may need to clean ourselves in other ways: we get a graze, mud on our hands, bird poo on our body or spill a drink. We may want to wash our hands before eating, or simply because we have not for some time, especially post-pandemic when regular handwashing has become habitual for many. We may practise ritual washing before prayer. Public toilets can also meet other health needs such as a clean, safe space to take medication or to access drinking water.

We use public toilets to check, adjust or change our clothing without being seen or judged by others and to protect them from seeing us exposed. Some items we may feel comfortable removing or adjusting in public such as removing an outer layer. For others we need the privacy of the cubicle, like adding or removing a vest or tights. Perhaps our clothing has become uncomfortable, soiled or the weather has changed, or we are changing activity. Muslim women wearing a hijab or niqab wear these as part of their public appearance and would only remove them in public space when out of sight or in the company of women (for some, this might only be other Muslim women). We might check or alter our appearance in other ways, such as our hair or make-up if we no longer feel comfortable in public looking the way we do. For these other physical needs, it is not the features of the toilet itself that we seek but the basin, soap and mirror, a flat surface and the privacy of the facility or the cubicle (see Chapter 10).

These examples are not absolute. Whether we want to pick our nose, adjust our underwear or go for a wee, we each have slightly different boundaries when it comes to what we are comfortable doing in public. Public toilets, including those in workplaces and businesses, are almost unique in offering visual privacy away from home, sharing parallels with changing rooms in shops, changing rooms in leisure centres and rented space like hotel rooms.

As a society, many bodily functions are still more acceptable for men than women; however, even if someone is comfortable doing something, it does not mean others are comfortable seeing it. A place away from home that offers this privacy will both protect us from being seen and protects others from seeing us (see Chapter 7).

The public toilet does not decide where the line is in terms of acceptable behaviour. This happens organically, by social behaviour and people's changing attitudes and reactions. There needs to be a balance, but by providing enough public toilets and helping people to find them, we are offering the opportunity for private activities in public space should people need or want it.

## The mind's needs

A trip to the toilet is also a transition from the space that we were in to a wholly different one. From the chaos of the city streets to the ennui of the workplace, a toilet can be an escape for the mind where we can go when we feel uncomfortable in front of other people. We may be feeling overwhelmed, upset or panicked. If we are in the middle of a task, a toilet break allows our brains to switch off. It can be just what we need to move thoughts on or shift our energy in a new direction. We may be angry and need to cool off, or in tears, or feeling vulnerable. Big emotions can be hard to deal with when in public. They may be caused by the presence or actions of other people or the wider environment itself.[11] A smaller, private, personal space can help restore a sense of control and to process whatever experience we are going through so that we are able to return to our day and our public face.

In a town or city, we are never alone. Simply being around other people can be mentally tiring whether they are familiar to us or strangers. The public gaze is constant and even if we find ourselves alone, CCTV coverage means we are observed from afar. In a surveillance society, opportunities to be anonymous are disappearing.

## The writing on the wall

A toilet cubicle is one of the few places where graffiti endures. Whether it is a name, a quote or joke, a phone number or something more artistic, these messages are written knowing something of their audience: a one-to-one dialogue with the next visitor and the next. Communications in public toilets are not always routed in illegal activity. Transdisciplinary researcher Ailo Ribas Goody observed how public toilets in Berlin were used as 'an informal living archive for local queer, creative and immigrant communities' through the 'layering of posters, call-outs, ads, stickers, event flyers and scrawled messages'.[12] Through informal, organic co-opting of a (private) public space, minority communities that might be hidden or excluded from society can connect and grow.

Most toilets serve a local community of regular visitors and can provide a space for formal or information communication. This can be about and between the community (Figure 4.2) or about sensitive issues where organizations wish to reach people away from their peers (Figure 4.3). Campaigns around domestic abuse, suicide prevention or incontinence have been posted on the backs of cubicle doors where charities know they will reach an extensive captive audience

**Figure 4.2** Community notices in a café toilet aimed at locals, particularly families. Note that the basin, soap and paper towels can all be reached by a four-year-old (see Chapter 9).

**Figure 4.3** Information poster in direct line of sight for anyone using the hand dryer. This one offers help if experiencing harassment, sexism, homophobia or transphobia.

able to take a note in private. Between friends and acquaintances, toilets also offer an opportunity for direct conversation in noisy or hectic environments, particularly conversations of a private nature where we can check who is or is not within earshot. These opportunities to control our environment are surprisingly rare once we are out of our homes.

Fundamentally, the public toilet – in particular the cubicle – offers a moment of solitude, a refuge, a rare withdrawal from public view that allows us to press on without returning home. Sometimes we just need a break.

## What if our needs are not met?

Sometimes my mum will go and see what new places are like and report back to me … because it would just be a disaster if I went somewhere and they didn't have loos there. I would just come home again. I don't go places I don't know.
**YOUNG ADULT WITH CONTINENCE CONDITION**

The Royal Society for Public Health (RSPH) survey found that a lack of knowledge about public toilets stopped one in five of those surveyed from going out as often as they wished, and over two in five of those who needed frequent access due to medical conditions.[13] Disabled participants in our research have reported feeling like 'little animals who keep to their tracks' by going back to the same toilets and never venturing further afield.

People limit themselves in other ways too, such as not taking their diuretic medication or limiting how much they drink. This deliberate dehydration was reported by over half (56 per cent) of participants in the RSPH survey as something they do occasionally or frequently, with 11 per cent restricting fluids on a weekly basis, even though it can 'seriously affect health and exacerbate existing medical problems'.[14]

> Say I'm going on a long bus trip … I'll make sure I don't drink. That's not good for your health in terms of MS. You're meant to keep hydrated but you end up not drinking because you worry there won't be any toilets.
>
> **ADULT WITH MULTIPLE SCLEROSIS**

> As a person with IBS I am constantly anxious, particularly when I have to travel … and I'll be honest, I wear all sorts of protection just in case, and eat and drink only the bare essentials if I know I am travelling anywhere.
>
> **FEEDBACK TO THE TOILET MAP**

## Community connections

In 2008 the charity Help the Aged (now AgeUK) conducted a survey amongst older people where 52 per cent said a lack of access to toilets stopped them from going out as often as they would like, running the risk of increased isolation.[15]

> Very seldom do I go out unless I know there are going to be toilets somewhere.
>
> **MEMBER OF AN OLDER PEOPLE'S FORUM**

Fifteen years later, AgeUK in London launched a campaign, London Loos, for more and better public toilets, part of their larger campaign, Out and About, to address social isolation through better community infrastructure. Their 2022 survey found that public toilets were a particular problem on the high street, where 70 per cent of respondents said toilet provision was not good enough, as opposed to parks (58 per cent).[16] This was reflected in our own survey which we ran with the Mayor of London. Of those Londoners who reported no public toilets in their local town centre or high street, 59 per cent said this restricted the amount of time they spent there.[17]

Poor toilet access in commercial and retail space was also a feature of the government's pilot programme Open Doors to offer empty premises in town centres and high streets for community use. The programme aimed to provide spaces for groups at risk of loneliness, identifying young adults and older people specifically, as well as increasing high street footfall and building socially and economically stronger communities. The evaluation found that the inaccessibility of some premises, including those where there were no toilets or the toilets were not safe or accessible, excluded people from attending what was otherwise a successful activity.[18] A lack of public toilets reduces our ability to participate in our local community.

> To be honest, that's why I don't suggest that she joins a local pensioners group [for excursions]. Because I know finding a toilet is the overriding thing – it's her one big concern.
>
> **OLDER PARTICIPANT WITH ELDERLY MOTHER**

## *Getting out and about*

A lack of public toilets affects our ability to spend times outdoors (Figure 4.4). Contrary to the London surveys, the RSPH study *Taking the P\*\*\*: The Decline of the Great British Public Toilet* found that nationally, most people felt that the place where there was a need for more toilets was in parks (over 60 per cent of participants).[19] Current public policy is to encourage us to be more active whether for wellbeing, to keep us in physical health and reduce obesity, to walk and cycle as greener methods of transport or for social and community connectivity. The pedestrian charity Living Streets UK regularly recognizes the need for more public toilets within their community campaigns, and public toilets feature repeatedly in the World Health Organization's guide to age-friendly cities as an 'important age-friendly feature of the built environment',[20] a concept picked up by local authorities and charities in the UK as 'age-friendly communities'.

> I try to run 5 km each day, you know. I go around the houses and then up past the Tesco, because at my age you need a toilet break.
>
> **OLDER PERSON**

Anxiety around finding toilets on a journey impacts the modes and routes that people can access.[21] A study by Roger Mackett, which investigated gender differences in transport behaviour amongst people with mental health conditions,

**Figure 4.4** A publicly accessible standard toilet with a view near the South West Coast Path, St Ives, Cornwall.

found that more toilet facilities would help men and women alike. It was the only factor within the study that would encourage men to use train travel specifically. Access to toilets was a greater source of stress for women, and one that increased with age.

> I take these furosemide tablets and if you take it, you 'go' every five or ten minutes. So, I'm scared to go to the high street because I'd have to take a bus and I don't know where the toilets are.
> 
> **OLDER PERSON IN CITY SUBURB**

## The mobile workforce

As well as affecting social isolation, community participation, economic activity, modes of transportation and physical and mental health, access to public toilets can limit the means of employment available to us. Many people work in environments without dedicated toilet facilities including people who work outdoors (for example street cleaners, maintenance crew, market traders, gardeners), people whose job has no fixed base (community nurses, tradespeople, film crew, other mobile workers) and people working in transportation (bus, train and lorry drivers, taxi drivers, couriers, delivery drivers, driving instructors).

This is by no means an exhaustive list, and many mobile workforces need access to toilets throughout the day and night (see Chapter 6). Through our work on The Toilet Map, we have been contacted by many organizations over the years who are seeking better toilet data to support their mobile workforces, including those employing or representing supermarket delivery drivers, rail maintenance crew, taxi drivers, driving instructors and bus drivers.

> As someone who works outside all day, a toilet stop is part of the normal routine.
> **FEEDBACK SENT TO THE TOILET MAP**

> I'm a diabetic so I drink a lot of water. I have a bladder problem as well and they put me on these tablets. So I want a wee every 10 to 15 minutes.
> **TAXI DRIVER**

Mobile workers are not a homogeneous group; this workforce is also affected by continence and other health conditions that make finding a toilet even more important. The impact of ageing, the increased risk we will have more than one health condition and the consequential impact on our need for a toilet affects people when at work. This complexity – where we are each made up of multiple characteristics that include our age, disability, gender, occupation and health – means that improving public toilets for any one context will have a positive impact on many others too. Yet it is difficult to say how many. We know we are an increasingly ageing population but statistics around people affected by continence are vague, with different definitions around levels of severity or permanence; in 2023 the NHS put urinary continence in the 'millions'.[22] Similarly, there is no clear data around the size of our mobile workforce. However, through the range of reasons people have for visiting public toilets and the number of factors that increase our reliance on them, making public toilets more inclusive through design will have benefits for everyone's needs.

## Covid-19 and national incontinence

As a nation, we experienced what it meant to have no access to toilets during the Covid-19 pandemic. On 23 March 2020 the United Kingdom was told to 'stay at home'. The government's instruction,[23] published on 25 March 2020, ordered all retail to close with a few listed exceptions. These exceptions included supermarkets, petrol stations, post offices and public toilets. Yet despite this exception, almost all councils closed their loos (Figure 4.5). A key essential service to support keyworkers, outdoor exercise and grocery shopping had been overlooked. An email to us during lockdown captured the worries of many people.

> I am seeing some councils saying all [toilets] are closed. This is really detrimental to my mum who has bladder problems. She is not old and frail but has a medical condition. Because of this, she is now afraid to go to the supermarket, go for her hourly walk (as toilets seem to be closed), or even drink now when doing her exercise or shopping.
> 
> **EMAIL TO PUBLIC CONVENIENCE LTD 11/05/2020**

This was a major concern for key workers, especially if they themselves managed bladder or bowel conditions such as urinary incontinence or IBS.[24] Local papers featured reports of key workers campaigning for councils to reopen toilets, with one worker on the south coast quoted as having to walk for over an hour to their care home, making for an anxious journey whilst managing IBS.[25]

**Figure 4.5** Information poster reading 'Our public toilets remain closed', for residents and visitors to a seaside town.

Councils felt it was too difficult to keep public toilets covid-secure. Reasons given related to protecting their own cleaning staff, encouraging the stay-at-home order by removing toilet access, lack of cleaning guidance and unknowns around the risk of infection.[26]

At least two councils did recognize how critical toilets were for essential workers to be able to get to work or carry their work out. Westminster City Council never closed their toilets for this reason, and Orkney Council reopened some after key workers explained their importance as part of their commute.[27]

With the shift of much toilet provision already falling into the private sector, the closure of nearly all businesses (shops, cafés) made finding a publicly accessible toilet impossible.

By June 2020, lockdown began to ease, and people began leaving their homes and travelling further under social distancing rules. Although guidance published in May 2020 encouraged the safe reopening of toilets,[28] it was July before most councils began to act, to support the public to spend time outdoors. This was following a joint letter from the Department for the Environment, Food and Rural Affairs and the Ministry of Housing, Communities and Local Government to all local authorities specifically drawing attention to the need for public toilet access.[29] The public had already suffered months of increased isolation due to a lack of toilet access, as reported in the House of Commons.[30] If a loss of continence can be considered the result of being denied access to toilets, the UK effectively became incontinent.

As lockdown-easing continued, allowing people to travel further and for longer, many businesses that would have once extended toilet provision beyond customer-only were still closed. This severely impacted councils who now relied on community toilet schemes. The London Borough of Richmond-upon-Thames' community toilet scheme had seventy participants pre-pandemic with an annual budget of £66,000. However, they spent £250,000 in the summer of 2020 on temporary toilets in three parks to meet the footfall and demand.[31] Equally, reports of open urination and defecation made headlines that included break-ins to use toilets, as well as evidence of toileting found in private gardens, bus stops and cemeteries.[32]

The newspaper *The i* reported that the lack of toilets were hampering the government's attempts to 'bolster the free-falling economy'.[33] Frances Newton in the *Tribune*[34] noted that whilst politics has traditionally focused on concerns around the toileting aspects of public toilets, and what exposed bodies might get up to in private spaces, it is the 'public' part that is in real danger, with public toilets being closed down or privatized. There is no estimate on the cost to the councils of open defecation, discarded nappies and underwear that littered parks, countryside and beaches during this period, or on the number of toilets that closed during lockdown and remain closed. With a level of foresight, the RSPH's report[35] stated in 2018 that the lack of public toilets 'is a threat to health, mobility and equality'. The pandemic and resulting lockdowns brought into sharp relief how important toilet provision is for public health, especially handwashing. This is an important shift for the perception of public toilets from public service to public health facilitator. For design, this opens up opportunities to think creatively about how public toilet provision might be met from the wider standpoint of public health, especially for the predicted one in four chances of a future pandemic in the next decade.[36]

Revisiting the experience of the Covid-19 pandemic reminds us how essential public toilets are for so many aspects of public life. Being able to use a toilet when away from home is one aspect of our public infrastructure on which all of us rely. Yet the pandemic experience of not being able to use a toilet is, for some, their post-pandemic experience too. If a public toilet is not designed to meet someone's needs, it is not one that they can use. If they cannot use the toilets around them, this limits many aspects of their life. Public toilets influence our social, cultural, active and working lives. They provide space to check in on our physical and mental health. The Victorians introduced the modern public toilet as a part of public health, something that the pandemic reinforced. Without public toilets, both our streets and our hands will be less clean. We cannot emphasize enough how the value of public toilets extends far, far beyond the cleaning costs of a public wee.

In the first half of this book, we looked at the recent history of inclusive design in public toilets, and how we approach inclusive design today. Now we have made the case for why public toilets matter: because everybody goes. In the second half, we will cover each aspect of toilet design in turn, from the point of needing the toilet, to finding, entering, using the loo and leaving the facility how we would wish to find it. We also look at managing, cleaning and maintaining toilets. We will do this by using examples from our research and the world around us.

Let us begin our journey, with the first step of designing inclusive public toilets: knowing where and how to find them.

# Notes

**1**   Bladder & Bowel Community (2024), 'Urinary frequency – How often should you pee?' Available online: https://www.bladderandbowel.org/bladder/bladder-conditions-and-symptoms/frequency/ (accessed 10 January 2024).

2. NHS, 'About furosemide', 21 February 2022. Available online: https://www.nhs.uk/medicines/furosemide/about-furosemide/ (accessed 10 January 2024).
3. Bladder & Bowel Community (2024), 'Stress urinary incontinence (SUI)'. Available online: https://www.bladderandbowel.org/bladder/bladder-conditions-and-symptoms/stress-urinary-incontinence/ (accessed 10 January 2024).
4. Prostate Cancer UK (2022), *Urinary problems after prostate cancer treatment* [pdf]. Available online: https://shop.prostatecanceruk.org/pdf/publication/urinary_problems-ifm.pdf (accessed 10 January 2024).
5. Bupa (2023), 'Irritable Bowel Syndrome (IBS)'. Available online: https://www.bupa.co.uk/health-information/digestive-gut-health/irritable-bowel-syndrome (accessed 10 January 2024).
6. Bupa (2021), 'Crohn's disease'. Available online: https://www.bupa.co.uk/health-information/digestive-gut-health/crohns-disease (accessed 10 January 2024); Bupa (2021), 'Ulcerative colitis'. Available online: https://www.bupa.co.uk/health-information/digestive-gut-health/ulcerative-colitis (accessed 10 January 2024).
7. Bupa, 'Crohn's disease'.
   NHS (2021), 'Overview: Bowel incontinence'. Available online: https://www.nhs.uk/conditions/bowel-incontinence/ (accessed 10 January 2024).
8. Bladder & Bowel Community (2024), 'Stoma care'. Available online: https://www.bladderandbowel.org/bowel/stoma/ (accessed 10 January 2024).
9. M. Chavez-MacGregor, C. H. C. van Gils, Y. T. van der Schouw, E. Monninkhof, P. A. van Noord and P. H. Peeters, 'Lifetime cumulative number of menstrual cycles and serum sex hormone levels in postmenopausal women', *Breast Cancer Research and Treatment* 108(1) (2008): 101–12.
10. S. Kale, 'The rise of period pants: Are they the answer to menstrual landfill – and women's prayers?' *The Guardian*, 1 September 2021. Available online: https://www.theguardian.com/society/2021/sep/01/the-rise-of-period-pants-are-they-the-answer-to-menstrual-landfill-and-womens-prayers (accessed 10 January 2024).
11. British Standards Institute, *PAS 6463: Design for the mind – Neurodiversity and the Built Environment – guide*.
12. A. Ribas Goody, 'Living archives', in *Matrix Open: Feminist Architecture Archive*, 2021. Available online: https://web.archive.org/web/20231210235140/http://www.matrixfeministarchitecturearchive.co.uk/explore/living-archives/ (accessed 20 June 2024).
13. Royal Society for Public Health, *Taking the P\*\*\*: The Decline of the Great British Public Toilet*.
14. Ibid., 3.
15. Help the Aged (2008), 'Memorandum by Help the Aged', *The Communities and Local Government Provision of Public Toilets Inquiry*. Available online: https://publications.parliament.uk/pa/cm200708/cmselect/cmcomloc/memo/public/ucm1302.htm (accessed 10 January 2024).

16. AgeUK London (2022), *Public toilets in London: The views of older Londoners* [pdf]. Available online: https://www.ageuk.org.uk/bp-assets/globalassets/london/campaigns/out-and-about/ageuk_london_loos_final.pdf (accessed 10 January 2024).
17. Greater London Authority (2023), 'Designing London's recovery: Improving public toilets', *Talk London*. Available online: https://www.london.gov.uk/talk-london/topics/recovery-covid-19/designing-londons-recovery/surveys/938# (accessed 10 January 2024).
18. Ministry of Housing, Communities and Local Government (2020), *Open doors pilot programme: Evaluation report* [pdf]. Available online: https://assets.publishing.service.gov.uk/media/5fb65741e90e0720929a03ce/Open_Doors_Evaluation_Report.pdf (accessed 10 January 2024).
19. Royal Society for Public Health, *Taking the P\*\*\**.
20. World Health Organization (2007), *Global age-friendly cities: A guide* [pdf]. Available online: https://iris.who.int/bitstream/handle/10665/43755/9789241547307_eng.pdf?sequence=1 (accessed 10 January 2024).
21. R. L. Mackett, 'Mental health and travel behaviour', *Journal of Transport & Health* 22. (2021).
22. NHS (2023), 'Urinary incontinence'. Available online: https://www.nhs.uk/conditions/urinary-incontinence/ (accessed 10 January 2024).
23. Ministry of Housing, Communities and Local Government (2020), 'Further businesses and premises to close: Guidance'. Available online: https://web.archive.org/web/20200325165536/https://www.gov.uk/government/publications/further-businesses-and-premises-to-close/further-businesses-and-premises-to-close-guidance (accessed 23 January 2024).
24. J. Bichard and G. Ramster, 'A mighty inconvenience: How covid-19 tested a nation's continence', *Built Environment* 47(3) (2021): 402–16.
25. S. Wynn-Davis, 'Hastings key worker asks for publicly accessible toilets to be reopened', *Hastings Observer*, 28 April 2020. Available online: https://www.sussexexpress.co.uk/news/politics/hastings-key-worker-asks-for-publicly-accessible-toilets-to-be-reopened-2552845 (accessed 23 January 2024).
26. Bichard and Ramster, 'A mighty inconvenience'.
27. Ibid.
28. HM Government (2020), *COVID-19 Secure: Safer Public Places – Urban Centres and Green Spaces* [pdf]. Available online: https://assets.publishing.service.gov.uk/media/5fa31272d3bf7f03acd139fc/201102_PDF_ready_CO_updates_Guidance_Safer_Public_Places_During_Covid_v7.7.pdf (accessed 12 December 2023).
29. Ministry of Housing, Communities and Local Government, Simon Clarke MP and Department of Environment and Rural Affairs, Rebecca Pow MP, *Public Access to Tips and Toilets* [pdf], 28 June 2020. Available online: https://assets.publishing.service.gov.uk/media/5f803d5e8fa8f51e81ae0084/Joint_letter_Simon_Clarke_MP_and_Rebecca_Pow_MP.pdf (accessed 12 December 2023).

**30** UK Parliament (2020), 'Public Lavatories: Coronavirus'. Available online: https://questions-statements.parliament.uk/written-questions/detail/2020-07-07/70519 (accessed 12 December 2023).

**31** London Assembly Health Committee, *Transcript of Agenda Item 7 – Access to Public Toilets in London*, 14 September 2021. Available online: https://www.london.gov.uk/about-us/londonassembly/meetings/documents/s92736/Minutes%20Appendix%201%20Transcript%20Health%20Committee%20September%202021.pdf (accessed 20 January 2023).

**32** Bichard and Ramster, 'A mighty inconvenience'.

**33** C. Beanland, 'Coronavirus: Lack of public toilets in lockdown and social distancing will change the way we use loos', *The i*, 19 May 2020. Available online: https://inews.co.uk/news/coronavirus-lockdown-public-toilets-429370 (accessed 8 June 2024).

**34** F. Newton, 'Let the people piss', *Tribune*, 26 April 2021. Available online: https://tribunemag.co.uk/2021/04/let-the-people-piss (accessed 20 December 2023).

**35** Royal Society for Public Health, *Taking the P\*\*\**.

**36** B. Riley-Smith and N. Gutteridge, 'One in four chance of a "catastrophic" pandemic in five years', *The Telegraph*, 3 August 2023. Available online: https://www.telegraph.co.uk/politics/2023/08/03/national-risk-register-danger-of-pandemic-in-five-years/ (accessed 12 December 2023).
R. Bech Hansen, 'The West should be on war footing for the next pandemic', *The Telegraph*, 22 May 2024. Available online: https://www.telegraph.co.uk/global-health/science-and-disease/defence-against-next-pandemic-needs-more-than-global-treaty/ (accessed 8 June 2024).

# 5   The journey

**Publicly accessible toilets** allow us 'to go' when away from home. So where are we going? Having toilets at destinations, en route and as part of a wider network will open our choices of where we can go, how we get there and how much time we can spend there.

Once we have toilets in the right places, next we need to know about them. Maps, leaflets and online information can reassure us in advance that our needs will be met. Once on our journey, we will need help finding the toilet, through clear signs that tell us enough about what is available to know that the detour will be worth the effort.

## Where do we need toilets?

The simplest journey we could be making is from A to B. This is even simpler if it is a familiar journey, where we know we will not need a toilet en route and we know toilets are available at our destination for however long we stay. If any of these things change, other toilets will come into play.

### *Large destinations*

A destination that has toilets will attract more people, for longer than one that does not. Eventually, we all need the loo. Approved Document M[1] specifies that a Changing Places toilet is provided in the largest publicly accessible spaces including assembly, recreation and entertainment buildings over a certain capacity; large shopping centres; large retail premises and leisure buildings; hospitals and primary care centres; and crematoria and cemeteries. Larger transport hubs can support transiting passengers, those waiting or using hospitality or retail venues, and the wider local area (Figure 5.1). In the capital, Policy S6 of the London Plan[2] encourages public toilets in all large developments open to the public. These should also include gender-neutral and Changing Places provision.

**Figure 5.1** Publicly accessible toilets at a major train station. These toilets include accessible, baby-changing and Changing Places facilities.

## Smaller destinations

Public toilets in major destinations seems like a no brainer, though in some places like beaches and public parks (Figure 5.2), it is not guaranteed. When we think about smaller destinations, our confidence around whether there will be a toilet for public use diminishes. Shopping parades and arcades, retail parks, children's playgrounds, recreation fields, markets or cemeteries may not have provision. Whilst national supermarket chains often have customer toilets, their 'local' or 'express' outlets are much less likely to. Service stations have toilets, but do petrol stations? Sometimes. In short, major destinations such a city centres, tourist attractions and big shopping centres can be expected to have publicly accessible toilets but with minor destinations it is much more hit or miss.

> The out-of-town shopping centre is sterile and not a great shopping experience, but if you have a kid it is easier and makes you suddenly go less into town.
> **PARENT**

**Figure 5.2** Well-signposted public toilets in a city park. Most parks should have toilets to help people spend longer outdoors.

## *Eat in or take away?*

Even customer-only toilets are not as predictable as we would like. Cafes must have a customer toilet as a planning condition, but the point at which this applies is debatable and has been challenged. In 2011, two outlets of Greggs in Kingston-upon-Hull were told they needed to have a toilet as they sold food to eat-in.[3] The dispute was between the local authority where the branches were located which tried to enforce a customer toilet, and Greggs' 'home' local authority responsible for overseeing their health and safety approach, which had already said they did not need them. In 2015 the Department for Business, Skills and Innovation supported the home local authority, saying that Greggs was predominately for takeaway, 'a sandwich shop that happens to provide some seats',[4] only for the High Court, in 2016, to overrule in favour of the branch local authority.[5] This was then appealed by Greggs before eventually being dropped in 2017.[6] The debate centred on the number of seats provided, whether takeaway or eat-in was the establishment's primary customer base, and whether the branch local authority should have followed the home authority's interpretation of the law.[7]

With the proliferation of coffee shops and sandwich shops over the last twenty years, this is an important and ongoing point, where clarity could lead to vastly more toilets for people to access when away from home. Instead, with the dwindling consistency over whether we can expect to find a toilet at many destinations even for customers, our confidence ebbs away.

## Trip-chaining

Not all journeys go from A to B. Rather than going from home to work and back again five days a week, many people have other responsibilities or errands to run. We may go from home to a place of study then on to another part of town. We may visit a supermarket, pick up a prescription, visit a relative, go to an appointment or to play sports, all on a circular route. We may go out to meet a friend after enjoying a hobby or collect the kids from the nursery on our way home from work before going onwards to the playground.

Multi-destination trips like this are known as 'trip-chaining'. This type of travel is done more often by women, who are more likely to be the primary carers for children and older adults, and more likely to be users of public transport.[8] Trip-chaining increases the time spent 'in public' and the likelihood of needing to find a toilet when out, particularly where the stop-offs are not a private home or workplace. To assist with this, toilets for public use should be provided in predictable locations to support us in our day-to-day lives: bus station, supermarket, high street, park, doctor's surgery.

## Transportation

When making a journey, what if we need a toilet break en route? The journey may be too long, unpredictable or subject to delays. Travelling with others will also increase the likelihood that someone will need 'a rest stop'. By car or bike, we can make a diversion to somewhere we expect to find a loo. By public transport, we are at the mercy of the network's infrastructure and timetable. Needing to change buses and having to do so at a place where there are no toilets is an unnecessary stress and may limit or remove someone's ability to make that journey.

Any transport hub where a lot of passengers are interchanging between lines or from one type of transport to another needs toilets, especially if, as in the case of buses or regional train services, there are not toilets on board (Figure 5.3). This includes train, ferry, bus and coach stations. When on board, information about which stops have toilets would help us to plan or deal with emergencies.

**Figure 5.3** Regional Thameslink train service overhead display. This informs passengers where toilets are, what types are where and whether they are vacant.

## Trains and tubes

The extent of the UK's rail network and the strength of its branding make train stations a recognizable feature and the gateway through which many people arrive in a town or city. They are a place to sit, stay dry and keep warm. They often have (or had) common features like pay phones and cash machines. Toilets form part of the necessities that we come to expect at train stations.

> Transport terminals are generally good, but my local station doesn't have one [a toilet].
>
> **OLDER PERSON**

Access improvements have been made to train stations through an increase in toilets for wheelchair users along with ramp and lift access. The only backwards step for access has been the introduction of gate lines, introducing a barrier so only paying passengers can reach the platform. If stations have a toilet, it could be either in the ticket office or on the platform-side, depending on the station design. By limiting who can access different parts of the station, we have also limited who can access the toilet. The gate line has turned a platform-side toilet from one that was publicly accessible into a customer-only facility (Figure 5.4).

This access could be made better use of by passengers already on board but without a toilet. In London, some tube lines including the Elizabeth Line have a journey time of over an hour from end to end. With frequent services, it would be useful for route maps to show at which station a passenger can hop off, use the toilet on the platform-side and hop back on, without needing to exit the station and be charged for separate journeys.

Back in the ticket office, anyone collecting or dropping off a passenger or just in the local area must seek a gatekeeper (in the most literal sense) and ask for access to platform-side facilities, running the risk that they will be denied. In 2022, Transport for London (TfL) said that people visiting one of their stations could ask at the gate line to use platform-side toilets without needing to be a passenger, but access would be at the discretion of TfL staff. Staff would receive training to 'understand what the circumstances are and to make an appropriate judgement'.[9] Whilst this human presence could help reduce ensuing problems like fare-dodging, it puts in place a level of 'gatekeeping' for platform toilets that

**Figure 5.4** Sign informing passengers within a London Underground station that toilets are provided, in the ticket hall.

does not exist for ticket office loos. On the other hand, this human interaction might build relationships between local people and station staff and further justifies effective access and inclusion training.

In other city and regional transport networks different approaches will apply. We received an email from someone denied access to the locked accessible toilet at their local train station by the ticket office staff member. This was reinforced with a sign that read 'toilet facilities are only for customers with a disability'. They learnt that the station no longer had toilets for non-disabled people due to vandalism and drug use. It is a challenging balance to strike and better to have toilets that need overseeing than no toilet at all, but the intention of the staff members should be to reduce the anonymity and opportunism of anyone intent in antisocial non-toileting behaviour rather than to make judgements over who looks most in need of the loo.

## Within a network

We now know where people expect to find toilets. How do these toilets relate to each other and how do we find the gaps in both the geographic area and the time of day? In a village, town or city, a good distribution of toilets will help people to visit and explore, whilst keeping the streets clean. Providing toilets at the gateways to an area (e.g. transport hubs, car parks and bike parking) (Figure 5.5), the meeting points within it (e.g. town square) (Figure 5.6), and its popular destinations (high street, seafront, city park) (Figure 5.7) will create a reliable network of toilets.

Establishing and sustaining this network is not easy. The publicly accessible toilets might consist of the ones at the bus station, the library, the car park and a council-owned block. This patchwork of provision shifts when one business shuts or a plot of land is redeveloped. It must also meet temporary or seasonal demand: markets, public squares, festivals and events. It is the council's role to oversee this and to find both the gaps and a way to fill them. Does the toilet provision match up with who the local area serves and attracts, and how it wishes to grow? It might seem at first glance that there is a good spread of toilets, but what if only one set is accessible? Are they well distributed or are they all in the same corner of town? Is there anything open after 6:00 pm? Perhaps there are several small sets of toilets, but seasonal tourism leaves these overwhelmed, or they are closed for residents in the winter months. In 2023, a district council in East Sussex decided to trial closing many of their public toilets across several towns during the winter.[10] Residents launched a petition and one smaller town council was able to reopen some of the toilets.[11] How can councils take a more holistic approach,

**Figure 5.5** Disabled parking bays outside a toilet block in a car park, Newborough Forest, Anglesey. Credit: Realimage/Alamy Stock Photo.

**Figure 5.6** Public toilets in Matlock, Derbyshire. These serve the park and are adjacent to the retail centre. Credit: NorthScape/Alamy Stock Photo.

**Figure 5.7** Public toilets on the seafront promenade, Clacton-on-Sea, Essex.

factoring in all publicly accessible toilets rather than just those that they maintain? What we need is a plan, or more specifically, a 'strategy'.

## A toilet strategy

Toilet Strategies have been statutory for Welsh councils since 2017,[12] whilst councils in other parts of the UK might choose to develop one. The legislation focuses on providing facilities for the transport network including on active travel routes and at destinations for 'cultural, sporting, historic, popular or national interest'.[13]

In producing a toilet strategy, the local council evaluates what exists and where more provision is needed. It will first bring together information from different council departments: transport and streets, community facilities, parks and cemeteries, libraries, leisure centres and other public-facing buildings (Figure 5.8); each of which might have toilets but who run them as peripheral aspects of their primary function. Because of this, it is common for councils to be unaware of the toilets they have in their own portfolio.

**Figure 5.8** Public toilets within a town hall complex. These are next to new play fountains and serve a café, in North East London.

An effective toilet strategy will not stop here. It should be created from the public's perspective, by including all publicly accessible toilets to build a true representation of available toilets when away from home. Each can be assessed on how it meets different needs, including medical conditions, different physical abilities, gender, age (including babies and children), neurodiversity and faith.

Significant differences will highlight how some people's toilet networks are vastly reduced compared to others, creating no-go areas and giving an inequitable experience of public life.

By creating a strategy, we also increase the visibility of public toilets within the council. Both a council officer and council member should recognize toilets as within their responsibility. This simple act of identifying toilets as a coordinated public service and raising its profile within the council will improve toilet provision over time. Guidance from the Welsh government also makes the link that publicly funded premises should have publicly accessible toilets. This recommends writing the provision of publicly accessible toilets into the planning conditions of buildings that are (partly or wholly) publicly funded and making the management of these an aspect of the leasing of public buildings.[14] Toilets can be written into local plans, so when a new development, redevelopment or regeneration project is proposed, toilets are written in at an inclusive urban design level.

When a building with a publicly accessible toilet closes, the impact of losing its toilets must be recognized. In 2017, a council on the south coast voted to close a set of public toilets, with one reason given being the availability of publicly accessible toilets in a nearby department store. In 2021, the department store closed. A strategy would flag the shortfall and make the case for funding to provide temporary or alternative facilities. If vacant premises are redeveloped, or a development site becomes available, the requirement can be part of the planning conditions. This could also have implications for how buildings – particularly those that receive public funding – are designed. By providing toilets in publicly accessible parts of a building, we are creating more welcoming architecture for visitors, those making deliveries and the public at large whilst extending the network of critical infrastructure through our healthcare, education, leisure and cultural settings, and beyond.

## Finding toilets

Finding a toilet starts at home. Many people need to know that a toilet will be available before they can make a trip out of their house. Planning journeys around suitable toilets becomes second nature, whereas the anxiety from not being certain of finding a toilet can mean not going to new places.

Simply knowing a toilet exists is not always enough information. Some people need to spend a considerable amount of time enquiring about accessible toilet facilities before they leave home. Even then, participants found that a toilet advertised as 'accessible' might be too small for their wheelchair or cannot accommodate a caregiver or assistant.

When visiting new places, finding information in advance can mean looking online or in maps or guidebooks. It can mean confining ourselves to the types of places certain to have a toilet, such as a theme park rather than the seaside, or scheduling-in detours to places like service stations. It can also mean asking friends or family to visit beforehand to make sure the toilets meet our needs, including whether it is currently in a good state of maintenance and cleanliness. It might also influence our choice of transport, such as driving instead of taking the bus, to make detours easier. So how can we make toilet information more inclusive? How do we help people to find the information, and what do we include?

## Online information

To plan journeys, we expect to be able to type 'public toilet near me' into Google and have a complete map of toilets we can access. However, just as toilets do not always exist where we expect to find them, toilet data is also missing from leading online maps and applications.

This is partly because of the fractured way in which toilets are provided. There are more than 400 councils responsible for public toilets, with the number growing as more town and parish councils take over management. If we consider all publicly accessible toilets then the number grows to thousands of different organizations each holding their own toilets' information. An online search for a public toilet in a certain area will often lead to the local council webpage. Currently these vary significantly in terms of what is included: some have maps with details about what is provided and opening times; others simply state that they have toilets. There are also councils who do not publish information about their toilets online. What does that tell the visitor? Are there no public toilets or is the council just keeping them a secret?

> I went into the info centre and said, 'Can you tell me where your loos are, there are no signs', and she said 'No, we don't put up signs. We don't want people to use the loo', and I said, 'Well why not?' She said, 'Well we only have one and we don't want it overwhelmed with people.'
> 
> **VISITOR TO A SOUTH LONDON TOURIST AREA**

Once out and about, council webpages are not the best place to look for toilet details, though it is helpful for residents who wish to report a problem. Most visitors will not know which council area they are in, so knowing that we have made the right online search is hit or miss. In London, for example, there are thirty-three local authorities, with major tourist attractions spread across the central half a dozen. In rural England, the multiple tiers of local authority mean that we must first know whether the county, district or parish council maintain the toilets. These webpages typically only capture council-maintained public toilets with limited information about each facility, though the best council webpages include both public toilets and toilets in public buildings.

As discussed in Chapter 2, The Toilet Map addresses this problem (Figure 5.9).[15] The current database of over 14,000 publicly accessible toilets in the UK far exceeds figures for public toilets alone.[16]

The Toilet Map project was inspired by the National Public Toilet Map of Australia. This was a government project funded by the Department of Health and Care, as part of a national continence programme.[17] Launched in 2001, their map of publicly accessible toilets shows what is achievable, with more than 23,000 entries from thousands of providers.[18]

These websites include details about each toilet to help people decide if it will meet their needs. Just the name of the toilet can tell people a lot about the type of facility they will find (e.g. Lower Village public toilet, West End urinal, Townsville train station). Other data fields on The Toilet Map include whether there is an accessible toilet, a gender-neutral standard toilet or baby-changing facilities, and the opening hours. With more data, specifically the means to collect and enter it, fields could be added to help those with other needs, such as information on steps, parking, bins or images of the facilities.

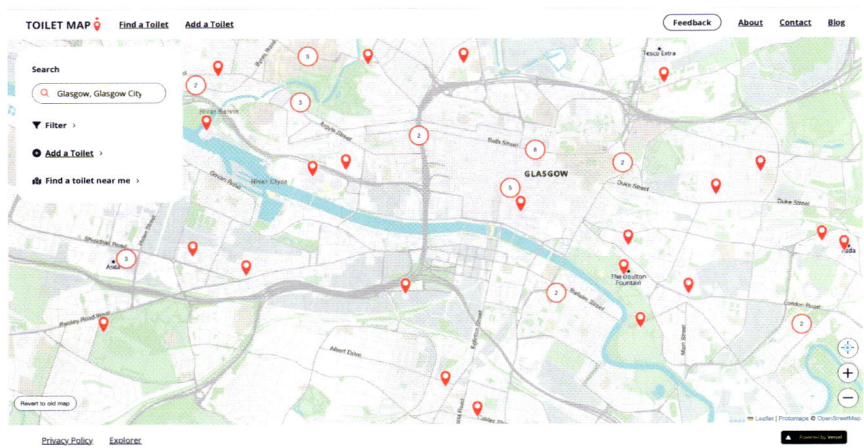

**Figure 5.9** The Toilet Map, centred on Glasgow. Credit: Public Convenience Ltd.

I've suffered from Crohn's Disease for the last five and a half years, so [The Toilet Map] certainly makes visiting new places a heck of a lot less daunting. It's especially important as public toilets are being closed left, right and centre, and many businesses are not always particularly welcoming to those in my situation.

**FEEDBACK SENT TO THE TOILET MAP**

Like with the National Toilet Map of Australia, the data from The Toilet Map is available under open licence meaning it is free to reuse in other applications, such as transport planning apps or sat-nav devices. This will help people to find toilets through methods they are already using and familiar with.

Ordnance Survey maps the location of public toilets in its Points of Interest dataset but is perhaps less likely to have information about each one, such as opening times. The National Rail Access Map includes toilets across UK train stations.[19] This was produced by Network Rail and the train operating companies, in collaboration with the Department for Transport. The Changing Places consortium has mapped all Changing Places facilities in the UK, and at time of writing celebrated their 2000th entry.[20] Like the National Toilet Map of Australia, these also include photos of each facility. Rather than a growing list of tick boxes and measurements, an image can give most people an instant idea of whether the access and arrangement of a toilet will meet their personal needs.

## *Looking for toilets*

Away from our screens, we look for toilets in the world around us. What cues do people look for when looking for the toilet?

Many of us check for destinations where we know there will be a toilet: a service station, a shopping centre, a fast-food restaurant. In both VivaCity and TACT3 research projects, most participants said they would find a toilet in this way when in an unfamiliar area. This was both due to a preference for privately run toilets and an assumption that there would not be any public toilets. The destination signs outside these places could advertise a toilet, particularly when there is inconsistency in whether toilets will be found. Large retail units (including supermarkets), train, bus and tube stations do not always have toilets. The sign at the entrance to the car park, station or at the supermarket door could include toilets in the list of facilities available, alongside things like a café or cash machine (Figure 5.10).

**Figure 5.10** Destination sign at a car park listing the available facilities. Alongside toilets, this sign lists beach facilities, café and promenade access. Kent.

## Maps and directional signs

Schemes such as Legible London or Bristol's Legible City position maps on totem signs which include public toilets and indicates the walking time to a loo. It is also important to show toilets on local area maps in places like coastal areas, open spaces and parks (Figure 5.11). There might be few, if any, businesses around that provide alternatives, and it helps people to plan their routes.

Fingerpost signs came in for public criticism in our research, when poorly sited or not maintained. Some participants found that 'the tops of poles get swung in the wrong direction'. Others who used wheelchairs found that fingerpost signs were far too high to read. Directional signs should be low and legible enough to be read by all, with clear colour contrast and without obstructing accessible routes (Figure 5.12).

Directional signs have another important function: to confirm you are still going the right way. Making sure a directional sign is regularly monitored, up-to-date

**Figure 5.11** Hastings local map of toilets. This shows the facilities, the distance in metres and how toilets are spread across this coastal town.

**Figure 5.12** A temporary low-level directional sign. This can be viewed by all users, and is bold enough to be spotted from a distance, signposting to temporary public toilets at Kings Cross, London.

and not missing along key routes from the entry point to the destination is vital to not abandon someone in a toilet desert. These are one of the first aspects of design that people will meet when interacting with the public service of toilet provision, and first impressions count.

> Often you see a sign and your spirits will be raised and then you can't find it.
> **YOUNG ADULT**

## What information do we include?

Different information becomes useful at different points in the journey. Once out in the world, it is difficult for maps and signs to show all the details that can be included online. The most obvious categories of information to show are the symbols for standard toilets, accessible toilets, Changing Places toilets and baby-changing facilities, and the distance or walking time. As with online information, the name of the toilet (e.g. High Street Public Toilet, The Big Supermarket, On-street Superloo) can tell the visitor a lot about what they expect to find (Figure 5.13). Finding room for opening hours will save a wasted journey.

> Generally, you don't see the disabled symbol associated with toilet signs, just signs for toilets and then you're hoping there's a disabled loo. I've followed signs for toilets and when you get there you can't use them.
> **WHEELCHAIR USER**

## Community toilet signs

**Community Toilet Schemes** can have between ten and a hundred participants. Each year, businesses might join or leave the scheme, or close their doors. Providing fingerposts or maps for this more volatile information can become more expensive. Councils have taken different approaches. Some have directional signs, some have printed maps at prominent locations such as local area information boards (Figure 5.14), and others share the information as a leaflet available to residents and tourists. Could there be another solution? Directional signage needs to be both hard-wearing and easy to update, whilst making use of existing street furniture.[21] This could also match each scheme's destination signs, which is consistently a window sticker in the shopfront of the business, though even this can be a challenge to enforce.

**Figure 5.13** Fingerpost sign specifically for toilets. Toilets include those on high streets, in parks and at the town hall and library. Each arm gives the types of toilet, the destination and the walking distance in metres. Kensington, London.

**Figure 5.14** Map of community toilets. This has venues, types of toilets and opening hours listed on the left, and doubles as a local area map for Walthamstow, North East London.

If (the business provider) has got a big poster for 'Hen's Nights' then next to it a Community Toilet Scheme sticker, they think it doesn't really go.
**COUNCIL OFFICER RESPONSIBLE FOR COMMUNITY TOILET SCHEME**

One challenge with community toilet schemes is that every scheme has its own branding, making it difficult for people, particularly non-residents, to know what to look for or even realize a scheme exists. A national toilet logo was developed as part of the guidance that accompanied the Public Health Act (Wales) 2017 to bring consistency across the country (Figure 5.15).[22] A similar approach could be implemented in the rest of the UK, or across metropolitan regions or counties.

**Figure 5.15** The Welsh national toilet logo. Crown copyright, image used by permission of the Welsh government.

## Signs at the door

Finally, we arrive at the toilet facility. Our journey to the toilet is almost over. What information is there left to convey?

We need to know which door to access. Door signs need to be clear and recognizable, especially for people with cognitive impairments and some neurodiverse people. Designs which play with the design of the male and female pictograms, use W and M or male and female animals can cause a lot of confusion and mistakes when this is at the expense of clear communication. Participants were embarrassed when they used the wrong facility, with one saying she was 'ashamed to say I walked into a Gents by mistake' after not correctly discerning the signs and blaming herself for being 'in a fluster … it's the most embarrassing thing I have ever done'. Another mentioned the signs being confusing particularly with reduced vision: 'it could get worse if my vision deteriorated'. When children are visiting the toilets by themselves, their confidence in their ability to be independent is undermined if they cannot understand which toilet to use.

Whilst we widely understand the standard male, female and disabled person pictograms[23] to indicate toilets, they could still be reconsidered. The first two rely on cultural stereotypes (and as my son said, 'why has the woman only got one leg?', which I now notice in many female pictograms yet is quite easy to avoid (Figure 5.16)). They also reinforce a binary approach to gender, not representing anyone who may not fit these definitions but who still needs to access a set of loos. More recently, a pictogram of a wheelchair user in a more active position

**Figure 5.16** Women's toilet symbol, on the toilet roof at the London Stadium (formerly the Olympic Stadium). This is visible from the top of the staircase on exiting the seating area, providing easy orientation.

**Figure 5.17** Active symbol for wheelchair-user/accessible toilet. This one also includes baby-changing facilities.

has been used to symbolize the **accessible toilet** (Figure 5.17). This active symbol suggests a more independent person, rather than portraying a disabled person as passive, disadvantaged or in need of help.

The depiction of the accessible toilet with a pictogram of a person using a wheelchair has had a role in creating conflict around who this toilet is for. Whilst the wheelchair-accessible unisex toilet[24] is an essential facility for people who cannot get about without their wheelchair, or who need it with them within the cubicle, the facility was also designed for other disabled people whose physical needs are not met by the standard toilet. The hand basin within reach of the toilet, a shelf, a full-size mirror, larger levers on the flush, tap and door lock are all features that help people who are disabled in other ways. Crohn's and Colitis UK's campaign 'Not Every Disability Is Visible'[25] has led to many providers adding this phrase on the door sign of the accessible toilet as a helpful reminder. Another campaign, Grace's Sign,[26] adds a heart to the standing pictograms, as seen at V&A Dundee. These recent efforts remind people that not everyone using the accessible toilet has a visible need and give confidence and legitimacy to people who know they do not look like the symbol of a wheelchair user (Figure 5.18).

**Figure 5.18** Grace's Sign toilets at V&A Dundee. Credit: Chris Keatch and V&A Dundee.

By using people to depict toilets, we have also taken the symbol of a standing man, standing woman and non-gender-specific wheelchair user out of circulation for other purposes. In other settings, the wheelchair user is shown within a context: a person using a wheelchair next to a ramp or a person in a wheelchair directed to a fire exit. The Changing Places symbol adds context, by creating a symbol that shows the wheelchair user alongside the hoist, changing bench and carer (Figure 5.19). How has a symbol of a wheelchair user alone, along with the standing male and female symbols, come to signify the toilet?

## Objects not people

The Old Vic Theatre in London revamped their men's and women's toilets to increase the number of toilets available for their audience. As part of this refit, they relabelled the toilets by using 'cubicles' and 'cubicles with urinals' to move away from a binary approach to gender. By describing facilities instead of people, they were not intending to create all-gender access, as they had provided 'gender-neutral' toilets elsewhere.[27] The instruction they provide online in their accessibility information is 'please choose the loo that feels most appropriate to you'.[28]

This is an interesting experimental design, though to be effective will depend on other factors. Will people know all the types of facilities when looking for the toilet? Are both sets next to each other? To understand what the signs mean, both options need to be apparent; 'toilets with cubicles' can sound like all-gender provision

**Figure 5.19** The Changing Places toilet sign. This symbol (centre) shows the facilities of the hoist and changing bench. Victoria Station, London.

when seen on its own. This could also fill the toilets with cubicles up to capacity. Whilst those comfortable in spaces with urinals can be directed elsewhere, might those who are not be left with a busier facility? Only by observing how these toilets are used can we understand their effectiveness, and this should be considered alongside wider evaluation on the change such as the impact on inclusivity and accessibility. For new developments and refurbishments, Building Regulations *Approved Document T* (or 'Part T') (2024) may apply. This guidance suggests male and female symbols are used to make access in future designs like this clearer.[29]

We encounter all-gender, unisex or **gender-neutral toilets** every day, on trains, aeroplanes and in many coffee shop chains. These facilities are essentially for everyone. The standard symbol for this toilet shows male and female pictograms side by side, sticking with the binary approach to gender. This is also the approach recommended in Part T for gender-neutral universal toilets. Recent alternatives have tried to indicate a gender-neutral provision with new pictograms; where one half is wearing a skirt, or using alternative versions of the less familiar male and female symbols that have an arrow or cross off a circle. This adds complexity, non-standardization and confusion, including for some neurodiverse people and those with neurodegenerative conditions.[30]

Sometimes the intention behind alternative symbols is about more than labelling the toilet door. Continuing to use established but adapted symbols of gender to depict new gender-neutral facilities is a way to communicate the perspectives of the organization, to make a point of saying 'this is a trans-inclusive space'. This helps to welcome people who are excluded in other parts of society. Figure 6.4 (see Chapter 6) does this subtly, by using a familiar unisex symbol of male and female pictograms with the friendlier wording 'mixed gender toilets'.

However, as our world becomes more inclusive of gender, and all-gender toilets become more common, why use gender at all, when gender is no longer relevant when determining if it is a space we can access? These are now *non-gendered* toilets. More providers and designers are using a symbol of a toilet either at the entrance to the facility or on the door of the cubicle (Figure 5.20), particularly at cultural and educational institutions (museums, theatres and universities). This can be reinforced with words to help people, including those who are neurodiverse, to interpret new symbols.[31] For this type of facility, the

**Figure 5.20** A toilet symbol for a standard facility. Words can give meaning to new symbols, until familiarity or standardization develops.

depiction of the toilet makes more sense than alluding to redundant references to gender.[32] One popular symbol is designer Sam Killermann's open-source All Gender Restroom sign from 2014,[33] as shown adapted for an ambulant toilet in Figure 5.21.

**Figure 5.21** Ambulant toilet symbol depicted by showing grab rails.

It is a symbol of a toilet rather than male and female pictograms that was chosen for the Welsh national toilet logo (Figure 5.15). It is also recommended for helping those with dementia.[34] This communicates very simply what the door leads to and fits better with other typographical language where the facility is depicted rather than the person accessing it, such as lifts, cash machines or car parks. **Ambulant toilets** can be shown with grab rails either side of the toilet (Figure 5.21), which is an interesting alternative to the term *ambulant* or the depiction of a person with a walking stick. Signs for family toilets should avoid depictions of traditional families since many do not look like this. A toilet symbol might not seem like the most important place for representation, but when families are nearly always depicted in books, TV and society as having a mum and a dad, it becomes another instance where people are positioned outside the norm. Family toilets have an adult toilet, a child-sized toilet and a baby-changing table: easy things to show on a sign.

It is a tricky but exciting challenge for designers to change established symbols for toilets. Signs need to be simple and clear enough to be understandable by everyone, which is helped by familiarity and consistency. Yet our familiar signage represents a time when we were perhaps too embarrassed to use a symbol of a toilet to indicate a toilet, and where men and women adhered to stronger stereotypes, occupying different roles in public space. A more pragmatic, less gender-based approach could lead to clearer signs for everyone.

## Anything else?

What other information is needed? We will need some signs within the toilet, to find our way out again (see Chapter 6). Back at the entrance, we need details of who to contact if there is a problem (see Chapter 10). We should also include the opening hours so that visitors know if it is about to open (Figure 5.22), or about to close (Figure 5.23), or because they hope to revisit later; but also, because it is expected. Where else would we find the opening times for a building, if not at the entrance to the building itself.

Finally, what if the toilet is closed when we arrive, whether temporarily or permanently? Inclusive public toilet provision will not leave us stranded, in desperate need of the loo. We need details of where to find the nearest alternative (Figure 5.24), via a link, QR code or local area map. Each public toilet is part of a

**Figure 5.22** Clear opening hours at the entrance to a public toilet. These city toilets in a business district are open until midnight in the week and 7:00 pm at the weekend.

**Figure 5.23** Opening hours sign on the back of the toilet door. This is an effective way to reach the relevant audience.

**Figure 5.24** Sign listing alternative toilets at a department store. This can help if one set is very busy, or to plan ahead. The accessible toilet symbol also shows this particular facility is right-hand transfer.

network of publicly accessible toilet infrastructure, with facilities open at different times of day, meeting different needs. The more we share this, the more we help people to go, when they need to go.

## Notes

1. Building Regulations, *Approved Document M: Access to and use of buildings. Vol. 2: Buildings other than dwellings*.
2. Greater London Authority (2021), `The London Plan: The Spatial Development Strategy for Greater London'. Available online: https://www.london.gov.uk/programmes-strategies/planning/london-plan/the-london-plan-2021-table-contents (accessed 23 May 2024).
3. L. Foottit, 'Greggs ducks toilet provision following council dispute', *British Baker*, 23 February 2015. Available online: https://bakeryinfo.co.uk/news/greggs-ducks-toilet-provision-following-council-dispute/619849.article (accessed 24 January 2024).
4. Foottit, 'Greggs ducks toilet provision following council dispute'.
5. BBC News, 'Greggs loses takeaway battle in Hull', 18 May 2016. Available online: https://www.bbc.co.uk/news/uk-england-humber-36320384 (accessed 20 January 2024).
6. BBC News, 'Greggs withdraws loo legal challenge', 13 June 2017. Available online: https://www.bbc.co.uk/news/uk-england-humber-40262371 (accessed 24 January 2024).
7. BBC News, 'Greggs withdraws loo legal challenge'.
8. F. Bellmann, L. Ypma and D. Polack, 'Women move differently – what everyone working in mobility should know', *World Economic Forum*, 12 January 2020. Available online: https://www.weforum.org/agenda/2020/01/mobility-in-2020-a-female-perspective/ (accessed 19 June 2024).
9. London Assembly Health Committee, *Transcript of Agenda Item 7 – Access to Public Toilets in London*.
10. C. Fuller, 'Council to close public toilets in cost cutting trial', *BBC News*, 18 October 2023. Available online: https://www.bbc.co.uk/news/articles/crg171rv1d0o (accessed 19 December 2023).
11. E. Crabbe, 'Bexhill: Public toilets closed in cost-cutting trial reopen', *The Argus*, 13 December 2023. Available online: https://www.theargus.co.uk/news/23984007.bexhill-public-toilets-closed-cost-cutting-trial-reopen/ (accessed 19 December 2023).
12. *Public Health (Wales) Act 2017*.
13. Ibid.
14. Welsh Government, *The Provision of Toilets in Wales. Statuary Guidance*.

15  The Toilet Map.
16  The current figure for public toilets in England and Wales (3990) is taken from Hansard (2021) *Non-Domestic Rating (Public Lavatories) Bill. H.L. Vol. 811*, col. 432. Available online: https://hansard.parliament.uk/lords/2021-03-17/debates/90B02AA3-684B-4374-A2D1-22520CBFE582/Non-DomesticRating(PublicLavatories)Bill# (accessed 16 October 2024).
17  The National Public Toilet Map. 'About the Toilet Map' (2024). Available online: https://toiletmap.gov.au/about (accessed 18 January 2024).
18  Department of Health and Ageing, 'Minister puts public toilets on the map', 19 September 2001. Available online: https://archive.ph/20121126224046/http://www.health.gov.au/internet/main/publishing.nsf/Content/health-mediarel-yr2001-bb-bb01080.htm (accessed 18 January 2024).
19  *National Rail Access Map*, (2024). Available online: http://accessmap.nationalrail.co.uk/ (accessed 18 January 2024).
20  Changing Places, '2,000 Changing Places toilets milestone reached in UK', 15 November 2023. Available online: https://www.changing-places.org/news/view/2-000-changing-places-toilets-milestone-reached-in-uk (accessed 19 December 2023).
21  Knight and Bichard, *Publicly Accessible Toilets: An Inclusive Design Guide*.
22  Welsh Government, *The Provision of Toilets in Wales. Statuary Guidance*.
23  The wheelchair figure is currently under review by the Guild of Architectural Ironmongers; Guild of Architectural Ironmongers (no date), 'Replacing the accessibility symbol – a GAI survey'. Available online: https://www.gai.org.uk/GAI/News/News-Items/2023/Replacing-the-accessibility-symbol-a-GAI-survey.aspx (accessed 29 January 2024).
24  Knight and Bichard, *Publicly Accessible Toilets: An Inclusive Design Guide*.
25  Crohn's and Colitis UK (2024), 'Not Every Disability Is Visible'. Available online: https://crohnsandcolitis.org.uk/our-work/campaigns/not-every-disability-is-visible (accessed 18 January 2024).
26  C. Wilson, 'Grace Warnock – A sign to change attitudes', The V&A Blog, 8 August 2018. Available online: https://www.vam.ac.uk/blog/projects/grace-warnock-a-sign-to-change-attitudes (accessed 18 January 2024).
27  The Old Vic, 'Our loos now offer "self-selection" rather than being labelled male or female. This takes a descriptive, rather than prescriptive, approach following advice from surveys conducted with focus groups. When you arrive in the theatre, you will see labels signposting which blocks contain cubicles and which contain urinals. We also have one specifically designed gender neutral loo', Twitter, 2 October 2019. Available online: https://twitter.com/oldvictheatre/status/1179336786537005057?s=20 (accessed 18 January 2024).
28  The Old Vic (2024), 'What to expect at the Old Vic: Loos'. Available online: https://www.oldvictheatre.com/visit/when-you-visit/ (accessed 18 January 2024).

**29** Building Regulations, *Approved Document T: Toilet Accommodation*.
**30** British Standards Institute, *PAS 6463: Design for the mind – Neurodiversity and the Built Environment – guide*.
**31** British Standards Institute, PAS 6463.
**32** Endpoint, 'Exploring the design implications of gender-neutral wayfinding signage', 10 February 2022. Available online: https://www.weareendpoint.com/wayfinding-news-and-views/exploring-the-design-implications-of-gender-neutral-wayfinding-signage (accessed 18 January 2024).
D. Hoskin, 'Toilet Talk: Looking for non-gender-specific toilets?' The V&A Blog, 9 March 2017. Available online: https://www.vam.ac.uk/blog/news/toilet-talk-looking-for-non-gender-specific-toilets (accessed 18 January 2024).
Nazerali, Ramster and Bichard, *Publicly Accessible Toilets after COVID-19*.
**33** S. Killermann (2014), 'All gender restroom sign: AKA my doodle of a toilet that became A Thing'. Available online: https://www.samkillermann.com/work/all-gender-restroom-sign/ (accessed 20 June 2024).
**34** A. Taylor, 'Why public toilets need to be more dementia friendly', Alzheimer's Society, 31 August 2017. Available online: https://www.alzheimers.org.uk/blog/why-public-toilets-be-more-dementia-friendly (accessed 22 January 2024).

# 6 Crossing the threshold

You have found a toilet, you are waiting outside, about to enter, and nothing will stand in your way ... except having nowhere to park, or a door too heavy to open, or the sinking realization the toilet is shut for the night. Once inside, what else might stop us from proceeding? Does the toilet offend our sense of smell, safety or comfort? Here we look at how inclusive design can help more people to take this next step, to cross the threshold.

We will also present the cubicle designs that those who commission public toilets can consider. For larger buildings, a combination of toilet provision would be better suited, to include ambulant, family and accessible provision, with ambulant provision replacing standard toilets for a more inclusive service.

## The toilet's situation

### *A sense of safety*

Arriving at the public toilet there is a question of safety and security that we will mentally go through when deciding whether to use it. Firstly, as we may be partially undressing, we want to sense that we are safe and secure from the street, neither too exposed nor hidden away. Some older self-contained public toilets are built out of the way. This may result in many people avoiding such provision.

> I feel it's important that they are positioned in good places ... you might have to walk ten minutes to get there and might not want to go to that part of town.
> **TEENAGER**

Such personal safety concerns can also be considered in toilets situated in car parks or off main walkways in shopping centres and parks.

> The men's are on the level but the ladies' toilets are down these stairs and it's really, really dark and there are all these hedges ... and these steps. It's really dangerous not only cause it's dark but it's steep.
> **OLDER PERSON WITH CHRONIC HEALTH CONDITION**

For everyone's management of continence, it is important that we are relaxed when using the toilet. So, siting toilet provision in spaces where there is good footfall, level access and good lighting will increase the sense of safety people have when using the facilities.

Such considerations have been important aspects of toilet provision internationally, especially in New Zealand and Japan. In both instances there has been a recognition of the importance of public toilets for visitors as well as residents, and imaginative designs have been put in place that also ensure provision is well situated and easy to identify. Making toilets stand out through architecture can turn them into visitor attractions. In addition, public toilets that are attractively designed may experience less opposition from local neighbours in their proposed sites. Whilst many people are in favour of public toilets, often they do not want to live next door to one.

Part of people's reluctance to have public toilets in their neighbourhoods stems from their association with antisocial behaviour (see Chapter 2). A toilet that is well used will counter this through increased footfall and natural surveillance, reducing opportunities for antisocial behaviour. Will a public toilet's value in society also be enhanced from that of a publicly owned amenity, an easy target for vandals, if we create something curious, interesting, and of community interest and benefit? The following two examples from Japan and New Zealand highlight the opportunities interesting public toilets can bring.

## *The Tokyo Toilet project*

The Tokyo Toilet project created seventeen public toilets in the Shibuya district, initially inspired by the 2020 Olympics, and featured in the 2023 film *Perfect Days* directed by Wim Wenders. Each facility was striking, unique and designed with the help of a respected 'creator' which included international architects and designers. The Hatagaya Toilet (Figure 6.1) was created by Miles Pennington with architectural design by Kotaro Imai laboratory and Kentaro Honma laboratory, University of Tokyo. Titled '… with toilet', it aims to show how a toilet can be a valued centrepiece of a community rather than hidden away. The Hatagaya Toilet also provides shelter, public seating and a wall for projections for film screenings or other events. By bringing value to the local area through a high-quality spatial design, an inclusive facility and a service that is an asset to the community (see Chapter 10), public toilets will be received more positively.

**Figure 6.1** Hatagaya Public Toilet, Tokyo, Miles Pennington/UTokyo DLX Design Lab. Architectural Design: Kotaro Imai Laboratory and Kentaro Honma Laboratory from Institute of Industrial Science at The University of Tokyo. Credit: Satoshi Nagare, Courtesy of Shibuya City.

## *Hundertwasser public toilets, Kawakawa, New Zealand*

The Hundertwasser public toilets (Figure 6.2) have placed the town of Kawakawa on the tourist trail as a major visitor attraction, and according to Knox (2018)[1] 'sparked the toilet transformation movement' inspiring other towns in New Zealand to create their own 'focal point flushers'. Designed by Austrian artist and architect Friedensreich Hundertwasser, the toilets were gifted to Kawakawa. In return the local community volunteered in the construction process. The toilets were built around a living tree that continues to grow through the ceiling into a rooftop garden. The majority of the materials used in the building are recycled and include multi-sized and multi-coloured ceramic tiles, bottles, steel and copper. It is the only structure of Hundertwasser's to be found in the Southern Hemisphere.

## *Stopping at the toilet*

A key consideration when siting a toilet is to think of bicycle, mobility scooter and other vehicle parking. As well as the general public, many delivery drivers, taxi

**Figure 6.2** Public toilets designed and gifted to the town of Kawakawa, New Zealand by Friendensreich Hundertwasser. Credit: Wirestock, Inc/Alamy Stock Photo.

drivers and motorcycle couriers rely on public toilets to be able to stop for a wee, so it's important that parking is close by.

> Cabbies often complain about a lack of toilets but are really objecting to a lack of toilets with parking.
> **CITY COUNCIL OFFICER**

Similarly, cyclists need to stop and use the loo, so safe and secure bicycle parking is important, especially if we are to encourage more people to cycle (Figure 6.3). Our growing cycling delivery economy can be supported by including parking accessible to cargo bikes. Bicycle parking should be in a well-lit and in an accessible area. Thought might also be given to parking and securing mobility scooters near any separate accessible toilets. All facilities should have level access. With no drop-curb access, toilets can be difficult to negotiate and even hazardous for some people.

One way to think of this, especially for toilets in train and bus stations, ferry ports and key roadways, is that public toilets are an essential part of the transport infrastructure. It is unthinkable to not have toilets on our motorways, and yet on large cycle routes and main roads around our towns and cities, there is very little provision.

**Figure 6.3** Public toilet at a cycle park in Gävle, Sweden. Design and construction: Danfo. Credit: Fotograf Stefan Estassy 2019, courtesy of Danfo AB.

## Making an entrance

Doors at the entrance to facilities are difficult for many users, whether young, old, carrying bags, pushing pushchairs or for those using walking frames, sticks, crutches or wheelchairs. When toilets are within larger buildings, there may be multiple doors to navigate, where we first enter a lobby or passageway that leads to all toilets, followed by additional doors to men's, women's or accessible provision. If these are required for fire regulations, they can still be adjusted for access and ease of opening.[2] Opening a solid door can be intimidating when we do not know what to expect on the other side. When doors lead to circulation space off which we find one or more fully enclosed toilets, they can have a glass panel (see Figure 6.4). This has two benefits. Firstly, it tells us that this door marked 'toilet' is not a locked door to a single cubicle, an easy mistake to make. It also allows people to know what to expect in terms of the toilet design before they enter, particularly useful for gender-neutral toilets where designs are new and unfamiliar.

Doors are also a physical barrier due to their need to be opened and closed and therefore touched. A door that can be pushed with our body or elbow in one direction must usually be pulled in the other. This requires dexterity, strength and touching handles. Such dexterity and strength might be difficult for older

**Figure 6.4** Glass panel in external door. As well as the glass, the plural use of 'toilets' and the door's push panel are other design cues that tell us we are not yet at the door to the cubicle.

people, children and those with walking aids and wheelchairs. Since the Covid-19 pandemic, touching so many things in public spaces has become a concern. As with any external doors or doors en route, a consideration for designers would be to assess if internal doors other than the door to the cubicle are necessary.

Thought should also be given to the door colour. Having a contrasting colour from the floor and wall will help everyone, but especially those with visual impairments and those who are neurodiverse.[3]

To reduce barriers further, and remove another surface we must touch, many toilets are now designed with a privacy wall instead of a door. This provides a shield from directly seeing into the toilet space (Figure 6.5) and increases natural ventilation.

## Is it open?

One of the most frustrating things is to know that the toilet is there but you cannot access it. In the early morning and late evening, anyone wanting to commute, walk the dog or go for a run will be limited in their route or the length of time

**Figure 6.5** Toilet entrance with privacy wall.

they spend outdoors if toilets are closed. In urban centres, this access is needed throughout the night to support a twenty-four-hour city. If no toilet is available, someone might be left with no choice but to urinate and defecate in the open. Studies have shown that this is a particular problem for the night-time economy where there is not enough provision to cater to people who have been drinking alcohol.[4] A lack of public toilets and the antisocial impact of people urinating in the street inspired a campaign by the Brixton Business Improvement District (BID) in South London called 'Go before you go',[5] reminding people in the clubs and bars of Brixton to visit the toilet before beginning their journey home.

Not everyone out at night is at a hospitality venue, and with less transport running, night-time journeys in the city can be long and complex. In London, whilst two-thirds of trips at night (by all modes) are for leisure, 17 per cent are work-related.[6] The rapid growth in online delivery of shopping and takeaways and new models for taxis has increased the number of professional drivers, riders and cyclists, with no fixed base or infrastructure to support them. People need toilet access for their commute or during work activities, even at night.

As with all public toilets, this infrastructure must be inclusive. Those out at dawn, dusk or at night, whether for work or leisure, have the same diversity of identities, needs and preferences; toilet provision must not assume a user base of non-disabled men. Night-time toilet infrastructure has in the past consisted of on-street urinals or no infrastructure at all, restricting the city to those willing to urinate in public. Night-time public toilet infrastructure must meet demand, be hygienic, safe, inclusive and open all hours or the right hours to support those who rely on it.

Finally, existing provision can use lighting to clearly indicate if it is open or closed. Well-lit toilets are an indicator of an open facility, helping people to spot them from a distance (Figure 6.6). This is an important factor even for standard opening hours on a winter afternoon. Conversely, when toilets are closed, they should not be lit the same, else people will be drawn to them only to find them locked, so don't forget to turn out the lights!

**Figure 6.6** Public toilets after dark, Kings Cross, London. Having exterior or interior lights on is a simple way to show if a public toilet is still open.

## Turnstiles and stairs

In Chapter 2 we gave an overview as to why turnstiles may be returning to some public toilets. Our research participants commented that they either 'don't do turnstiles' or they were 'a complete faff'.

> [turnstiles are a] bad thing … they are not all big enough if someone is overweight or even if you have a bag.
>
> **OLDER PERSON**

They also found turnstiles unreliable.

> At the turnstiles … it ate my money and if there's no-one there to serve you, it's really frustrating.
>
> **OLDER PERSON**

Facilities that have turnstiles require a payment to access. This can introduce an economic barrier as well as a physical one. Some providers charge up to 50p at the turnstile, quite costly for a family day out or for those with no or low-incomes.[7] For international tourists, turnstiles may be difficult through not having the right change, yet they can be more reliant on public toilets due to unfamiliarity with the local alternatives such as chain and department stores. We go into more depth on the reasons and barriers to charging people to use toilets in Chapter 10.

Participants found that provision located up or downstairs was especially difficult to get to.

> [this] loo that has the best changing facilities but they're down a huge flight of stairs which is mad.
>
> **PARENT USING A PUSHCHAIR**

> I took one of the residents out and she wanted to go to the toilet, but the toilet was downstairs … going down the stairs was quite a struggle … she found it quite hard to get down and come up.
>
> **CARER**

> I was thinking 'I want to go to the loo' hoping there would be a sign saying the loo is at least on the same level … it was down four flights of stairs … it wasn't great. That may well have been the last time I used a public toilet and I just remember thinking 'God I wish these stairs weren't here.' It's just a design thing really.
>
> **DISABLED ADULT**

> I can't manage stairs very well. I certainly won't go to anything below ground.
>
> **OLDER ADULT**

Where stairs exist, guidance should follow the Building Regulations *Approved Document M* and the British Standards BS8300. Handrails are necessary even if it is a few stairs or stairs to different levels. It is also recommended to have handrails at two heights to help children and people of short stature. Signage directing the way to the toilets could include the number of steps to the loos. This would give people a sense of how many stairs there are to get there, and if they may or may not be able to reach the toilets. Signage could also include directions to the nearest alternative level access toilet for those who feel they could not manage the number of stairs.

## Navigating the space

We have (finally) crossed the threshold of the public toilet building. Now there are more door choices to navigate, to men's, women's, gender-neutral and accessible toilets, and doors to cubicles alongside those to an attendant's room or cleaning closets, etc. Unmarked doors can cause further confusion which leads to panic, particularly when it is time to leave.

> I had to climb out of a window because I couldn't find the exit. I tried what I thought was the door, but it was locked, and I panicked. I shouted out but no one responded so I climbed out of the window. I made a complaint to the manager, and they came back with me and showed me that the door was open. It turns out I got the exit confused with a cupboard.
> **YOUNG ADULT**

> My son, he's seven, insists on going in the men's toilets, he doesn't want to go into the ladies anymore, 'I'm a man I'm not going in the women's loos'. I was in the ladies with my daughter, and I heard a howl of complete terror 'mummy', and I panicked, I thought there was someone in there, somebody was doing something, so I rushed into the gents' loos and found him trying to open a cupboard door. There were all these doors around, and he couldn't remember which one he'd come in from. For children learning to use toilets on their own it can be completely terrifying.
> **PARENT OF YOUNG CHILD**

Such confusion can be very distressing especially for those who are neurodiverse and those with neurodegenerative conditions. Providing signage and colour contrast on doors, especially the exit, makes the space safer and easier to navigate for many people (Figure 6.7), as adopted by Sainsbury's across their stores.[8]

**Figure 6.7** Sainsbury's signage to show the way out of the toilets.

## A sense of cleanliness

One of the key aspects that makes us feel comfortable and confident in a public toilet is the sense that it is clean. For many people this will be on sight but can also be on reputation. The smell of the toilet may help assess how clean it is, particularly for those with sight loss. For autistic and other neurodivergent groups, hypersensitivity to odour is common. Poor ventilation coupled with the odours of cleaning materials or artificial air fresheners can become a key sensual barrier to using the toilet on par with physical barriers.[9]

This presents an interesting conundrum for design. Firstly, to prevent antisocial behaviour, toilets need to be well used with a fairly high footfall to discourage behaviour that takes place when there are opportunities to be alone (see Chapter 2). Yet more people using the toilet will also increase the likelihood of perceived dirtiness from others, especially through smells (see Chapter 9).

When crossing the threshold, bad smells have a strong impact, and create strong reactions. Comments from a range of older, younger, disabled and non-disabled participants focused on how unpleasant bad smells and poor ventilation could be:

'I do get concerned about odours.'
'I certainly think there should be good ventilation.'
'It can really stink if there's bad ventilation.'
'With no ventilation, the smell lingers. All those multiple users, you get bad smells.'
'It reeks in there sometimes.'
'Is there some way of removing smell?'
'I like good ventilation but would also think it's important for the attendants.'
'I like good ventilation because sometimes I find the cubicle a bit claustrophobic.'
'I myself hate using stinky loos, it's not a pleasant experience.'

For many the experience of poor ventilation leaves a bad impression, namely that the toilet is dirty despite what the visual cues might be. It can also be uncomfortable to use and reinforce the perspective that public toilets are unpleasant. Although poor ventilation and the resulting bad smells do not always inhibit use, they remove the sense of toileting in comfort.

## A sense of comfort

Comfort is difficult to define as it is often subjective, with people experiencing different levels of comfort and therefore tolerance of a public toilet. There are key elements of the public toilet that may make the experience of using it more comfortable. This includes the sense of security and cleanliness, as well as features such as shelves, coat hooks, sensor flushes and good placements of wash basins, taps, soap and hand dryers.

In historian John Crowley's (2001) *The Invention of Comfort* he states that the modern incarnation of comfort is the 'self-conscious satisfaction with the relationship between one's body and its immediate physical environment'.[10] Sociologist Elizabeth Shove[11] suggests that comfort can be a state to be achieved as well as a state of being, which reflects the relationships between people as well as the relationships between people and objects that may enhance physical and mental wellbeing.

There is a key distinction in thinking about comfort in public space from that in the home. In our homes our design choices are made by us. In public space they are made by others, who choose the technologies of comfort for us. Whilst we may tolerate lower levels of comfort in a public facility than we would in our homes, comfort should not be side-lined in the design of public toilets.

One of the main cues to comfort will be the sense of cleanliness the provision affords. For design, this means that all aspects of servicing the toilets (and the toilet paper, soap and hand towels) should be understood, so that the provision can be cleaned thoroughly and efficiently and kept in good order without impinging on access, comfort, security and dignity (see Chapter 10).

## The toilet queue

In the UK, the women's toilet queue is ubiquitous (Figure 6.8). In many situations women express surprise if there is no queue. To explain the phenomenon, a number of stereotypes have emerged on the mystery of why women spend so long in the toilet. Is the queue because they are doing their hair and make-up or gossiping? The reality is more mundane.

**Figure 6.8** A typical queue for the women's toilets, at a train station.

Due to our cultural perceptions of privacy and dignity, women need to use the toilet out of sight, so individual cubicles are required. Women need to pull down or pull up their clothes, whether trousers, skirts and dresses, tights, a second layer and finally underwear.

Despite progression in childcare roles, women still make up the majority of those responsible for children, so they may also have to help a child or children use the loo. Along with bags and outer garments, pushchairs and other items, all this takes time to negotiate.

Research has estimated it takes a woman on average 90 seconds to use the toilet.[12] It can take several minutes if the woman is also toileting a child. It could take a couple of minutes if a woman is changing a sanitary pad or tampon (and around a fifth of women of menstruating age will be having their period at any one time).[13] Women are also more likely to experience urinary tract infections and incontinence both of which take time to manage.[14] In contrast, men will spend an average of 35 seconds at the urinal and a minute overall in the facility.[15] It has also been observed that women are more likely to wash their hands after using the toilet then men,[16] therefore spending longer in the toilet facility.

So part of the explanation for the toilet queue is that women tend to take longer to use toilets then men for these biological and social reasons. This could be eradicated if more toilets were provided. This brings us to an important secondary factor. The allocation of space for toilets is too often divided equally between the men's and women's facility. In space divided equally, however many cubicles are provided in the women's, some can be substituted in the men's for a greater number of urinals. Consequently, a men's toilet facility will frequently have more places to 'go', yet they take less time to do so. This is a serious underrepresentation of a biological need.[17]

In the United States there has been a move towards 'potty parity', with campaigns for the number of toilets in women's and men's facilities to be provided at a 2:1 ratio. The American Restroom Association notes a few problems with this, where it does not address the minimum levels needed for either gender, or significant differences exist in the gender of users, at a venue, which may not be a 50:50 split. They argue that to improve provision for women, building codes need to ensure minimum levels for everyone, that older buildings need to be brought up to this minimum, and that more toilets should be gender neutral, which have 'intrinsic potty parity'.[18]

This final suggestion would alleviate the women's queue. **Fully enclosed, gender-neutral cubicles** would meet everyone's privacy needs. By providing cubicles that include washbasins too, we will provide for more needs and alleviate any discomfort or stress from sharing the handwashing space across genders in a way we are culturally not used to. Research by Luc Bovens and Alexandru Marcoci simulated changes in queue times between gender-separate and gender-neutral provision. They found gender-neutral toilets consistently cut wait times for women, whilst for men it was found to be the same or slightly increased. This depended on 'usage intensity, occupancy time and presence of urinals'. They observed that toilet providers could reduce costs and number of facilities without increasing overall wait times by changing to gender-neutral toilets.[19]

Such single-user cubicles require a new design. Instead of partitioned cubicles, a fully enclosed toilet gives complete privacy (see Chapter 7). It could be further improved, to include washbasins and have a bin for menstrual and incontinence products. This would save embarrassment for men who use continence or period products from not having a bin in the cubicle (see Chapter 8).

One criticism against gender-neutral provision focuses on concerns of women's safety. Well-designed gender-neutral toilets would increase the user numbers and natural surveillance around the facility. This would decrease the risk that comes with 'being alone and out of sight'.[20] People looking after children would not have the worry of their children toileting on their own in a separate-gender facility.

Gender-neutral toilets are already found in many areas of public life. It is the only provision offered on trains and planes. It is often the only provision in many coffee stores, cafés and restaurants, and it is already the norm for the accessible toilet which is deemed acceptable. Here one of the complexities of having a wee in public is revealed: change from what we are used to is resisted, even though it is an established design in another facility, context or culture.

# Which cubicle?

After navigating doors and turnstiles and possibly queueing for the loo, we then come to the next stage in this journey: which cubicle to use?

## Accessible toilet

Many people do not have a choice in the type of toilet they can access and use. The **accessible toilet** has become symbolic of disabled people's access to our built environment. In 2004, Part 3 of the 1995 Disability Discrimination Act[21] (DDA) came into law. This section of the act required service providers (shops, restaurants, cafés, transport stations, etc.) to ensure access to disabled customers. The implementation of the act (which is now superseded by the Equality Act 2010),[22] led to a huge increase in adjustments to buildings to meet the requirements.

This included providing accessible toilets. As noted in Chapter 3, guidance for the design of the accessible toilet is given in *Approved Document M* of the Building Regulations[23] and the British Standards BS8300.[24] Many accessible toilets that were built in response to Part 3 of the DDA at the turn of the millennium will have followed the guidance of Part M (see Figure 6.9) and BS8300. These documents have subsequently been revised so newer buildings may differ slightly in the design of the accessible toilet.

The Building Regulations for England and Wales ensure that, in principle, buildings have adequate toilet provision, yet the choice of what kind of provision is often overlooked. Despite the requirements of the Equality Act, many small

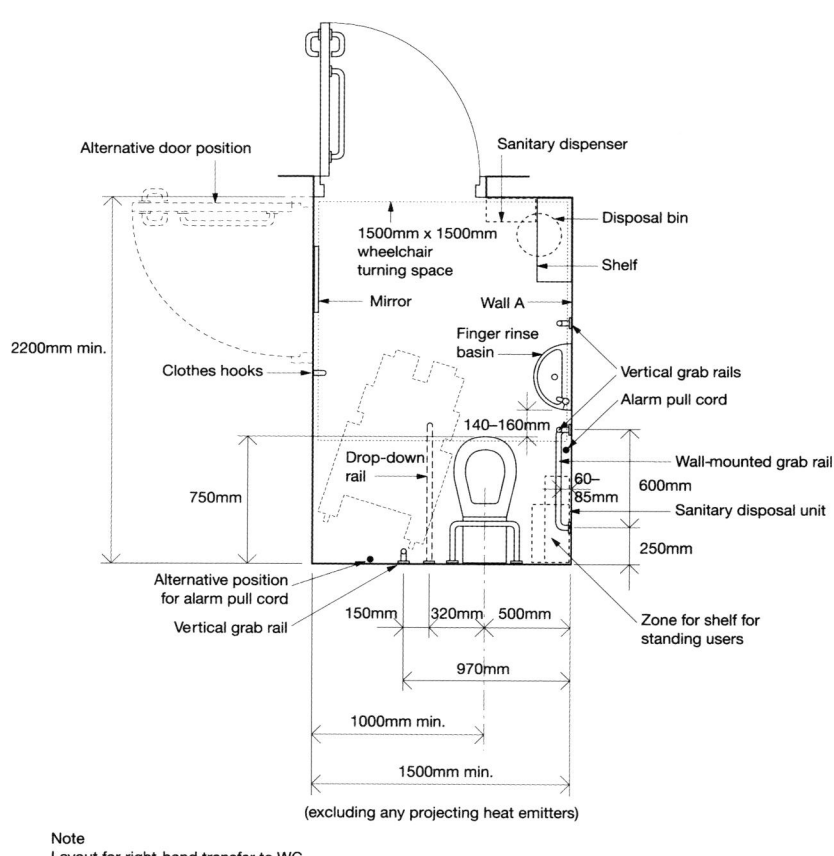

**Figure 6.9** Unisex wheelchair-accessible toilet with corner WC – plan view (Diagram 18 of Building Regulations: *Approved Document M* Vol. 2. 2015, 2020).[25] Crown Copyright 2021.

enterprises do not have an accessible toilet. A single accessible gender-neutral toilet that includes accessible baby-change would meet this requirement.

## Changing Places toilet

A Changing Places toilet is a larger accessible toilet that includes an adult changing bench, a hoist, a toilet, washbasin, screens and space for one or two carers (Figure 6.10).

In 2020 the government announced that Changing Places toilets would become compulsory in all new public buildings including 'art galleries, cinemas, concert halls, conference centres, further education colleges, universities, hotels that include leisure facilities, libraries, motorway services, museums, places of worship, and theatres, shopping centres and retail parks with gross floor areas of 30,000 m$^2$ or more, retail premises of 2,500 m$^2$ or more, sport and leisure buildings over 5,000 m$^2$, and stadia, theme parks, zoos and exhibition centres with a capacity above 2,000 people'.[26] This was amended into Building Regulations Part M (2020). The British Standards BS8300 provided full best practice design guidance for Changing Places toilets in 2018. Both the Building Regulations and British Standards refer back to *Changing Places: The practical guide*[27] for further information and guidance.

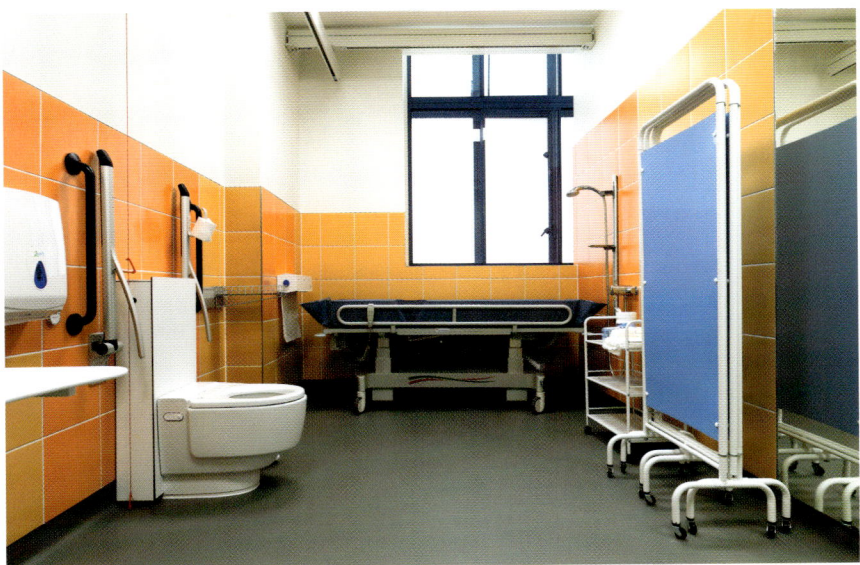

**Figure 6.10** Changing Places facility. In this example, the changing table can be rotated to allow carers to assist from both sides. Credit: Wellcome Collection/Eva Herzog.

The government has estimated that the spending power of disabled people and their carers is around £249 billion[28] yet still some disabled people are excluded due to a lack of infrastructure. The latest Building Regulations amendment helps to increase access to the UK's destinations and transport infrastructure for those who need the provision of a Changing Places facility.

The government set aside a £30 million fund to help install Changing Places toilets in existing buildings.[29] These changes are estimated to help over 250,000 people and their carers access toilets that require the extra space for toileting. It is a landmark adjustment to the need for wider access in our towns and cities.

## Ambulant cubicle

Requirements for **ambulant toilets** are also found in the Building Regulations Part M[30] and Part T, which provides guidance for an 'ambulant single-sex toilet cubicle' (see Figure 6.11) and an alternative design of a 'fully enclosed self-contained ambulant universal toilet'.[31] These toilets are designed to meet the needs of older and disabled people who may need a little more support than the standard cubicle offers but who do not require the full fixtures and fittings of the accessible toilet. They are often found at the end of a row of standard toilet cubicles as they require an outwards-opening door, grab rails and slightly more space (although this means further to walk for the 'ambulant').

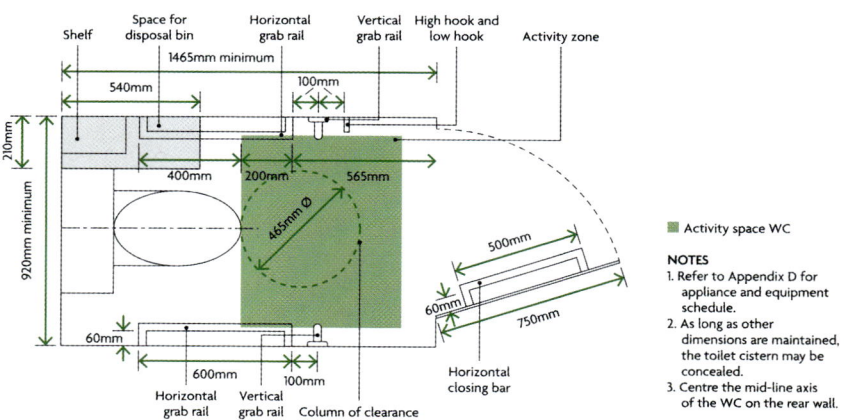

**Figure 6.11** Ambulant single-sex toilet cubicle (not self-contained), plan view showing minimum dimensions (Diagram 5.1 of Building Regulations: *Approved Document T*, 2024).[36] Crown Copyright 2024.

Both Building Regulations[32] and British Standards[33] require a minimum of one ambulant cubicle in each set of toilets. However, the London Legacy Development Corporation (LLDC) 2019 Inclusive Design Standard,[34] developed as a legacy of the 2012 London Olympic and Paralympic Games, goes further in this and many other areas. For ambulant provision, LLDC recommend 10 per cent of cubicles are ambulant cubicles in both separate-gender and gender-neutral provision, with one as a minimum requirement.[35]

The one key problem of the ambulant toilet is that it is part of the standard provision and can be missed when queueing for the loo: do we wait until this becomes free, interrupting the flow of the queue or do we just go with the vacant option?

The ambulant cubicle can also help those with children, as there is no internal door swing to manoeuvre around. Even then, some find themselves sacrificing their privacy for the safety of their children.

> I don't want to leave him in the pushchair so either you take the baby out of his pushchair and you carry them while you go to the toilet, which is quite hard as you can imagine but you have to do it quite a lot of the time, so I learnt a technique which is to go to the end toilet put the pushchair sticking out because obviously it wouldn't fit in and just go to the toilet with the door open thinking that everybody would see the pushchair there and wouldn't come and look into the toilet.

**PARENT OF TODDLER**

## Standard cubicle

Most people will use the **standard cubicle**. Guidance on the design of this can be found in British Standards BS6465 Part 2,[37] Approved Document G of the Building Regulations[38] and *Approved Document T* where it is named 'single-sex toilet cubicle', alongside the alternative 'fully enclosed self-contained universal toilet' (see Figure 6.12).[39] With so many design variations, it is important that the correct configuration is considered for the type of building the toilet will be in and the service it will be supporting.

We can also design beyond the minimum requirements of the Building Regulations. If the provision is part of a transport hub then all cubicles should be larger to fit luggage. No one will want to leave their bags outside and doing so could be a security threat. If the service attracts parents with young children, a larger standard cubicle that includes baby-changing would work well.

The current recommendations in Part 2 of the British Standard 6465 focus on toilet design in banks of cubicles and are mostly found in the configuration of a row of standard cubicles with an ambulant cubicle at the end. Yet with the numbers of older people increasing and with them more likely to use the toilet frequently, a more inclusive approach would be to have a configuration for a higher proportion of ambulant cubicles, if not all.

> It would be great if every toilet had grab rails so that they became an everyday bit of equipment and not medical and scary.
> 
> **CARER**

When separate-gender toilet provision is reached, we will make the decision on which one to use. For people who are non-binary, or whose gender is misread or misunderstood by others, this can cause anxiety or carry the risk of verbal or physical abuse from other users, of being denied access or of being told they are in the wrong facility for them.[40] Some people may opt for the accessible toilet due to its non-gendered designation rather than because of its design features. Removing gender separation from the standard and ambulant toilet designs, in line with accessible and Changing Places toilets, can make facilities more accessible for all.

## Universal toilet

In 2024 the government issued a new Building Regulation Approved Document T, also known as Part T,[41] that would cover all standard and ambulant non-domestic toilets with very few exceptions. Part T states that all new buildings must have 'single sex' toilets. It also says, if space allows, a gender-neutral **universal toilet** should be provided, or be the only provision if there is no space for separate-gender facilities. The regulations for universal toilets define them as gender neutral or gender separate, fully enclosed with floor-to-ceiling walls and containing wash basins (Figure 6.12). Standard and ambulant designs are provided. Whilst fully enclosed cubicles improve privacy for everyone, the need for handwashing in all cubicles could limit the benefits of gender-neutral toilets in high usage settings to reduce queue times compared to separate-gender toilets with communal handwashing. Yet the design for fully enclosed gender-neutral toilets without handwashing in the cubicle does not seem to be an option. Striking a balance between these competing pressures of inclusive cubicles and a high throughput of users is critical for better toilet provision.

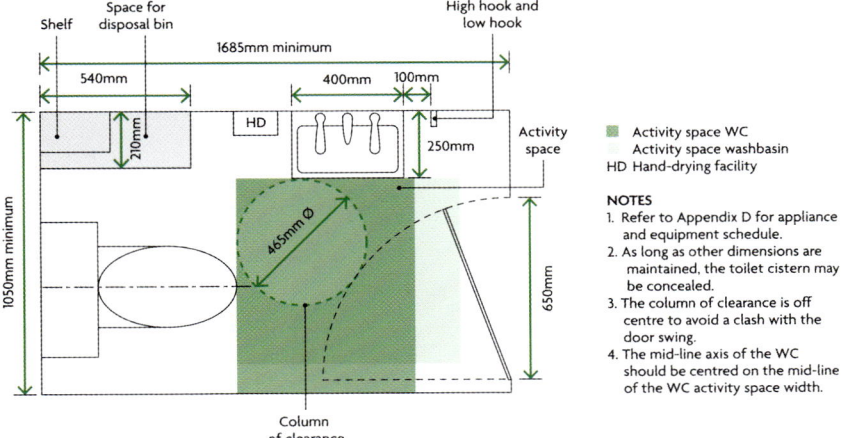

**Figure 6.12** Fully enclosed self-contained universal toilet, plan view showing minimum dimensions (Diagram 4.1 of Building Regulations: *Approved Document T*, 2024).[42] Crown Copyright 2024.

## Which urinal?

Are urinals essential? Urinals are a specific furnishing of public space and are not commonly found in homes, nor are they generally a feature of the accessible toilet, or of gender-neutral provision on trains, planes or in cafés and restaurants. However, they can help in high usage settings or where there is a surge in user numbers. Urinals could even be provided alongside gender-neutral toilets, either in single-user, lockable cubicles or a multi-person urinal that is in a separate room or location from the toilet provision.

When designing urinals, there is the added consideration of urinal etiquette which dictates which urinal to use. These tend to be the ones furthest from any existing users. For some men, if both the end urinals are being used, they will use a cubicle instead. Some men avoid urinals entirely, either due to paruresis (see Chapter 7) or other aspects of use.

For example, for many men who conduct faith observances when toileting, the cubicle is preferential as they might prefer to sit to urinate.

> I'm not comfortable using urinals because of my faith. There is not enough privacy and splash back makes prayer and going to the mosque invalid.
> **YOUNG PERSON**

Urinals can also be difficult for tall men.

> I have problems due to my height. I'm 6'3" so when I use a urinal, I get really bad splash back.
> **MIDDLE-AGED PERSON**

They can also be difficult for men with visual impairments.

> I don't like the idea of standing next to men, especially as I might have difficulty locating the urinal, it's usually white on white.
> **PERSON WITH VISUAL IMPAIRMENTS**

Ambulant urinals have handrails to help those who need support when standing. The LLDC Inclusive Design Standard recommends one ambulant urinal for every four urinals.[43] We discuss more ways to make urinal design more inclusive in the next chapter.

## Won't somebody think of the children?

Baby-changing facilities in gender-neutral spaces make a more inclusive facility. They also require more room, for the table, the bin, any pushchairs and access to the toilet for the guardian or other children in the group. These reasons often lead to them being placed in the accessible toilet. Of course, this also gives access to baby-changing for disabled adults who need to tend to their children. Wheelchair-accessible baby-changing would be of adjustable height and enable a wheelchair user to access the table.[44]

However, changing a baby's nappy can take time. While in smaller venues the accessible toilet may be the only toilet, where space allows we can offer alternatives. A second accessible toilet without baby-changing facilities will increase the availability of accessible facilities to disabled people. We could also provide additional baby-changing facilities in the standard toilets (with provision in both facilities if separate-gender toilets are provided), or in a dedicated, accessible, baby-changing area outside the cubicles. How space is divided will be location specific. How many infants or families are you expecting to attract? Most children are in nappies until three years old, so bear this in mind when selecting changing tables, to meet the size and weight needs of more children.

> Sometimes there seems like there's a lot of baby change but nothing once the child is older. My daughter is getting bigger, and her legs are hanging down

[from the changing table]. Children are not toilet trained until two or three, but baby change excludes after the first year.
**PARENT OF YOUNG CHILD**

Once children are toilet trained, there is a need for more family-friendly toilet provision. This could include child toilet seats that can drop down onto standard toilets to help children use the toilet comfortably, or family-specific cubicles with a lower toilet alongside a standard-height toilet. These family toilets also have baby-changing tables and accommodate space for a pushchair within the cubicle, allowing an adult to keep a sleeping child with them whilst they or other children use the loo.

In many men's toilets there might be a urinal set at a lower height, designed for boys but also convenient for men of short stature. In contrast, there are practically no lower toilet pans in the women's or men's toilets for children.

Many child-sized features can be provided alongside adult-sized equivalents in the standard, ambulant and accessible toilets. Sometimes a lower height basin or hand dryer would be better for everyone. That is why we have shown child-sized or child-height toilets, basin, hand dryers and urinals alongside so called 'standard' facilities in the remaining chapters. Provision for children does not always mean an additional family toilet or child-specific facility. Designing all toilet facilities to be inclusive of children makes them more inclusive for everybody.

When children are not considered, this makes toileting them difficult. Feminists and disability activists assert that the lack of women's and disabled public toilets is symbolic of restricting their access to public space. This can be extended to the lack of provision that meets the need of children and goes against UNICEF's Child Friendly Cities initiative.[45] Those looking after children are not exclusively non-disabled or young adults. Disabled adults, those with medical conditions and older people also care for children, so family facilities would also benefit from other inclusive features, including a grab rail near the toilet or a height-adjustable baby-changing table.

## *We're there ...*

On this journey we have considered if the toilets give us a sense of safety and comfort, whether these are in a stand-alone building or down a long corridor away from the general public. There have been numerous obstacles to manage such as steps and turnstiles, opening hours, overall cleanliness and then the decision on which provision to use for our physical, cultural and social access. We may have had to queue or think about how best to signal a need for a specific cubicle, such as the ambulant facility or a cubicle with a bin or baby-changing table. We may be accompanied by older or younger family members or others who need assistance, further limiting choice and possible comfort in toileting. These are some of the many decisions we will have made before we reach the ultimate destination, the toilet cubicle and the next step: entering the cubicle and closing the door.

# Notes

1. J. Knox, *Kiwi-As Toilets: Where to Go When You Need to Go in New Zealand* (New Zealand: BookPrint Ltd, 2018), 14.
2. Department of Levelling Up, Housing and Communities and Ministry of Housing, Communities and Local Government (updated 2022), *Building Regulations Fire Safety Approved Document B. Building regulation in England covering fire safety matters within and around buildings* [pdf]. Available online: https://www.gov.uk/government/publications/fire-safety-approved-document-b (accessed 12 December 2023).
3. British Standards Institute, *PAS 6463: Design for the mind – Neurodiversity and the Built Environment – guide.*
4. S. Thomson, M. M. Smith and S. Hulley, *CivicWatch Good Practice Guide: Street Urination. London* (Jill Dando Institute of Crime Science, University College London, 2004).
5. Brixton Business Improvement District, 'Brixton BID launches new Go Before You Go campaign', 20 December 2017. Available online: https://brixtonbid.co.uk/go-before-you-go/ (accessed 20 December 2023).
6. Greater London Authority (2018) *London at night: An evidence base for a 24-hour city* [pdf]. Available online: https://www.london.gov.uk/sites/default/files/london-at-night-full-final.pdf (accessed 12 December 2023).
7. A. Johnson, 'Brits left raging at 50p public toilets – but there's a cheeky plan to get it free', *The Mirror*, 1 June 2024. Available online: https://www.mirror.co.uk/news/weird-news/brits-left-raging-50p-public-32937741 (accessed 8 June 2024).
8. Alzheimer's Society (2018), *Dementia-friendly retail guide* [pdf]. Available online: https://www.alzheimers.org.uk/sites/default/files/2019-07/AS_NEW_DF_Retail_Guide_Online_09_07_19.pdf (accessed 30 January 2024).
9. British Standards Institute, *PAS 6463: Design for the mind – Neurodiversity and the Built Environment – guide.*
10. J. Crowley, *The Invention of Comfort: Sensibility and Design in Early Modern Britain and Early America* (Baltimore: Johns Hopkins University Press, 2001), 142.

11  E. Shove, *Comfort, Cleanliness and Convenience: The Social Organisation of Normality* (Oxford/New York: Berg, 2003).
12  Greed, *Inclusive Urban Design: Public Toilets*; K. Van Hautegem and W. Rogiest, 'No more queueing at the ladies' room', *People Queue Magazine*, 13 July 2017. Available online: http://peopleqm.blogspot.com/2017/07/no-more-queueing-at-ladies-room.html (accessed 21 December 2023).
13  L. O'Dwyer, 'Why queues for women's toilets are longer than men's', *The Conversation*, 23 August 2018. Available online: https://theconversation.com/why-queues-for-womens-toilets-are-longer-than-mens-99763 (accessed 21 December 2023).
14  K. Czajkowski, M. Broś-Konopielko and J. Teliga-Czajkowska, 'Urinary tract infection in women', *Menopause Review* 20(1) (2021): 40–47, doi: https://doi.org/10.5114/pm.2021.105382.
15  Greed, *Inclusive Urban Design*.
    Van Hautegem and Rogiest, 'No more queueing at the ladies' room'.
16  Greed, *Inclusive Urban Design*.
17  J. Stromberg, 'Everybody poops. But here are 9 surprising facts about feces you may not know', *Vox*, 22 January 2015. Available online: https://www.vox.com/2015/1/22/7871579/poop-feces (accessed 28 December 2023).
18  American Restroom Association (no date), 'Potty parity'. Available online: https://americanrestroom.org/potty-parity/ (accessed 12 December 2023).
19  L. Bovens and A. Marcoci, 'The gender-neutral bathroom: A new frame and some nudges', *Behavioural Public Policy* 7(1) (2020): 1–24, doi:10.1017/bpp2020.23.
20  J. Sanders and S. Stryker, 'Stalled: gender-neutral public bathrooms', *The South Atlantic Quarterly* 115(4) (2016): 783.
21  *Disability Discrimination Act 1995 Part III*.
22  *Equality Act 2010*.
23  Building Regulations, *Approved Document M: Access to and use of buildings. Vol. 2: Buildings other than dwellings*.
24  British Standards Institute, *BS8300-2 Design of an accessible and inclusive built environment*.
25  Building Regulations, *Approved Document M: Access to and use of buildings. Vol. 2: Buildings other than dwellings*.
26  Ministry of Housing, Communities and Local Government, 'Changing Places toilets for severely disabled people to be compulsory in new public buildings', 19 July 2020. Available online: https://www.gov.uk/government/news/changing-places-toilets-for-severely-disabled-people-to-be-compulsory-in-new-public-buildings (accessed 28 June 2024).
27  Changing Places Consortium (2021), *Changing Places: A Practical Guide*. Available online: https://toiletmap.s3.eu-west-1.amazonaws.com/content/Changing%20Places%20a%20Practical%20Guide.pdf (accessed 28 June 2024).

28. BBC News, 'The power of the "purple pound" explained', 21 February 2017. Available online: https://www.bbc.co.uk/news/av/business-39040760 (accessed 21 December 2023).
29. Ministry of Housing Communities and Local Government, '£30 million investment to provide Changing places toilets', 4 March 2021. Available online: https://www.gov.uk/government/news/30-million-investment-to-provide-changing-places-toilets (accessed 21 December 2023).
30. Building Regulations, *Approved Document M: Access to and use of buildings. Vol. 2: Buildings other than dwellings*.
31. Building Regulations, *Approved Document T: Toilet Accommodation*.
32. Building Regulations, *Approved Document M: Access to and use of buildings. Vol. 2: Buildings other than dwellings*.
33. British Standards Institute, *BS8300-2 Design of an accessible and inclusive built environment*.
34. London Legacy Development Corporation (2019), *Inclusive Design Standards* [pdf]. Available online: https://cdn.disabilityinnovation.com/uploads/documents/Inclusive-Design-Standards.pdf?v=1572970889 (accessed 24 June 2024).
35. London Legacy Development Corporation, *Inclusive Design Standards*.
36. Building Regulations, *Approved Document T: Toilet Accommodation*.
37. British Standards Institute, *BS6465 Sanitary Installations: Part 2 Code of Practice for Space Requirements for Sanitary Appliances*.
38. Building Regulations, *Approved Document G: Sanitation, hot water safety and water efficiency* (2015). Available online: https://www.gov.uk/government/publications/sanitation-hot-water-safety-and-water-efficiency-approved-document-g (accessed 21 December 2023).
39. Building Regulations, *Approved Document T: Toilet Accommodation*.
40. S. Cavanagh, *Queering Bathrooms: Gender, Sexuality and the Hygienic Imagination* (Toronto: University of Toronto Press, 2010).
41. Building Regulations, *Approved Document T: Toilet Accommodation*.
42. Ibid.
43. London Legacy Development Corporation, *Inclusive Design Standards*.
44. Ibid.
45. UNICEF (2023), 'About child friendly cities and communities'. Available online: https://www.unicef.org.uk/child-friendly-cities/about-child-friendly-cities-communities/ (accessed 20 January 2024).

# 7 Closing the door

A toilet cubicle has become available, but will we enter it? Before we use the toilet, what are we looking for in the design of this new space? We look for dignity, by being able to shield our bodies and the sounds and smells we make during this private act. We look for comfort, by having enough room to move and undress or to help or be helped by someone else. We look for safety, through a lockable space.

This chapter shares how to create a space that will give people the safety, comfort and dignity to use a toilet through the design of the cubicle itself: its walls, doors, hinges, locks, handles, hooks and shelves.

> You need a cubicle which is a little more generous with space for people, to allow people the space to hang their coats up and things like that because no one likes to have their clothes draping around places where other people's urine might have dripped.
> **PERSON WITH CHRONIC HEALTH CONDITION**

## Designing privacy

Using a public toilet is an unusual activity for interior design, in that we are doing one of our most private acts in a shared, public space, in very close proximity to strangers. We need to create a sense of privacy to forget about those beyond the door, and to convince ourselves that they are not aware of our actions either. This level of privacy is not just for the comfort of the user. Our culture of the toilet taboo creates feelings of disgust, embarrassment or violation both if we are exposed when using a toilet and if we are exposed to others during their toileting acts or to the sight of their bodies against our choice. As Alexander Kira explains in *The Bathroom*[1] (see Chapter 2), the design must provide both 'privacy for' the user to undress and eliminate without being detected and 'privacy from' awareness of these acts for other people in the facility.

**Figure 7.1** Fully enclosed cubicle. This one has handwashing facilities within the cubicle.

## *Walls or partitions?*

The construction of the space helps create this two-way privacy by preventing visual, audio and olfactory clues – what we see, hear and smell – both during use and for those who visit before and after us. There are two distinct designs for the space construction. The first has the toilet in its own lockable room; the walls and door extend from the floor to the ceiling. We refer to this as a **fully enclosed cubicle** (Figure 7.1). The second has the toilet in a cubicle where the walls and door provide visual privacy within a certain height range, with gaps at the top and bottom: a **partitioned cubicle** (Figure 7.2).

The difference in these two constructions affects how comfortable we feel to use the facility, due to the different levels of privacy they provide. Cubicle walls stop people from seeing the parts of our body that are private to us. A fully enclosed cubicle stops people from seeing any part of us (or even knowing there is someone in there) and keeps any sounds or smells that we may emit during the act contained within the room. This can cause a different problem later, of odours still lingering when the next person enters. Ventilation is key. Whilst separate-gender toilets can be built with partitioned cubicles,[2] users may prefer solid walls, or gaps kept to a minimum, to help block sounds from escaping. Any gaps would be for ventilation or light (Figure 7.3).

**Figure 7.2** Partitioned cubicles.

**Figure 7.3** A partitioned cubicle with minimal gaps. This single-gender cubicle gives the feel of a fully enclosed toilet, with a small gap at the ceiling for light and ventilation.

It's quite embarrassing when you've got something like IBS … you just want your privacy and you're more able to get that in an [accessible] toilet.
**PERSON WITH CONTINENCE CONDITION**

I would prefer a fully enclosed cubicle with good ventilation, so that you don't feel like you're sat right next to the person on the other side. [A partition] is a visual screen as opposed to a screen from all the other senses that come with going to the loo.
**PERSON WITH CHRONIC HEALTH CONDITION**

He's fascinated by gaps underneath the door. He tries to crawl underneath especially when I'm on the loo. Or he peers under the gap and upsets the person next door. It's an issue at crawling age; I can't put him on the floor, he'll just head for the gap, so I have 'to go' with him on my lap.
**PARENT OF YOUNG CHILD**

The physical structure of the toilet cubicle is not the only means to create 'privacy from'. Removing evidence of our actions, by leaving the cubicle in a clean state free from soiling, is another way to protect those who follow us from seeing evidence of shared use (see Chapter 8). Another is to avoid eye contact or verbal communication, particularly during any toilet activities, also practised at the urinals.

## *A note on urinals*

Many men will use a urinal without visual privacy, and how absolute this need for privacy is will vary between cultures and individually. Some people experience a social phobia of urinating in public called *paruresis*, or *shy bladder syndrome*. There are different severities of paruresis. For many it is the presence of people within visual or audio range that stops them from being able to wee. Whilst paruresis can affect all genders it is more apparent in men due to the social expectation to use a urinal without privacy.[3]

Urinal design in the UK rarely gives the user visual or audio privacy for urination or privacy from the weeing of others. Instead, privacy is created through social behaviour, by not looking, making eye contact or conversation. However, variations in design to create more privacy can ease the onset of paruresis for some. The two common designs are a trough urinal, either raised or along the floor, and an individual urinal. The latter spaces out the distance between users to a minimum, rather than leaving this to individual comfort levels, which may

**Figure 7.4** Individual urinals with partitions. Credit: VPales/Alamy Stock Photo.

be very different (Figure 7.4). The curvature of the bowl can also give more visual privacy from whoever is adjacent. According to Part T, partition screens should also be used between individual urinals.[4]

Trough urinals can also be improved through partition screens. This increases the user's comfort by offering minimum spacing and more visual privacy in an undressed state. The Victorian urinals in Figure 7.5 and in Chapter 2 (Figure 2.1) show how even the earlier public urinals had dividers to help people space themselves with more comfort and privacy.

The position of the urinal within the facility can also affect use. The urinal should not be in view of those walking past when there is no external door or when the door to the facility is open. This includes reflections in mirrors. Comfort can also be increased by having enough space between those at the urinal and those who are handwashing, queueing or accessing the toilet cubicles.

Public toilets that only have gender-neutral fully enclosed cubicles with washbasins have a few options should designers wish to include urinals. Whilst many designs do away with them, some have a separate multi-user urinal away from general view, and some have a one-person urinal behind a lockable door (Figure 7.6).

**Figure 7.5** Trough urinal with partitions.

**Figure 7.6** An individual, lockable urinal on the left next to a gender-neutral public toilet.

# A comfortable size

Whether created through solid walls or partitions, the physical space within the toilet cubicle affects how comfortable and usable it is. To be inclusive, the standard cubicle needs to be big enough for more than the average person (a cubicle designed for the average person will be too small for half the population). Not only are people different sizes, but some are less stable or flexible, or have a mobility aid like a walking stick. Some are pregnant or have a child in a baby carrier. Some may be using the toilet accompanied, such as small children or their guardians. Excluding these people from the standard cubicle will increase the pressure on the **accessible toilet**, where space is given to allow someone to turn their wheelchair, far more space than most people require.

So how much space is enough? Enough space in a toilet cubicle means being able to turn around and close the door without being squeezed, knocked off balance or brushing against the toilet seat. Enough space allows someone to hang up a bag and take off their coat without hitting the walls. A big enough toilet allows a child to stand without hurting themselves on fixtures and fittings whilst their grown-up uses the toilet, and vice-versa. Part T sets different minimum dimensions for 'activity spaces' in front of the toilet and any other fixtures such as the basin. These spaces may overlap and can be temporarily obstructed by the swing of the door. A column of clearance of diameter 465 mm in front of the toilet bowl is also specified. This must not overlap the door swing. This column is the minimum dimension to work towards or exceed, to allow people to get in and out of the cubicle.[5]

The bigger the toilet is, the more groups it includes. Adults with a carer may have their needs met in a more spacious standard toilet rather than the accessible toilet. A toilet with room for a pushchair or buggy, or luggage, increases the user group further. Both the LLDC Inclusive Design Standard (2019) and Building Regulations *Approved Document M* (2015) require at least one enlarged cubicle in separate-gender toilets for every four or more cubicles.[6]

> I absolutely hate those toilets where you've got a sanitary bin squashed up against one leg and a toilet roll dispenser squashed against the other. An extra 10 cm would mean I don't have to touch those things.
> **PARENT WITH YOUNG CHILD**

> I look after my three-year-old grandson. There's not enough room to see a toddler in the toilet, you've got to leave the door open … the cubicles are too small.
> **GRANDPARENT**

The challenge of design is to balance competing demands. We want to increase the size of cubicle to increase the number of people who can use it; we want to increase the total number of cubicles needed to meet the volume of people visiting (remembering queues also take up room); and we need to achieve this in the minimum floor space or use it as an argument to increase the size of the toilets. There is value in understanding the needs of existing users and the needs of those whom we wish to attract. However, in terms of cubicle size, it would be unusual for someone to walk into a toilet cubicle and say 'oh this is a bit big …'.

## Drips and slips

> Some are just too dirty to use. Sitting there with your feet in a pool is worse. It could be a leak or cleaning but it's still very unpleasant. Slippery floors are a risk.
> **PARTICIPANT WITH CHRONIC HEALTH CONDITION**

Let's take a quick look at the floor. A wet toilet floor invites questions: has it been cleaned, is the toilet leaking, or has someone been careless or had an accident? In this context, pooling water on the floor will make the facility appear less clean even if it is a recently cleaned floor that is drying. The toilet will always be an environment that carries the risk of a wet floor, but we can design out drips from handwashing (see Chapter 9) and minimize the risk of slips by making flooring slip-resistant. This is recommended in the accessible cubicle but could be applied more widely as we make all toilets more inclusive.

> At the garden centre the accessible loo is in the ladies so my husband goes back to the car to get my crutches so that I can walk into the loo. When I get in there the floor is wet, but I just have to manage on my own. Then the crutches skidded, and I fell on the floor. I could hear people coming in but was too embarrassed to say I needed help. There was no alarm. It's only that I was in there for so long that my husband shouted, 'are you OK?' I said no and my husband came in and had to unlock the door with a coin
> **WHEELCHAIR AND WALKING-AID USER**

## Doors and hinges

When we choose which cubicle to use, our decision-making process is influenced by the design of the door, and in particular, the hinge. The choice of hinge decides two things: which way the door opens, and whether it stays open or swings shut.

These factors influence, in turn, the size of the cubicle, the use of the circulation space outside the door and how we read whether the toilet is available.

## Reading the room

When entering a toilet facility, we look for a vacant cubicle. This is where self-closing hinges, such as sprung hinges and gravity hinges that cause doors to swing shut, cause problems. The first way that someone can know – in a split second – that a cubicle is available is by seeing that the door is ajar (Figure 7.7). One door ajar in a row of others can be spotted from the end of a corridor, and no further information is needed. When doors close independently of whether there is anyone inside, this clue is lost and new sources are needed. With partitioned cubicles, we might look for changes in the light under the door as the occupant moves about or the sounds of activity. The formal design intervention – the lock indicator – is not as reliable as an open door. In many cases, lock indicators are too small (or non-existent), inconsistent in the colour that means open or closed, or inaccurate (a locked door is indicated as unlocked, or vice-versa). We go into detail on locks in the next section of this chapter.

**Figure 7.7** A row of cubicles with self-closing doors. Spot the available cubicle.

After reading the lock indicator, and sometimes irrespective of what it says, the next thing we do to find an empty cubicle is try the handle or push on each door. This is uncomfortable for many people. The occupant is fearful that the lock has failed and that the door will open. The person waiting does not want to appear impatient, to cause embarrassment or to be shouted at and feel the door of a cubicle with a broken lock be slammed shut against their arm. The constructed privacy we give people when using a public toilet by blocking senses and denying thoughts of what is happening inside is now fracturing between these two people through a brief unwanted interaction, and the continued discomfort of meeting face-to-face when the user leaves the toilet.

What is often observed in the women's toilets is that many people delay checking all the doors to see if one is vacant, preferring to wait a moment until someone emerges from one of the line of cubicles. Once a queue has formed, this becomes a problem. Depending on the layout of a facility, and particularly in larger facilities, the head of the queue becomes more reluctant to perform this check as this risks them losing their place.

In any case, a queue implies to all who join it that all toilets are engaged. The front of the queue waits until someone leaves a cubicle, and so on and so on. Far too often, and always in facilities with self-closing doors, we find it is only a small proportion of the cubicles that people are exiting and entering, and several other cubicles have been vacant the whole time. No one goes into them because no one has come out.

Why do self-closing hinges persist in cubicle design? One reason is aesthetics: as we can see in Figure 7.7, a row of closed doors is a clean, modern, sleek look; something for us to admire as we wait for a cubicle that had no one in it. Another reason might be ignorance: hinges are bought, or going spare, and the installers use them not knowing how this hinders the visible clues that we rely on to find an available loo, particularly if they do not regularly experience it themselves.

If the cubicle has an outwards-opening door, self-closing hinges do have the benefit of stopping it from swinging open into someone's path. This arrangement allows for far more movement within the cubicle where there is a lot of pressure on space, and the Building Regulations Part T (2024) encourages outward-opening doors.[7] Now our locks need to be even better designed, for there is nothing the occupant can do should the door open whilst they are on the loo.

We also need to think about where the cubicle is positioned. With current toilet design, it is often only the **ambulant cubicle** that has an outwards-opening door, positioned at the end of the row where people will not be passing or queueing (Figure 7.8). This space must also be free from handwashing, drying and baby-changing facilities. We could also increase the corridor width so that people are

**Figure 7.8** Ambulant cubicle with outwards-opening door, indicated by a handle.

not forced into the door's swing. This would allow outwards-opening doors for more than just the ambulant toilet, or more than one ambulant toilet.

As our cubicles get larger and the doors extend from floor-to-ceiling, so doors get heavier. The right hinges will allow a door – including fire doors – to be used without significant force. The Building Regulations Part M also gives the maximum force to open entrance and internal doors.[8] To operate a door, and to indicate which way a door opens from the outside, a handle is needed on the side that we pull, and a push plate on the side that we push. On the inside, the lock sometimes doubles as a handle, but not always, as we shall see in the next section.

## Locks

'Yes, that'll do it,' said the doctor looking at my infected finger, after I told her how I had scratched it a fortnight earlier on the lock of a toilet door in a wine bar. It was one of those fiddly locks with a bolt that slides across except that the knob of the bolt was missing, exposing the end of a screw that would have held it in place. In trying to slide what was left, my finger slipped. The tiny scrape had grown redder and redder until it was an inch in diameter and I was unable to bend the joint. The doctor prescribed antibiotics, and it took another week for the skin to dry out, scab over and flake off. This was by no means an **accessible lock** or even a functioning one. How hard is it to get a lock right? What do people need from a lock?

## We need a lock to stop the door from opening

This may be obvious, but a surprising number do not work and are not routinely checked. When a cubicle does not lock, many people will not use that cubicle, which makes the queue longer. Those that are prepared to 'risk it' might do so if they can hold the door shut whilst using the toilet, but if someone should push against the unlocked door, it could cause a shock or injury. Checking that locks are working could become part of daily cleaning routines, or when toilets are opened or closed. Alternatively, users could be provided with a means to easily report minor but critical malfunctions like this, through a QR code for the cubicle.

## We need to know that the lock is working

If we cannot tell if the door is locked, we must perform a few trial runs where we lock and unlock it, trying the door to see when it is effectively locked. Some internal thumbnail locks are designed to unlock when the handle is tried from the inside, rendering this action futile. Being able to see that a mechanical barrier is holding the door shut – a bolt, a latch, a hook – gives us reassuring feedback that we have used the lock correctly (Figure 7.9).

## We need the lock to show others that the door is locked

Lock indicators are surprisingly ineffective. An inclusive indicator will be visible from a distance, for example from the furthest point at which a queue might form (Figure 7.10). It will have clear colour distinction between open and closed that considers those with colour-blindness. Red and green can appear the same, whereas a blue or green-blue provides more contrast with red. An inclusive lock will have intuitive meaning through these colours as to what they indicate. Does white mean locked or unlocked, or was it once another colour that's rubbed off through wear? There would also be words or symbols on the indicator: locked/unlocked, engaged/vacant; as a second level of information (Figure 7.11).

**Figure 7.9** A mechanical, inclusive lock where we can see the door cannot be opened.

**Figure 7.10** Colour-coded lighting showing from a distance if a toilet is available. The left handle is glowing green, the right handle glows red.

**Figure 7.11** Lock indicator with colour-coding and labels. Engaged is written in red; vacant in green. The words communicate the meaning for those with red-green colour-blindness.

Not having this information means that, as we have already covered, cubicles with a shut door can appear occupied whilst toilets that are locked do not appear to be. If the indicators fail, do we assume cubicles are vacant or occupied? Poor design leaves us in a no-win situation.

## We need to be able to open and close the lock

> I don't lock the door – I go in and just hope no-one comes in. I've been stuck in the loo too many times.
> **ADULT WITH ARTHRITIS**

Many of us come across toilet locks that we cannot physically open or close. This can be due to the high dexterity needed to operate small, fiddly sliders or bolts, or because we do not have the hand strength. A lock that can be locked easily but is tricky or stiff to unlock becomes a source of stress or distress.

> I have terrible trouble with door locks. Often they may be easy to close but rely on more grip and pressure to open in which case I get stuck in the toilet.
> **ADULT WITH CHRONIC HEALTH CONDITION**

I was trapped in the loo … they had to break the door down. I had to stand on the loo whilst they broke the door, I was crying.
**TEENAGER RECOUNTING AN EXPERIENCE AGED TWELVE**

A good test for an accessible lock is whether it can be operated with a closed fist, forearm or elbow. These are often seen in the accessible cubicle (Figure 7.12) as a feature of Part M of the Building Regulations and are now a recommendation in Part T for all cubicles.[9] Using these locks in standard cubicles (Figure 7.9) will make them inclusive to people who would only opt for the accessible toilet because of the lock and other features that rely on hand strength and dexterity, like taps and flushes. We need to fit a lock anyway, so awareness of these aspects of design will help us to make an inclusive choice at no extra cost.

Those locks with big handles, like levers, they're easy to use and they never seem to get stuck.
**YOUNG ADULT**

A big handle lock that slides across [is best], the bigger the better.
**DISABLED PERSON**

**Figure 7.12** Inclusive lock in accessible cubicle. This design allows the user to see that the lock is latched across the door.

## We need a way to open the door once we have unlocked it

Sometimes the lock doubles as a means to get the door open when leaving the cubicle. Not only do we need to slide, twist, unhook or lever the lock undone, we also need to push or pull on it. Not all locks give us much to pull on or are designed to make this comfortable. A handle or grab rail that allows us to pull, or a panel to push on, will allow us to get the door open as well as telling us whether it is push or pull that we are after. For outwards-opening doors, Part T requires a horizontal bar to pull the door closed in the first place.[10]

## We need a way to open the door if the lock cannot be unlocked

People can get locked in toilets. Maybe the mechanism fails, maybe they are physically or cognitively unable to open the door, or maybe they have fallen ill. This is a particular risk with fully enclosed cubicles where we cannot climb, see or communicate through the gaps around the door.

The easiest security measure is to use locks that can be unlocked from the outside. Many locks have a slot on the exterior of the door that allow them to be twisted and unlocked with a coin or screwdriver (Figure 7.11). If a door opens inwards, Part T requires an 'emergency release mechanism' to allow the door to open outwards in case someone has collapsed against it.[11] An electronic lock needs a means of overriding it. If we have not considered ways to open a locked door, we must find to a way to unhang or destroy it.

## We need to be able to get help if we are locked inside

As more toilets are built in fully enclosed cubicles, we must think about how someone will attract attention if stuck or unwell. We can check toilet cubicles regularly – at least twice a day at opening and closing – though some places check hourly. We can display information on who to contact and how, so someone can get help for themselves or for another user. We could fit alarms (see Chapter 8) in toilets other than the accessible cubicle particularly if we know users in this setting are more likely to fall unwell.

## Children and locks

Some young children like to play with locks and handles. It can be stressful to be using a toilet whilst our child does this, knowing that they or someone on the outside might open the now unlocked door. It would also be risky if the child left the cubicle whilst their grown-up was still on the toilet.

Whilst the guardian of a three-year-old might wish a toilet lock to be too difficult or out of reach for their child to unlock whilst they are weeing, a six-year-old using the toilet on their own may be locked in, frustrated or distressed by the same feature. Considering the needs of children will make a more inclusive environment for all. Children, their parents and guardians trying to support them, and other adult users who may have similar physical needs such as less reach or hand strength, will benefit from locks at a more accessible height.

> I sometimes have to stand on a stool to lock doors. Locks are often too high and you can sometimes reach the lock to lock it but don't have the strength to unlock it – so I can't get out.
> **PERSON OF RESTRICTED GROWTH**

## Electronic locks

Electronic locks are found on automatic public conveniences (APCs) as well as in many on-board train toilets (Figure 7.13). This adds a cognitive challenge to using the toilet, where we must follow a set of instructions and press a series of buttons to open and close, and lock and unlock the toilet door.

> You feel silly standing outside having to read instructions on how to go to the toilet.
> **ADULT**

> Those ones in the market [APCs], I don't like them … they're so in-your-face. There's no privacy or dignity there. I was in one and it opened!
> **OLDER PERSON**

> Those three-stage locking devices on trains are just counter-intuitive. I've accidentally pressed the emergency button in there.
> **DISABLED ADULT**

Train companies use different designs where some buttons have dual functions and others do not. Is the door locked automatically when it closes or is that a separate button? Must we press an unlock button before pressing the button to open the door? We cannot see if the door is locked. Instead, we have a light indicator displaying a colour or word. Is it working? What does the colour mean? It is displaying the same information for others in the carriage? Such high

**Figure 7.13** Electronic lock on a train. These can need instructions when each train has a slightly different design. This one has two buttons for four operations: open, close, lock and unlock.

cognitive load can be especially difficult for children, people with dementia and people who cannot read.

If this design can be simplified or standardized, then it does have benefits. An electronic button to activate the lock requires little to no force or dexterity compared to a mechanical lock.

## Toilets locked from the outside

Some toilets are locked from the outside even when empty. This is to control who has access. Some are customer-only toilets, some are for specific groups (bus drivers at the end of the line) or abilities (RADAR accessible toilets for disabled people). Some are at the recommendation of the police, to try to avoid people using the toilet for other activities (see Chapter 2). They can be unlocked with passcodes, universal keys or by gatekeepers whose permission we must seek. How can systems that are intended to exclude be made more inclusive?

## Locks with passcodes

The design of a passcode lock (Figure 7.14) can exclude more than it means to. The buttons are fiddly and give no feedback. Many would be unable to push them. Extra symbols like * are needed, and there is no instruction as to how to cancel the entry and start again. The coffee shop where I wrote some of this book has a toilet locked with a passcode. The instructions were nearly fifty words long. In a two-hour period whilst I was working, over a dozen people walked by to use the toilet. Two went back to the till to ask for the code (to be told the keypad is currently deactivated), one more could not lock the door once inside and two others walked in on someone else using the toilet. It took one man three visits before he gained access.

Once inside, the latch from the passcode lock will click across the door; however, it can still be unlocked by someone else with the right code. A second, mechanical lock (typically lower down in the usual lock position) stops people from coming in. When leaving, the user unlocks the familiar mechanical lock but the door does not open. Panic sets in. When someone does not understand that

**Figure 7.14** Passcode lock in a restaurant.

there is a second latch to release; or in the case of a child, they cannot reach it; the design of the lock has trapped them in the toilet. There must not be such a cognitive overload for simply locking and unlocking a door.

## Toilets locked with keys

> Another place has a public loo but they keep it shut and you have to go and knock on a door and get the key and go and unlock it. What they will claim is that if they leave them unlocked, they will get vandalised.
>
> **OLDER PERSON**

Some publicly accessible toilets are locked with keys. Having found the toilet, we must now find the key holder and have them escort us back. Even short distances can be difficult for many. This can also be embarrassing and stressful. We do not want to tell a stranger that we need the toilet, we do not know if we have any right to access, and do not know if permission will be granted. What if the toilet is not for us? What if we are who they are trying to exclude? Access becomes restricted to those privileged enough to expect it to be given.

> You have to go and ask someone and you are generally made to feel bad and by the time you wait for them to get the key, with my UI [urinary incontinence] it is already a problem, because you only have to think about going to the toilet and then it comes.
>
> **OLDER PERSON WITH CHRONIC HEALTH CONDITION**

## Toilets locked with RADAR keys

In some cases, we can carry our own keys. RADAR keys (officially known as the National Key Scheme) are available for people to access accessible toilets (Figure 7.15). Not all accessible toilets have a RADAR lock but when they do, it is a way of limiting access to disabled people so that the toilet is more likely to be available when they need it. RADAR keys can be obtained through the local council. They can also be purchased online with no evidence of need. The provider will also hold a key. It is very common to see accessible toilets with RADAR locks, particularly on the transport network. If demand far outstrips supply, this is one way to prioritize access to those with an urgent need.

As with any barrier, problems come from trying to define who is given (or gives themselves) access to what is a complex and changing need, and the design of the barrier itself, in this case the key.

**Figure 7.15** RADAR lock from the inside. An inclusive design, this both locks and opens the door. Credit: Wellcome Collection/Eva Herzog.

I said I needed to change my daughter's nappy and the station manager and everybody searched for the RADAR key and nobody could find one and in the end I had to change her in the middle of the station.
**PARENT OF INFANT**

[the] key is awful. I have a tremor in my right hand so can't possibly use a key in that hand. By the time I've got it out of my handbag and then trying to get it in the lock, it's too long and I worry I'll wet myself. I find locked toilets so frustrating.
**OLDER PERSON WITH CHRONIC HEALTH CONDITION**

There are other ways to limit access to toilets, such as payment systems or card-activated doors (see Chapter 10). We may need to seek help or permission from others, such as security guards or receptionists. We are also limited in more subtle ways through symbolic barriers, sometimes even self-imposed, where we tell ourselves a toilet is not intended for us. For some, a toilet in a public building is a public toilet; for others who have never crossed the threshold of a library or town hall, these are out of bounds. Publicly accessible toilets in businesses are not accessible to those not comfortable in those premises. To make a toilet inclusive, providers need to *say* everyone is welcome. If we cannot design physical barriers out, we must follow through with action, by being ready to help with locks, keys and doors that may stand in someone's way.

## Hooks and shelves

When we enter a public toilet we are dressed for the outdoors. We have coats, gloves and scarves, multiple bags and other items in our hands or our pockets that will fall out when we undress (and no bag of rice to hand should our mobile phone fall down the loo). We may also have items that form part of our toileting needs. Catheters, stoma bags, period products, nappies, plus water or wipes to wash ourselves, others or our equipment. So, where can they go?

### Hooks

> [the hook] must be six feet high … they've done a very silly thing. Nobody of five foot or under can hang a coat, sticks or shopping bag.
> **OLDER PERSON USING A WALKING AID**

Typically, a hook is found on the back of the door. How high to place it is a decision for inclusive design. A reasonable height for the average adult will be too high for many. Taller people can bend down, but shorter people, people unable to stand and children have a lower maximum reach. Coat hooks are not always strong enough or big enough to hold a bag as well as a coat and are often so high that if the bag were to fall, the contents would be damaged. Having two hooks, one lower and one higher, is a good option, and recommended in the Building Regulations. They can also be placed somewhere other than the back of the door (Figure 7.16).

A hook near the toilet, strong enough for a bag and near enough to reach, will help if we need items from inside the bag whilst on the loo. Tampons and sanitary towels are no good to us hanging 6 feet up on the back of the door. It is surprising a nearby bag hook is not seen more often considering the extent of the need. Would public toilets have more bag hooks if those designing and installing toilets carried handbags? Perhaps you have not tried to wee, poo or manage a period whilst clutching a bag (or a baby!) to your body. It's no picnic. As with the cultural norm of the toilet queue itself (see Chapter 6), women's needs are considered less important or not at all.

Why not place a bag on the floor? This can be dirty, wet or messy with toilet paper. Toilet cubicles with gaps under the doors and walls carry the risk of a bag

**Figure 7.16** Two hooks for coats and bags on the side wall.

being snatched from outside. Not everyone finds it easy or has the balance or flexibility to pick things up from the floor. A hook makes things more comfortable.

> You need somewhere to hang your bags when you're sitting on the loo so you need a hook at least, because I hate putting anything on the floor. You don't know how clean the floor is.
> **OLDER PERSON WITH CHRONIC HEALTH CONDITION**

> While you lift your skirt and pull your knickers down or undo your zip and pull your trousers down … I hold my handbag in my teeth, so I am holding onto my handbag, but if I have more shopping then that, what are you going to do?
> **ADULT PARTICIPANT**

What about that baby? Not everything we carry can be hung on a hook or popped on a shelf. Child seats (Figure 7.17) can be helpful for adults using baby carriers, or whose infants like to crawl around, touch or run out of the cubicle. Whilst we are getting better at providing baby-changing facilities, we still forget that grown-ups will need to use the loo whilst keeping an eye on one or more tots.

**Figure 7.17** A child seat in a larger cubicle. This is at a museum that attracts young families.

A child seat and cubicles large enough to take a pushchair are both thoughtful additions to venues that welcome young families.

Back at the baby-changing table, a hook here gives us somewhere to hang the changing bag. Some drop-down models have this integrated into the design. Now we can get the nappy, wipes, cream, spare clothes or anything else that becomes essential mid-change (Figure 7.18).

## Which hook do we choose?

A hook protrudes into the toilet space so we need to be careful that we cannot hurt ourselves on it. A metal hook with sharp edges or corners can cut skin. A protruding hook can injure an eye. People are of all heights, so it is not enough to say that hooks should not be at eye level; a child will often find themselves in a cramped cubicle waiting for their grown-up to use the toilet. They are encouraged out of the way, pressed up against a wall, where a hook can stick out. The rule with children is: if they can hurt themselves on it, they will. Hooks need to be curved and smooth, with a good colour contrast from the wall behind (Figure 7.19). The hook and fixings need to be strong enough not to break and curved enough to stop things falling off.

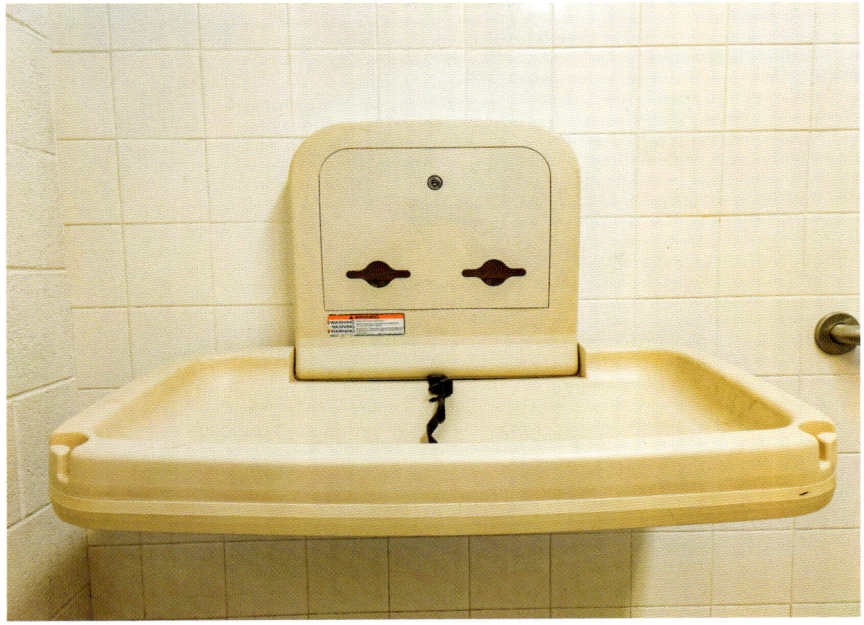

**Figure 7.18** A drop-down baby-changing table. The front corners are moulded to give somewhere to hang a bag. Credit: Chon Kit Leong/Alamy Stock Photo.

**Figure 7.19** An effective hook design. These are a curved, smooth, hard plastic with a strong colour contrast (orange on white). Credit: Wellcome Collection/Eva Herzog.

**Figure 7.20** Shelf in standard cubicle, above the cistern.

## Shelves

Shelves can perform some of the work of hooks, and more. Whilst of less use for coats, shelves allow us to put down all the loose objects that we might carry in our hands: phone, keys, gloves, water bottles, coffee cups and bags (Figure 7.20). A flat surface with space for belongings makes a good baby-changing area and is a good alternative to a hook next to a drop-down table (Figure 7.21).

Shelves also perform another important role by providing a surface for people with medical conditions who need to empty a catheter or replace or empty a stoma bag. Shelves are a requirement of an accessible toilet for this reason though they are often missing. They make a standard cubicle more inclusive too (Figure 7.22). The essential components of a stoma-friendly cubicle are a hook, a shelf, a mirror and a bin, all within the cubicle. Colostomy UK (2023) provide recommendations for the position and size of the shelf.[12]

Why don't more toilets have shelves? Some shelves disappeared through police intervention, as it can also be a place to prepare illegal drugs (Figure 7.23). The problem here is the illegal use, not the shelf. By designing out crime in this way, we design out our legitimate use, too.

**Figure 7.21** Bespoke baby-changing area with individual handwashing and surface space for belongings.

**Figure 7.22** Stoma-friendly standard cubicle. The design was planned so that the bin fit under the shelf, rather than as an afterthought, pushed up against the toilet.

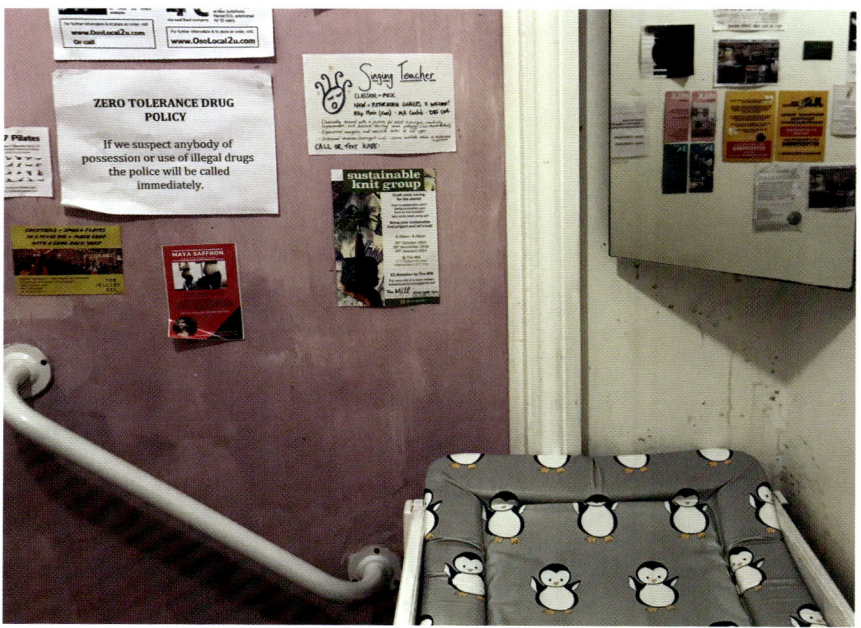

**Figure 7.23** Warning about drug use in a café toilet.

It is not only in the cubicle where we need a shelf. We also have items to set down when washing our hands or using a urinal. Whilst it is less essential to remove a coat when standing rather than sitting to wee, men do need their hands free to use a urinal and to be able to wash their hands afterwards. Once pockets are full, what do they do with the bags, bottles, phones or other objects they might be carrying? A shelf area and a few hooks close by would allow men to set down loose items before using them (Figure 7.24).

We might think that toilets meet a biological need, and that the paraphernalia that people carry with them is their choice to cope with, whether that's shopping, clothing or babies. But this is the reality of how we live our lives. By designing to help people with their day-to-day activities, we can create a better experience, and the design of the cubicle is the crux of creating comfort and privacy. Let's stop for a moment, take a breath and relax …

It's time to go to the toilet.

**Figure 7.24** Hooks opposite urinals. Credit: imageBROKER.com GmBH & Co. KG/Alamy Stock Photo.

## Notes

1. Kira, *The Bathroom*.
2. Building Regulations, *Approved Document T: Toilet Accommodation*.
3. UK Paruresis Trust (2023), 'Paruresis symptoms & problems'. Available online: https://www.ukpt.org.uk/what-is-paruresis/spectrum-of-severity (accessed 15 December 2023).
4. Building Regulations, *Approved Document T: Toilet Accommodation*.
5. Ibid.
6. London Legacy Development Corporation, *Inclusive Design Standards*. Building Regulations *Approved Document M: Access to and use of buildings. Vol. 2: Buildings other than dwellings*.
7. Building Regulations, *Approved Document T: Toilet Accommodation*.
8. Building Regulations, *Approved Document M: Access to and use of buildings. Vol. 2: Buildings other than dwellings*.
9. Building Regulations, *Approved Document T: Toilet Accommodation*.
10. Ibid.
11. Ibid.
12. Colostomy UK (2023), 'Guide to stoma-friendly accessible toilets'. Available online: https://www.colostomyuk.org/wp-content/uploads/2023/02/Colostomy-UK-Stoma-Friendly-Accessible-toilets-2.pdf (accessed 4 June 2024).

# 8  In the cubicle

On our journey so far we have felt the need to go to the loo and looked for a toilet we can access both legitimately and physically. We have negotiated doors and chosen which type of toilet to use. We have possibly had to queue but finally we are in the cubicle, maybe with a child (or two). Hopefully we have been able to lock the door, take off our coat and put down any shopping, luggage or loose items. These are all the considerations we have gone through just to get in the cubicle. If someone has a bladder or bowel urgency condition, there will no doubt be a certain amount of stress as well. It is no wonder some toilet signs show figures with their legs crossed (Figure 8.1).

In the cubicle with the door shut and hopefully locked, we are ready to 'go'. In the cubicle is a toilet pan (usually with a toilet seat), a toilet paper dispenser, a flush and perhaps a sanitary / disposal bin. We turn our attention to these features: is the toilet seat up or down? Can we find the flush? Is there toilet paper?

**Figure 8.1**  Toilet sign with legs crossed. Credit: Peter Cripps/Alamy Stock Photo.

> One of the biggest horrors for people who need to use public toilets and they've got some sort of disability; you know you get in there and often you don't have the chance to check that there's toilet roll and you know it's really annoying when there's none … it's the basics.
>
> **WHEELCHAIR USER**

What problems do people have with these items or the lack of them? How can our experience within the cubicle be more inclusively designed?

# The toilet

## The toilet pan

The toilet pan affords the collection of our products of excretion: our wee, poo and menstrual blood; and in the UK, the toilet paper we use to clean ourselves.

Guidance recommends that the toilet pan is set centrally in the cubicle. If the cubicle also includes a disposal bin, and depending on the size of the bin in relation to the pan, this can make it a particularly tight squeeze. This is not just an issue in the separate-gender women's toilets. As more calls are recognized for disposal bins in the men's toilets to meet the need of colostomy and urostomy users and trans men, designing in space around the pan to allow for this could be something to explore.

The orientation of toilet pans and urinals also needs some consideration. LLDC Inclusive Design Standard (2019) recommends at least 10–15 per cent of toilet pans and urinals do not align with Mecca. This has been part of their standard since the development of venues and other buildings for the 2012 London Olympic and Paralympic Games, and reflects the needs of both the then global audience and current local population.[1]

## Toilet pan height

The standard toilet pan can vary in height. This can pose issues for some users of the standard cubicle. If too low, people with knee and hip issues may have difficulty getting up. The NHS advises against using low toilets after hip replacement.[2] If too high, parents may have issues getting a child onto the toilet pan especially if there is not enough space to bend and lift a child on. *Approved Document T* of the Building Regulations (2024)[3] recommends a toilet pan height of 480 mm.

You still have to lift them, and trying to do this whilst pregnant is difficult in the space. Then when you're not pregnant and have a bad back trying to lift a larger child onto the toilet is also difficult. A four-year-old can be quite big but still not be able to get onto the loo unless she puts her hand on the loo and jumps up and I'd rather she didn't do this in public loos.

**PARENT OF YOUNG CHILD**

The toilet pan found in the accessible cubicle is also recommended to be a height of 480 mm to make it easier for people to transfer from their wheelchair to the pan. The 2005 VivaCity audit of 101 accessible toilets found that 66 per cent of toilet pans were the wrong height and considered 'the WC pan [as] one of the more controversial aspects of [accessible] toilet cubicle design'.[4] Many people commented that the toilet pan was too low.

If the toilet pan is too low, I just can't use the loo.

**WHEELCHAIR USER**

I don't sit on the loo … if I'm having a pee I hover and hold onto the chair … I might not be able to get off if I sit down.

**WHEELCHAIR USER**

The accessible cubicle has been primarily designed for wheelchair access, so the height of the toilet pan in relation to the ease of transfer from a wheelchair is critical. The Centre for Accessible Environments *Good Loo Design Guide* (2004)[5] provides good illustrations of the different ways people might transfer from their wheelchairs to the toilet pan. People develop their own methods for transference based on their body's needs and abilities.

## Toilet material

Most toilet pans are ceramic; however, some may be stainless steel (Figure 8.2) or a composite resin (Figure 8.3). These have been specifically designed to prevent vandalism. Stainless-steel toilets tend not to have a toilet seat, with bare metal or a small wooden or a plastic seat pad attached to the top of the pan. This can be very uncomfortable when trying to sit to have a poo, especially in cold weather. Stainless-steel toilets are unpopular with the public and often result in hovering over the pan or avoiding the provision altogether.

Those vandal-proof stainless steel loos with half-moon seats, I won't use them.

**OLDER PERSON**

**Figure 8.2** Stainless-steel toilet pan with small rimmed 'seat'.

**Figure 8.3** Resin composite toilet pan.

> Some train stations have stainless steel loos, I hate those.
> **YOUNGER PERSON**

Resin composite toilets have the top of the pan rounded and moulded into a seat shape. This makes them easier to clean but can be a bit off-putting at first for those who prefer the sight of a physical toilet seat. The resin has the look and feel of our more familiar ceramic toilet that we will have at home yet is still robust for the public toilet. They also feel more comfortable from a temperature perspective when sitting down.

## The toilet seat

Is the toilet seat (if there is one) up or down? For the majority of people the first step will be to put a raised toilet seat down but many recoil at the thought of touching it. As Kira (1976)[6] notes there is an element of 'stranger danger' at play where the stranger is microbe-based, which resonates with our feelings towards bodily waste. The irony of this situation is that a raised toilet seat can be because the toilet has been recently cleaned, and cleaners have been advised to leave the toilet seat up to dry the underside.

If down, is the seat clean? Many women hover over the seat either due to pre-existing drips or as a learned behaviour in the belief that the seat is inherently dirty. A lot of girls are taught to use public toilets this way. Some may put toilet paper around the seat to act as a barrier so that they can sit down.[7] However, we are more likely to drip urine on the seat if we are hovering. The intention to avoid contact with visible or microbial dirt leads to the toilet becoming dirtier and the behaviour being reinforced.

Hovering is also a less effective way to wee. A US study in 2020 of over 6,000 women found that hovering could increase the risk of urinary tract infections (UTI) due to the incomplete voiding of the bladder.[8]

> Squatting [hovering] over instead of sitting down on the toilet can change the mechanics of urinating; over time that can increase the risk of lower urinary tract symptoms including pelvic floor dysfunction and infections.[9]

Here the complex psychological interplay between our preconceptions of the public toilet as a dirty space coupled with the thought of direct contact with microbial 'stranger danger' can have real physical health ramifications.

UTIs, a common health issue that occur predominately in women, cost the NHS £386 million in 2017/18.[10] They are most commonly treated with antibiotics, contributing to antimicrobial resistance which the World Health Organization considers to be the 'top global health and development threat'.[11]

Is there a way to design hovering out? This is not how we would use a toilet at home. It may also be that the drips on the seat were not urine at all. An overpowerful flush can throw water onto the seat. When a toilet cubicle includes handwashing, there is a new source of water that might be mistaken for urine: a powerful tap splashes out of a small basin; water is shaken from hands and lands on the seat; the hand dryer blows water that lands as a spray of drips. Not only does this look untidy, the next person may now assume the worst of both the liquid and the previous user's behaviour, resulting in more people hovering when they may otherwise have chosen to sit.

Toilet seat design extends to the needs of children. A child-sized seat stops a child from needing to hold the toilet seat to avoid falling in. An adult seat can also lead to mistakes in positioning on the toilet.

> The toilet seat is too big for a toddler, sometimes she is not sitting back far enough because she has to hang onto the toilet seat and her wee shoots forward through the gap between the seat and the loo soaking her pants.
> **PARENT**

These spaces of everyday interactions seem oblivious to the needs of the child's body. Child-sized toilets (Figure 8.4) or child-sized seats (Figure 8.5) are an inclusive addition to facilities that attract families with very young children in particular.

Checking the fittings of the toilet seat so that it does not wobble or come loose should be part of a basic cleaning and maintenance routine. In the accessible toilet the toilet seat can be used for additional support, so it is essential that it is secure and robust.

> [Transfer is] a strain on the hinges, I've broken a few toilet seats in my time because of this.
> **WHEELCHAIR USER**

> [I've] broken a few toilet seats in my time … I'm 20 stone, I can come down with a bang so those plastic ones can be dangerous.
> **OLDER PARTICIPANT**

> One time … the toilet seat wobbled, and it really scared me so now I just try to hang on until I get home.
> **OLDER PARTICIPANT**

**Figure 8.4** Child-sized toilet next to standard toilet.

**Figure 8.5** Child-sized toilet seat on a standard toilet pan. A wall-mounted infant seat is also available. Credit: Maria Argutinskaya/Alamy Stock Photo.

A poorly fitted or maintained toilet seat in the accessible loo can have quite serious consequences as one of our participants recounted.

> I had a really nasty pressure sore from a loo seat in Brighton. I caught my skin on a sharp bit, it was only a little cut and I thought I'd be alright but after a couple of days it began to get nasty and now it's taken four to five months to heal. It went into a pressure sore because I was sitting on it. I have to have the district nurses come every day … just from a tiny cut when transferring from a toilet.
> **WHEELCHAIR USER**

For many involved in the design, fitting and management of public toilets it may seem as if it is just a toilet seat. Yet it is the one aspect of the toilet cubicle that will have direct physical contact with our bodies. It can carry traces of the previous user, not only in any residual left behind but also from body heat which can be off-putting.

## *The toilet lid*

There is no direct reference in design guides as to if a toilet lid should be included or not. However, this is another feature that will need to be put down or lifted up and so touched to use the toilet, as well as added to the cleaning routine and robustly secured to prevent vandalism.

Post-Covid-19 it has been recommended, where there is one, to put the toilet lid down before flushing to limit the spread of the flush plume although research was ongoing concerning just how unhygienic the flush plume might be.[12]

Toilet lids on the accessible toilet pan can be uncomfortable for people who need back support, either through a back rest (recommended prior to BS8300, 2018)[13] or the close-coupled cistern itself (now recommended in BS8300, 2018).

> [My] trunk control is very poor; the level of the spinal injury is T4 just under the armpit. My spinal support is not good, so I need a backrest … I sit far back on the loo as I need to wiggle out of my clothes and then I need to lean back to pull them up.
> **WHEELCHAIR USER**

Other users find the backrest problematic.

> That backrest is impossible. I can't sit back because of the way I sit on the loo.
> **WALKING-AID USER**

I often find the toilet seat has a cover which covers the backrest and prevents the toilet seat staying up.
**WHEELCHAIR USER**

I prefer to stand when urinating, but sometimes find the padded support at the back of the pan prevents the toilet seat from staying up.
**WHEELCHAIR USER**

Having a lid on a toilet that has a backrest can obstruct the use of the accessible loo for some users (Figure 8.6). New buildings will follow the current guidance in BS8300 (2018) which does not include a backrest but recommends a flat-top close-coupled cistern.

Back in the standard toilet, there have been recent innovations in toilet lids as a component of the flush system (Figure 8.7). This uses a mix of water and air to get rid of the waste once the lid has locked in place. They use less water in the flushing cycle and so are a sustainable alternative. If using this design is an option it should be checked to make sure the closure mechanism is not difficult for users with less hand strength or dexterity. Consideration should also be given to instructions

**Figure 8.6** Accessible toilet with a back rest, obstructed by the toilet lid.

**Figure 8.7** Combined air and water flush system that requires closing of toilet lid to work.

required to illustrate this new style of toilet flushing. Our familiarity with flushing the toilet is similar to the operation of the door lock. Having to read instructions on this action may be difficult again for people whose first language is not English or who cannot read. Those who are neurodiverse or have neurodegeneration may panic if they cannot simply flush the toilet.

Whether intentional or not, some toilet flushes are positioned behind the toilet lid. Not everyone wants to touch the lid or will think to look there. This could result in the toilet being left unflushed, a potential design barrier to keeping the cubicle clean (Figure 8.8).

## *Sit or squat?*

Most of the UK population will use a pedestal toilet pan designed for sitting. The World Design Organization[14] estimates that from the global population of 8 billion people, two-thirds (over 5 billion) use squat toilets (Figure 8.9). Squatting to use the toilet especially to poo has a number of health benefits. The Bladder and Bowel Foundation (2021)[15] promotes squatting to wee and poo as the heathier way to 'go'. Squatting uses gravity to help us release our wee and poo, and also

**Figure 8.8** A toilet lid that conceals the flush operation when open. The sign reads 'flush button located behind toilet seat.'

**Figure 8.9** Squat toilet in Japan.

makes key muscles relax and avoids straining.[16] A number of footstools are now on the domestic market to raise the legs to a squat-like position for healthier excretion.

Squatting is not something that is accommodated in UK toilet design, with some providers telling us that toilet seats can be broken due to people climbing on the pan to use as a squat toilet.

Squat toilets are also rare in public toilet provision in the UK. In 2010 a shopping centre in Rochdale made national news[17] after installing squat toilets in its public toilet facilities. These were soon closed down after 'public outrage'.[18]

If a toilet is to serve a community who would prefer squat toilets in addition to the UK's more familiar design, then user engagement during the design process should pick this up. They would also be suitable in international settings in the UK such as airport provision.

## Wiping or washing

### Toilet paper dispensers

> Big rolls get stuck, and you have to ferret for the paper end, and you end up tearing off confetti … then you give it a good tug and you end up with a stream of paper all over the floor which you then don't want to use.
> **OLDER PERSON**

Seat down, lid up, you are finally using the loo. Once you have finished your business you will reach for the toilet paper. Only now do you realize that there is none or that it is difficult to get hold of. Being able to clean ourselves after using the loo is one of the most important aspects of toileting. In the accessible loo it is recommended that the toilet paper can be used with just one hand. We would recommend this for all toilet cubicles as many people who do not require other features of the accessible loo may require an accessible toilet paper dispenser.

The British Standards BS6465 Part 4[19] recommends that due to the cost of labour for refilling toilet paper dispensers, larger models should be considered, but that these should not restrict the space of the cubicle. The reality of this recommendation is that large roll 'drums' have been installed in many public toilet facilities, where it is difficult to find the end of the toilet paper even for a dexterous person (Figure 8.10).

> That big toilet paper drum, I have problems with that. I can't unwind the paper. I can't really manage with just one hand.
> **DISABLED PERSON**

**Figure 8.10** Large drum toilet paper dispenser in the accessible toilet. This is difficult to use and difficult to reach.

You've got to be able to get hold of it and they [children] have to, too.
**PARENT**

The positioning of the dispenser, particularly large drum rolls can cause people difficulty, especially in the accessible loo.

[Toilet paper is] sometimes difficult to get to. I sometimes have to take the toilet paper before I sit down as I would not be able to reach it when on the pan. Polio affects my turning so I find it difficult to turn or go back in any way. So, toilet paper placing can be difficult and in an awkward position. Those big rolls are awful, trying to find the start. I would prefer a single-sheet dispenser.
**WHEELCHAIR USER**

It can be really awkward when it's a roll, the positioning where it's too far back and you have to turn around to reach it. Single paper dispenser would be easier.
**OLDER USER**

Single-sheet dispensers (Figure 8.11) are considered more accessible in all cubicles and less wasteful, with the option to take as many sheets as needed. Care needs to be taken when refilling these types of dispensers to make sure they are not too packed and difficult to pull the paper out.

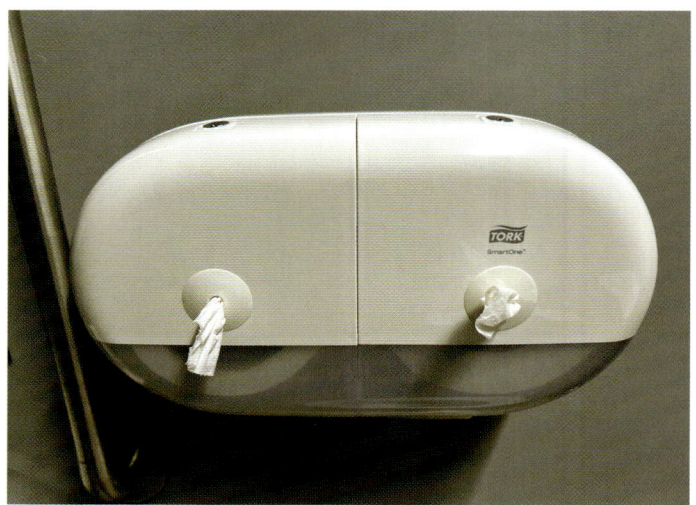

**Figure 8.11** Single-sheet double toilet roll dispenser.

For many users of the standard toilet cubicle, the toilet roll dispenser may also act as support when sitting down or getting off the toilet pan. This can put a lot of pressure on the dispenser's fittings and may result in it or part of it coming away from the wall. Providing more toilets with grab rails is a better alternative.

## Washing with water

Some people prefer to clean themselves afterwards with water instead of toilet paper. This is a common method of post-toilet hygiene in many countries and cultures. In the UK, people might use plastic water bottles in public toilets, which is one reason why (cleaners have shared with us) these are often found in the cubicles or in the rubbish. Providing a bin within the facility for plastic recycling, and for litter in general, might help keep it tidier. Some toilet designs, such as those in Japan, include water cleansing from a jet within the toilet pan. These can be very helpful for disabled people who may have difficulty cleaning themselves with paper but may be expensive for providers to install in the accessible public toilet. More affordable options are now available with a bidet function within the toilet seat lid. These have been fitted in some UK workplaces for people who need or prefer to clean with water, where the bidet seat is used on one or more toilets in a row of standard cubicles. Cleansing with water can also be included by supplying a hand-held sprayer or a water jug, called a 'lota' in Islamic culture.

Establishing the demand is something that can be revealed through people-centred research and community engagement with current and future users of a toilet facility.

# The flush

Flushing the toilet takes away the evidence of our body's waste. To not complete this action contravenes our deeply held social practices and a key element of our toilet training.[20] Sometimes our thoughts may be elsewhere and we completely forget: this happened to me recently causing me to rush back into the cubicle. Thankfully there wasn't a queue waiting to go in. What would they have thought of me! Yet for some users the type of flush operation may mean they cannot flush. This might be due to where it is positioned or the way the flush is activated.

## *Flush design*

**Sensor flush:** Post-pandemic, sensor-operated flushes have become popular as they limit the touchpoints within the toilet, especially those that do not include handwashing within the cubicle. They are generally accessible to all users as they do not require dexterity or hand strength (Figure 8.12). They are usually set within a panel system (not a cistern) and need to be positioned at a good height and space away from the toilet pan to avoid accidentally going off when using the loo, but not at such a height that they can't be reached by children.

> I set [sensor flushes] off with my backpack and sometimes it continuously flushes. It makes me feel uncomfortable and rushed. I really feel the need to control toilet flushing.
> **YOUNG ADULT**

> Children always want to flush the loo; they have to squeeze past the sanitary bin and then [the flush] is too hard for them. The push button is too difficult but waving your hand across [a sensor flush] is ideal because you don't have to touch anything.
> **PARENT**

Some sensor flushes have signage to indicate that it is sensor-operated. This helps people who may not recognize a sensor flush or be familiar with its

**Figure 8.12** A sensor flush in an accessible toilet. This has the instruction 'wave to flush' and is positioned within reach of the user. This toilet features strong colour contrast and both hand dryer and paper towel options (see Chapter 9).

operation. People with neurodegeneration and otherwise able to use the toilet independently may be confused by a lack of familiarity with a sensor flush. Don Norman, author of *The Design of Everyday Things* (1988),[21] has posited that if instructions are required the design can be considered to have failed. However, sensor flushes are a relatively new development in public toilet provision. Signage

**Figure 8.13** A sensor-flush sign. The sign should be rotated 90 degrees so that the hand is waving in front of the sensor, not underneath it. Credit: Topsy Page, 2023.

to aid people in their operation is helpful in the early stages as they transition to the more familiar (Figure 8.13).

**Push-button flush:** There are different types of push-button flushes that vary in the size of the button, the effort needed to push it and the volume of water released. They are often 'flush' with the cistern or wall. Some require a small amount of pressure to operate (Figure 8.14) (but if too small a button, will still be inaccessible to those who have limited dexterity). Larger versions can be equally difficult if they need too much force. Those that are inset into the top of cisterns can be inaccessible due to the reach across the toilet pan to access.

> I can't use those button flushes that they put on top of the cistern, I don't have the strength and it makes you feel really dirty when you can't flush.
> **USER WITH CHRONIC HEALTH CONDITION**

> I can't use the wall push button flushes with my nails.
> **YOUNG ADULT**

> They're very stiff but I can work it very well with my walking stick. I put it on there and lean on it and the thing flushes very well.
> **OLDER PERSON**

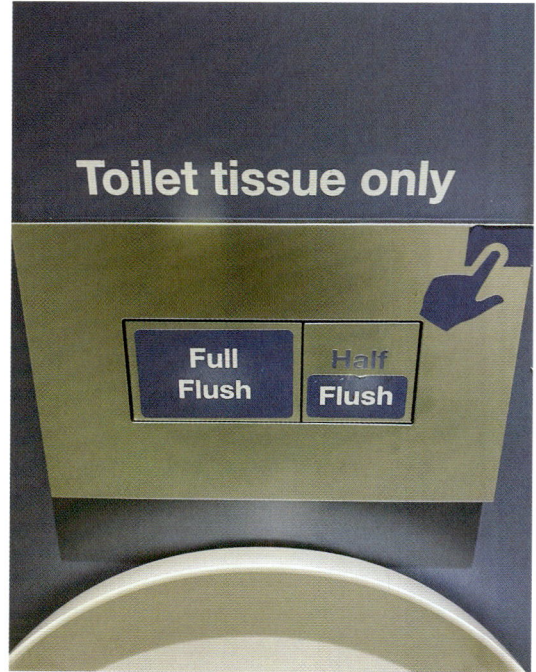

**Figure 8.14** An accessible push-button flush. This is large, labelled and requires little force.

> Push buttons don't work. I need a flush that responds to gentle touch. I have to throw my arm to grab a handle, so I need one to just touch.
> **DISABLED USER**

**Lever flush:** Lever-handled flushes have the benefit of familiarity as the typical flush design of the twentieth century, whether positioned in a panel or directly attached to a cistern. However, they still require touching a potentially dirty surface. We create our own techniques to operate flushes and other contact points in the toilet; perhaps we use toilet paper or cover our hands with our sleeve. We may use our wrist or elbow to keep fingers clean. An illuminating discussion on X, formally *Twitter*, revealed how some women used their feet to operate the flush. The most accessible design is the paddle-lever flush (Figure 8.15), which is the recommended flush for the accessible toilet. The paddle-lever flush (or other accessible flush designs) could be used in all standard facilities to make them more inclusive. As these can be pushed with an arm or elbow, this also helps people who do not wish to touch anything with bare fingers, without resorting to extreme measures.

**Figure 8.15** Paddle or spatula lever flush handle.

## Flush position

The location of the flush can stop us from using it, in different ways. Perhaps we cannot find it, hidden behind a toilet seat lid. Perhaps a sensor flush has activated while we are using the loo, leaving the cistern empty when we need it. Hand-operated flushes can be too high for someone of limited reach, including children, to access or apply pressure to.

The VivaCity study found this was a particular problem in the accessible toilet; nearly half of the toilet flushes audited were on the wrong side, especially when installed on a cistern. Paddle flushes should be installed on the transfer-side of the toilet, not on the side closest to the wall and the fixed grab rails, so that a wheelchair user does not have to reach over the toilet pan to operate it (Figures 8.16 and 8.17).

> So often you find the toilet flush on the wrong side, and you can't reach to flush it … it really does annoy me because you don't want to leave the toilet without it being flushed because there's nothing more off-putting than coming into a loo that hasn't been flushed.
> **WHEELCHAIR USER**

**Figure 8.16** Paddle flush installed on the correct side of the accessible toilet pan.

**Figure 8.17** Paddle flush installed on the wrong side of the accessible toilet pan.

[If the] flush is on the wrong side I can't stretch over the toilet as I can lose my balance and fall.
**WHEELCHAIR USER**

I often find flushes on the wrong side … I struggle to reach it. I once mentioned this to [large supermarket chain] but they didn't understand what I was talking about.
**WHEELCHAIR USER**

After going to the loo, I found I couldn't reach the flush. I had to go to customer services and apologise for the mess I'd left in the toilet but that I couldn't reach to flush it. It was so embarrassing, I hated leaving the loo like that and I hated having to ask a stranger to flush it for me.
**WHEELCHAIR USER**[22]

Setting the paddle flush too high also means people cannot use it, especially on a cistern that has been raised to accommodate a backrest. British Standards BS8300 recommend a paddle-lever flush to be set at 800–1,000 mm from the finished floor level.[23] The Building Regulations Part M[24] only gives instruction that the flush handle (on a cistern) should be on the side of the transfer space with no indication of a suggested height.

When they first plan these loos, I don't know how they start or what they're thinking of but the height for pushing a button or pulling the flush or whatever, it varies so much.
**WHEELCHAIR USER**

*PAS 6463: Design for the Mind* recommends quiet flush systems especially in Changing Places toilets and other settings where 'sensory sensitivities are likely to be experienced by some users'.[25]

# Sanitary and disposal bins

Maybe you have come to the toilet for another reason other than to have a wee or poo. Maybe you just want to check that you are not leaking from your tampon, sanitary or continence pad or ostomy bag. If you are a man and need a bin, currently you have very little option but to use the accessible loo as there tend not to be sanitary bins in the men's provision (or disposal bin as Part T[26] has reframed them).

> [Continence] pad disposal is always a problem because of a lack of disposal in men's toilets.
>
> **OLDER PERSON**

Bins help prevent period products (tampons and pads) being flushed down the toilet pan as these can often cause blockages to the plumbing.[27] Sanitary bins are found predominately in the women's, accessible and gender-neutral provision. They are a legal requirement in workplaces[28] but only in the women's and accessible toilets. The Boys need Bins campaign by Prostate Cancer UK highlighted the lack of a requirement for bins in the men's toilets within workplace legislation. Changes to this would be one step to allowing men to 'live well and have incontinence dignity'.[29] Therefore, bins are needed in all toilets, in most or all cubicles, for menstrual and continence products, and where there is a baby-changing table. When a toilet cubicle also includes baby-change provision, the larger nappy bin can be used for all sanitary and continence waste.

However, sanitary and nappy bins are not always accessible. It may be too difficult for those with limited dexterity to lift the lid or operate a pedal, or because they are out of reach of the toilet. Sanitary bins come in different dimensions, so should be selected and designed into all cubicles from the beginning to make sure there is enough space between toilet and wall for it to fit. Anyone sitting on the toilet does not want to be so close to the bin that they touch that too, nor must it stop people from getting close enough to use the flush (Figure 8.18). Parents commented that sanitary bins can, like flushes, turn the toilet into an adventure for children. Enclosed sanitary bins integrated into the layout would be preferable (Figure 8.19).

> Children seem to love touching bins … it would be good if they were out of toddler height.
>
> **PARENT**

> She likes to put things in the sanitary bin, she gets her hands right in there.
>
> **PARENT**

In this setting, all bodily waste is considered to be from a healthy population and can be thrown away in a regular bin and collected as municipal waste.[30] There does not need to be different bins for different types of waste. Bin selection should consider if the bin has a lid (to contain smells), if it is large enough for items like nappies and continence pads, its overall volume (factoring in how often it will be emptied), whether it will fit the space without blocking access (including the transfer space for wheelchair users), if the lid is accessible and if it is within reach

**Figure 8.18** Sanitary bin blocking access to the flush.

**Figure 8.19** Sanitary bin factored into the layout of the cubicle at design stage.

when needed. Some sanitary/disposal bins are sensor-operated which takes into consideration concerns about dexterity and hygiene. Making sure the bin's sensor operation is also legible to visually impaired users would also help. Current sanitary bins in the marketplace appear not to have considered the full range of abilities that may be needed or the space in which the bin will be placed.

# Grab rails

> [I] use to use the ordinary ladies, but I've found over the last couple of years that I have greater difficulty getting up and down from the loo seat. I now need the hand bars. I wouldn't use the disabled loo if standard toilets had hand bars.
> **OLDER PERSON**

Grab rails are essential in the accessible toilet (see Figure 8.20) with clearly laid out guidance in both the Building Regulations *Approved Document M* and the British Standard BS8300-2 (2018) (see Chapter 6). Despite such clear instructions, grab rails continue to be misplaced or misaligned with other features of the accessible

**Figure 8.20** Grab rails in unisex accessible toilet with corner toilet.

cubicle. Many disabled people require grab rails to use the toilet on their own. Not all of the grab rails may be used in the same way as people use the loo based on their abilities and experience, so the grab rails are there should additional support be needed. However, it is essential that they are fixed securely to the wall at the recommended heights from floor level.

Grab rails are also found in the ambulant cubicle. Guidance for the layout of the ambulant cubicle is also found in the Building Regulations ADM, the British Standards BS8300 and Part T (Figure 8.21). Whilst these diagrams may include the space for the waste/sanitary bin in the floor plan, this is not included in the elevation guidance. This can lead to poor choice in bin provision, as one that is too high might make using the grab rail awkward to use (Figure 8.22).

Normalizing grab rails and adding them to more standard facilities would make the toilet more inclusive, particularly in small settings like cafés where only one standard toilet is provided.

> I would be able to use a standard toilet if it had grab rails and was slightly bigger.
> **OLDER PARTICIPANT**

**Figure 8.21** Grab rails in an ambulant toilet, in Sainsburys.

**Figure 8.22** Grab rail in ambulant cubicle with large sanitary bin.

It would be great if every toilet had grab rails so that they became an everyday bit of equipment and not medical and scary.
**CARER**

The accessible loos … have more space than I actually need. It's more important that I have grab rails … so a larger standard cubicle would be ideal.
**PARTICIPANT WITH CHRONIC HEALTH CONDITION**

# Alarms

Many users of the accessible cubicle will never use the alarm (typically an emergency pull cord) but get an added sense of security and reassurance from knowing it is there. So, it is important that it is positioned and managed right. The Building Regulations (ADM) offer two options for the position of the emergency pull cord: on the side closest to the toilet pan or placed against the back wall of the transfer space. Both sides have positives and negatives. Placing the cord on the side closest to the toilet pan, and near the basin (Figure 8.23), might make it unreachable to someone fallen in the transfer space. It might also get in the way

**Figure 8.23** Alarm cord on the side closest to the toilet pan, between the grab rail and the basin.

of reaching from the toilet pan to the basin. If it is accidentally set off, there needs to be a reset button close by.

> If it's too near the sink and you're washing your hands you sometimes get caught up in it.
> **WHEELCHAIR USER**

> Sometimes it's in the transfer space [but] how do you reach it if it's on the other side? I fall on the floor, that's it – I can't slide over.
> **WHEELCHAIR USER**

An alternative position for the alarm cord in the Building Regulations (but not in the British Standard BS8300) is by the side of the toilet in the transfer space. This can get in the way for people transferring from the wheelchair to the toilet pan. Figure 8.20 shows an alarm cord on the side of the transfer space, close to the wall to avoid conflict with the drop-down grab rail.

> You do get frightened if you pull it by accident – I did do that once and no-one came. It's a problem when it's wrapped around the grab rails. You get scared to touch the rail.
> **WHEELCHAIR USER**

Regardless of which side it is placed, the alarm cords must reach to 100 mm from the floor in case someone has fallen and cannot get up. Yet they often end up being tied up to one of the grab rails making them completely useless. Euan's Guide has a campaign to remind people of this. Their labels are available to fit to alarm cords. These inform the public and help give people permission to fix any mistakes they might see, should they find cords are not hanging freely (Figure 8.24).

What is essential is that the alarm cord is visible and in good working order. Regular servicing of the accessible cubicle should ensure that the alarm cord has not been tied up or damaged.

**Figure 8.24** Euan's Guide card fitted to an alarm cord. The card reads 'This red emergency card must hang freely all the way to the floor. If it does not, it may prevent a disabled person from asking for help.'

## Leaving the cubicle

We have finished using the toilet. What is there left to consider before leaving? When we tidy up after ourselves, we are removing any evidence of our activities in the cubicle, to lessen the risk of embarrassment should we cross paths with the next user. Anything that is not where it should be is a sign of dirt or untidiness.

The most obvious of these is any waste still in the bowl after flushing, and some people will look for a toilet brush. Next is to wipe drips from the seat and by doing so, any judgement from the next user that we have not cleaned up after ourselves in this simplest of ways. If we have used toilet paper as a barrier between our thighs and the seat, or between our hand and the flush or lock, we must also dispose of this in the pan, along with any that fell onto the floor.

There is also evidence left in the form of smells. Some people bring air freshener with them, others look for it in the cubicle or wait a little longer before leaving until confident that the smell has dispersed. Bad smells can make the public toilet seem dirtier even without the presence of visible dirt.

> It's a matter of scrunching up your nose and getting on with it, leaving with a minimal amount of contact.
>
> **ADULT USER**

All of these symbols of how we might leave a cubicle match those that we check for when choosing a cubicle (see Chapter 6). If a cubicle is tidy when entered, then we will be able to see any changes that we make to the space. Conversely, if there is already paper on the floor, there is less chance that we will bother or even notice to pick up anything that we drop. An untidy cubicle will become untidier over time.

Whether it is drips on the seat or a smell that offends us, these visible signs of untidiness are not a danger to our health, but they are a simple reminder of other people's presence in what is now 'our' space. We have no way of knowing whether one or a hundred people have visited this cubicle since the last visit from the cleaner, or the levels of microbial dirt that have accumulated in that time. What good design choices can do is make a toilet easier for users to keep clean. Effective flushes, accessible bins, functioning toilet roll dispensers and good ventilation encourage and enable cleaner and tidier behaviour. We are more able to reset the cubicle for the next person, to leave the toilet as we would wish to find it.

So that's it! You have successfully had a wee or a poo (or both), changed a tampon or continence pad or helped a child. Pop your coat on and pick up your bags. Next, please wash your hands.

# Notes

1. London Legacy Development Corporation, *Inclusive Design Standards*.
2. NHS, 'Hip Replacement: Recovery', 6 March 2024. Available online: https://www.nhs.uk/conditions/hip-replacement/recovery/ (accessed 12 July 2024).

3. Building Regulations, *Approved Document T: Toilet Accommodation*.
4. Hanson, Bichard and Greed, *The Accessible Toilet Design Resource*.
5. Centre for Accessible Environments, *Good Loo Design Guide* (London: Centre for Accessible Environments, 2004).
6. Kira, *The Bathroom*.
7. K. Wang and M. H. Palmer, 'Women's toileting behaviour related to urinary elimination: Concept analysis', *Journal of Advanced Nursing* 66(8) (2010): 1874–84, https://doi.org/10.1111/j.1365-2648.2010.05341.x.
8. W. S. Reynolds, C. Kowalik, M. R. M. R. Kaufman, R. R. R. Dmochowski and J. H. Fowke, 'Women's perceptions of public restrooms and the relationship with toileting behaviours and bladder symptoms: A cross sectional study', *The Journal of Urology* 204(2) (2020): 310–15, https://doi.org/10.1097/JU.0000000000000812.
9. S. Bobinger, 'Women: Don't hover over the toilet seat', The Ohio State University Wexner Medical Centre, 24 July 2020. Available online: https://wexnermedical.osu.edu/blog/dont-hover-over-the-toilet-seat (accessed 12 July 2024).
10. UK Parliament (2021), 'Written Evidence Submitted by the Urology Trade Association'. Available online: https://committees.parliament.uk/writtenevidence/41388/pdf/#:~:text=In%202017%2F18%20alone%2C%20treating,diagnosis%2C%20and%20increased%20patient%20expectation (accessed 28 December 2023).
11. World Health Organization (2023), 'Antimicrobial resistance'. Available online: https://www.who.int/news-room/fact-sheets/detail/antimicrobial-resistance (accessed 28 December 2023).
12. J. Crimaldi, 'Toilets spew invisible aerosol plumes with every flush – here's the proof, captured by high-powered lasers', *The Conversation*, 8 December 2022. Available online: https://theconversation.com/toilets-spew-invisible-aerosol-plumes-with-every-flush-heres-the-proof-captured-by-high-powered-lasers-195717 (accessed 1 January 2024).
13. British Standards Institute, *BS8300-2 Design of an accessible and inclusive built environment*.
14. World Design Organization (2021), 'SquatEase'. Available online: https://wdo.org/programmes/wdip/shortlist-gallery/squatease/ (accessed 3 January 2024).
15. Bladder and Bowel UK (2021), 'Why squatting for toilet function is good for health'. Available online: https://www.bbuk.org.uk/squatting-for-toileting-health/ (accessed 3 January 2024).
16. There have been a number of theories that sitting instead of squatting to use the toilet can increase the risk of colon cancer. Although squatting is recognized as 'healthier' it remains unproved that using the toilet pedestal can increase the risk of colon cancer.

17  BBC News, 'Squat toilets in Rochdale shopping centre', 15 July 2010. Available online: https://www.bbc.co.uk/news/uk-england-manchester-10644118 (accessed 3 January 2024).
18  H. Johnson, '"Squat" toilets to be abandoned after public outrage', *Manchester Evening News*, 9 August 2010. Available online: https://www.manchestereveningnews.co.uk/news/local-news/squat-toilets-to-be-abandoned-after-public-895943 (accessed 3 January 2024).
19  British Standards Institute, *BS6465 Sanitary Installations: Code of Practice for the Provision of Public Toilets*.
20  T. R. Schum, T. M. Kolb, T. L. McAuliffe, M. D. M. v D. Simms, R. L. Underhill and M. Lewis, 'Sequential acquisition of toilet-training skills: A descriptive study of gender and age differences in normal children', *Pediatrics* (109) (2002): 48–54.
21  D. Norman, *The Design of Everyday Things* (New York: Basic Books, 1988).
22  Hanson, Bichard and Greed, *The Accessible Toilet Design Resource*.
23  British Standards Institute, *BS8300-2 Design of an accessible and inclusive built environment*.
24  Building Regulations, *Approved Document M: Access to and use of buildings. Vol. 2: Buildings other than dwellings*.
25  British Standards Institute, *PAS 6463: Design for the mind – Neurodiversity and the Built Environment – guide*, 85.
26  Building Regulations, *Approved Document T: Toilet Accommodation*.
27  The Water Industries Act (1991) specifically stipulates that sanitary waste should not be flushed due to the damage it can cause to sewers and drains. The Environment Protection Act (1990) imposes a duty of care that includes disposal of sanitary waste as 'controlled' waste.
28  Health and Safety Executive, *Workplace health, safety and welfare. Workplace (Health, Safety and Welfare) Regulations 1992. Approved Code of Practice and Guidance*. Available online: https://www.hse.gov.uk/pubns/books/l24.htm (accessed 28 December 2023).
29  Prostate Cancer UK (2023), *Lifting the lid on male incontinence* [pdf]. Available online: https://prostatecanceruk.org/media/r25l0esd/6999_boys_need_bins_brochure_digital_final-3.pdf (accessed 24 January 2024).
30  Waste Industry Safety and Health Forum (2015), *Managing Offensive/Hygiene Waste Safely. Formal Guidance Document* [pdf]. Available online: https://www.wishforum.org.uk/wp-content/uploads/2019/06/WASTE-22-.pdf (accessed 28 December 2023).

# 9 Water and wellness

How do we restore cleanliness after using the toilet, and leave feeling refreshed in both body and mind? Public toilets can provide a hygienic environment for our bodily functions and a moment of calm from the world outside, whether the chaos stems from the people, traffic, workplace or weather. The transition that occurs from stepping into the privacy of the public toilet and out again should mean we have emerged in a better state than we entered.

In this chapter, we think about how we wash and dry our hands, our sensory experience in this environment, and our final thoughts on how toilets can go further to support our physical and mental needs.

## Washing hands

The pandemic threw handwashing to the forefront of our minds. Whilst public toilets have always had water available for handwashing (though the soap or drying facilities might be less than desired), the pandemic elevated handwashing to an activity in its own right, worthy of public infrastructure (Figure 9.1). Providers began taking more of a role in encouraging handwashing by advising on effective techniques (at least twenty seconds, with soap) or reminders via a poster.

As well as being a public health issue, handwashing is a step towards making us feel not just relieved but refreshed by a visit to the public toilet. By washing our hands, we are already cleaner than when we went in. If we cannot wash our hands, we feel dirty. If we cannot understand how to perform such a natural task, we feel frustrated. If we cannot physically operate each step or cannot reach even to try, we feel unwelcome, overlooked and excluded. Like so much of the design of the public toilet, handwashing is a process, made difficult or impossible if one of the steps of basin, tap, water, soap and drying cannot be completed. It discourages good practice. Whilst handwashing signs might have their place, design can play a greater role in encouraging and helping people to wash their hands and wash them well than simply telling them to. Taps must be chosen, soap must be positioned and basins must be fixed in place, but the design decisions we make around each of these facilities can include or exclude.

**Figure 9.1** Sign pointing to toilets and handwashing facilities during the Covid-19 pandemic. South Terminal, Gatwick Airport. Credit: Alan Morris/Alamy Stock Photo.

Even a map of the town might tell you where [public toilets] are but it won't tell you what they're like, and if one was dirty but I have to go, well I have to go. I don't have a choice. So, it's really annoying when there's no toilet roll, no soap. It's basics.

**YOUNG PERSON WITH CONTINENCE CONDITION**

## Basins

Before we think about the design of the basin we must decide where handwashing will take place. There are three options for this: basins may be located within the cubicle, outside in a shared area, or both.

Having a basin within the cubicle is a requirement of the accessible toilet so that people can, for example, clean their hands before transferring to their wheelchair or clean their body or equipment if using continence products. A basin within the cubicle is a more inclusive option for standard or ambulant cubicles too. It allows people with medical or menstrual equipment (stoma bags, menstrual cups) to wash the items and their hands. Whilst not the ideal design, a basin in the cubicle can help Muslims perform ablution.[1] More generally, we might have a stain on our clothes or wish to wash our face or some other part of our body in a way that requires the privacy of the toilet cubicle.

There are reasons for providing communal handwashing outside the cubicle. This increases the number of people who pass through the facility in a set period as both basins and toilets can be in use at the same time, rather than one person having jurisdiction over both behind a locked door. This is important for high-volume, time-sensitive settings where space is limited such as theatres or sports venues. In settings where a high turnover of cubicles is essential, it would still be useful to provide a proportion of standard and ambulant cubicles with basins (and signed as such), for the needs mentioned before.

Shared handwashing is also handy for people who are visiting the toilet for access to water specifically. There are many situations that are made a bit better by water and soap. Communal handwashing could be provided even if there are basins in the cubicles (Figure 9.2). If we are about to eat, we have just come in off the street, or we live outdoors, we may wish to visit the toilet without needing the loo. Building Regulations Part T (2024) says 'there should be no shared hand-washing facilities in corridors, shared or enclosed spaces outside [its definition of] universal toilets' where the definition refers to 'individual use by either sex'.[2] There is no insight given into why a provider might have wished to provide shared handwashing when universal toilets already contain basins, nor any reasons

**Figure 9.2** Communal handwashing and drinking water outside gender-neutral toilets. The floating basin design is also accessible to wheelchair users. The toilets also have basins within the cubicle.

why it is advised against, should the need exist. Some places do provide shared handwashing within, near to or outside gender-neutral facilities, such as city farms, and without incident. In post-pandemic times, we should be increasing our opportunities for handwashing. Providing this as part of a public service that already has shelter and plumbing is a sensible option.

What about the position of the basin itself? If the room in which communal or individual handwashing takes place is accessible to wheelchair users then the basin itself must be too, by being of a low enough height and of a design that allows a wheelchair user to get close enough (Figure 9.2). A lower-height basin also helps children wash their hands independently. Whilst taller adults can reach down lower, children cannot reach higher than their size allows so if only one basin is provided, it should be positioned at the lower end of the guidance. To make an existing, non-wheelchair-accessible basin immediately more inclusive, a child's step stool is a thoughtful addition.

Whilst there are recommendations for basin height from the floor, what is overlooked yet more important is the height and distance to the tap. The height of the basin is irrelevant if the basin or any surround is so deep that the user still cannot reach the flowing water or tap controls (Figure 9.3). This

**Figure 9.3** Handwashing at a shopping centre. The sensor taps and soap are just about within reach of this five year old.

affects children in particular who often need to be lifted to reach handwashing facilities, limiting their independence. It might not always be possible for a child to be helped by their adult. What if they want to use a facility for a different gender? What if their adult is still in the cubicle themselves or is outside with other children who do not wish to visit the loo (particularly if they must pay per person for entry)? What if their adult is not able to lift them? What if the basin is within the cubicle? What if they are on a school trip? Placing basins at lower heights or set at different heights means that children are not designed out or forgotten. Instead, design enables them to practise good hand hygiene from a young age.

> Do I wash my own hands first then dry them, then pick up the child and wash their hands, and they always want soap, so you have to hold them up to the soap which is always higher. I have a bad back now because of all the lifting. So, do I wash my hands before all that or do all that and then wash my hands?
> **PARENT OF SEVEN-YEAR-OLD**

## *Taps*

> Some of them you are supposed to put your hands under the tap and the water comes on automatically, some of them you are supposed to push the top down, some of them you are supposed to turn round and some of them don't work.
> **ADULT PARTICIPANT**

The proliferation of tap designs means that we have two challenges when operating a tap. First, we need to understand how the tap works, then we need to have the strength to turn it on (and sometimes off). Turn, push, press, wave, or hold hands out and hope, the design of the tap does not always tell us which one will fit the bill.

**Twist:** Once we are old enough to know which way turns it on and which turns it off, a twist tap become intuitive. However, these can be fiddly or stiff. We also need to remember to turn it off, to not waste water or flood the basin.

**Lever:** Whilst this is a similar action to twisting, we are controlling the valve with much less force or purchase. A lever-arm tap is a more **accessible tap** design (Figure 9.4).

**Press:** Press taps began as a way to stop the problem of water waste from taps left on. Water flows until the tap has risen back to the start position. It can take a lot of pressure to press the tap down. Some press taps need to be held down whilst in use, which makes handwashing harder, particularly if we only have one

**Figure 9.4** Lever-arm tap. This one controls both on/off water flow and temperature.

hand or we are holding something else, such as a walking aid, bag or child in reach of an ill-positioned basin.

> I have difficulty using sinks especially those with push-button taps, when you let go and the water flow stops.
> **PARTICIPANT WITH CRUTCHES**

I hate using press taps – you have one knee up for them to sit on and you're trying to get the water to work and them to wash their hands – you do feel like giving up but it is important.

**PARENT OF TWINS**

**Push:** An electro-mechanical push button such as on a train or in an integrated wash system (where water, soap and hot air are released in a timed programme) do not require much hand strength. We are not physically controlling the valve that releases water at pressure, we are only activating the electronic switch that does this for us. Design needs to avoid the button being too small, out of reach, or hard to find. It can also be unclear if it is a push button or a sensor.

**Sensor:** sensor taps are hygienic and increasingly common. They work best when they are activated by the user placing their hands in a handwashing position, under a visible spout from which the water stream will appear. It also helps if the sensor is visible to us so we do not spend too much time looking for a way to turn the tap on. Sensors can sometimes be hidden from view in a recess or out of line with the tap making for a less intuitive or understandable arrangement (Figure 9.5). If this is unavoidable, a sensor symbol can help indicated where to place

**Figure 9.5** Unintuitive sensor tap layout. The tap sensor is both hidden underneath the shelf and out of line with the tap (to the left).

**Figure 9.6** Sensor tap instruction. The sign reads 'To operate place hands below tap spout. Please do not try to move tap body'. This suggests it is not obvious to people that the tap is sensor-operated from the design alone.

our hands. The more instructions we need to add to explain where and how to operate a tap, the more we as designers might question if the design itself could be improved (Figure 9.6).

Sensor and lever taps are a less familiar design compared to twist-operated taps, so their operation may be confusing for people with neurodegenerative conditions such as dementia. PAS 6465 makes recommendations here, such as lever taps that have a more intuitive side-to-side motion rather than up-and-down.[3] Familiar, intuitive design is an important consideration, and one that will shift with the generations, with the next more familiar with a wider range of tap controls.

## Spout

An aspect of handwashing design that is rarely mentioned is the projection and height of the spout in relation to both our hands and the basin. If the tap is too short, much higher than the basin, or too powerful for the size of basin, then putting our hands under it will divert water onto and behind the taps and any surrounding surface (Figure 9.7) or even onto the floor. A spout that falls further into the basin, or which forces our hands low enough so that water deflects into it and not onto the surrounding area (or ourselves), will keep the handwashing area

**Figure 9.7** A tap too short for the basin. This surround is of no use as a shelf for belongings as it is flooded from deflected water.

clean, free from water and stop it rotting or rusting over time. It will also stop the floor from becoming a slip hazard. This is a particular issue in the accessible toilet if just a small hand rinse basin is installed.

> The sink is too small … I end up covered in water and then there's water all over the floor which is dangerous when I'm using crutches.
> **PARTICIPANT WHO USES A WHEELCHAIR AND WALKING AIDS**

## Temperature

Effective handwashing needs hot water – but not too hot! The Health and Safety Executive[4] mandate that hot water taps reach 50°C within one minute to control the growth of legionella bacteria. However, the risk of scalding starts at 44°C for vulnerable people including the very young or very old and people with sensory loss.[5] The LLDC Inclusive Design Standard (2019) sets its limit for hot water temperature at no more than 43°C.[6] Temperature control is an important element of handwashing for neurodiverse adults and parents of neurodiverse children.[7] An adjustable lever-arm mixer tap with an intuitive means of control, including clear directions for hot and cold, is an inclusive option.

'I'm very sensitive to the cold, my fingers go numb then as they warm up they become incredibly painful, so in winter it's really important I have a decent temperature of water.'
**PERSON WITH REYNAUD'S SYNDROME**

## Soap

Now that we have made sure more people can reach the water spout and tap controls, we have increased our user group to include people of short stature, children and, depending on the accessibility of the basin area, people in wheelchairs. Soap is most conspicuous by its absence; however, when present, it also needs to be within reach (Figure 9.8). We will still exclude those we had intended to welcome if we now place the soap a foot higher.

Ideally there will be soap provided at every basin since everyone will need it. Positioning the soap at either end of a row of basins means an awkward dance

**Figure 9.8** Water and soap positioned at the same height. The soap is within reach of the basin, and both are sensor-operated (child aged four).

of people with wet hands squeezing past to reach it and dripping on the floor, or not bothering. To be more inclusive, soap dispensers must be usable with one hand or sensor-activated.

> I need to use both hands to use the dispenser, but I can't as I need one hand to support myself.
>
> **ADULT USING WALKING AID**

## Drying hands

Next, we want to dry our hands on something other than our clothes. This is both for our own comfort and to keep the facility nice for other people. If we exit the door to the facility with a wet hand, the door handle will be left damp leaving an unpleasant feeling for the next person who touches it. One option, of course, is not to have a door to exit the facility (see Chapter 6) but this is not always possible. Handwashing may even be within the cubicle. So when it comes to hand drying there are two options: absorbing the water with a towel or blowing the hands dry with air. Which is better?

### Paper towels

Paper towels are very good at drying hands; rarely does anyone complain that a paper towel has not worked. Paper towels can also dry other parts of the body that might need to be cleaned which is why they are recommended for the accessible toilet. We recommend paper towels for any toilet seeking to be more inclusive where handwashing is within the cubicle.

> When you go to the toilet there's no paper towels – there's not even a dispenser for paper towels – all there is, is a dryer and it's not acceptable. A dryer is no good. You can't cleanse yourself with a dryer … to turn around and dry yourself on the stomach or wherever. The paper towel is absolutely essential … it's absolutely ideal.
>
> **PERSON WITH CHRONIC HEALTH CONDITION**

The disadvantage of paper towels comes from the waste they create. This can be from user behaviour (people taking more than they need) or poor storage (towels falling out of a dispenser onto surfaces or the floor) but even used frugally this is still a single-use system. How they are sourced and disposed of will also affect how environmentally friendly paper towels are. They can also require more human resources: used towels go in a bin which then needs to be emptied and the towels restocked, requiring more regular management of the facility. The bin should be visible and close to the dispenser to allow a swift, intuitive disposal, keeping the facility tidy.

There are a few other problems with paper towels to look out for. If paper towels are in the toilet cubicle they may sometimes end up down the toilet, especially if the toilet paper has run out. This can cause blockages and put the cubicle out of service.

In the past, paper towels have also been seen as a fire risk, whether accidental or through arson. This is as much a risk of the bin as the towels, and whilst bins and towels go hand in hand, public toilets need bins regardless, for sanitary waste and litter. Addressing the cause of arson and reducing opportunities through surveillance, whether from other users, staff supervising or other nearby activity, would be a better solution than removing features like towels and bins that make public toilets inclusive.

## Hand dryers

*Dyson Airblades* and similar high-power dryers have the directional blast to blow hands dry. Some elements of the design can still be improved. As the water is blown off rather than heated into condensation, this sprays droplets down the wall underneath the dryer, ruining the surface and leading to stains or peeling paint. This could be minimized with a wipeable surface like tiles or a splashback that is regularly cleaned (Figure 9.9). If the hand dryer design has a base to it, water will collect in this part of the dryer. With no drainage system, this creates a puddle in the base where dirt and germs collect and which eventually overflows, dripping down the sides and onto the floor. Again, regular cleaning is required (Figure 9.10).

Hand dryers also have an environmental impact. The efficiency of the dryer needs to be considered as well as the use of an on-site renewable energy source or renewable energy supplier.

Whilst paper towels are useful for drying skin elsewhere on the body, hand dryers are sometimes used to dry clothing. This can be helpful in emergencies, such as wet weather or the need to clean stained clothing.

**Figure 9.9** High-power dryers with splashback to protect paintwork.

**Figure 9.10** High-power dryer with drip tray. Whilst water still overflows from the base of the dryer, it now collects somewhere other than the floor.

## Paper towels v. hand dryers: Who can use them?

A big problem with both options is access. Let's look at how each option stacks up.

**Dexterity:** Single-sheet paper towels are easier to use than ones with perforations. Paper towel dispensers can be fiddly to get the towel out. Sensor-operated paper towel dispensers could be used: whilst not currently common in the UK, on a recent trip to California practically every public toilet had one of these.

**Visibility:** Both hand dryers and paper towel dispensers are sometimes hidden, built into a false wall above the basin. Hiding facilities from view risks people missing the opportunity to use them. So why do it? In the case of paper towels, it hides the dispenser itself and makes it harder for the public to access the bulk of the supplies, which might reduce theft. Another reason is to create a clean, modern aesthetic. To alert people, we need extra signage (Figure 9.11) – 'paper towels hidden here' perhaps, or an appropriate icon. Without being certain of what they are interacting with, people bend down awkwardly to get a look. This is especially the case with paper towels, where someone might not like touching things they cannot see (who does?). If no paper towels are felt, we must also contort ourselves to figure out if the towels have run out or if they have not fed through the dispenser properly.

**Position:** Wall-mounted drying facilities, whether above the height of the basin or positioned too high on an end wall, can be out of reach to many. We must often walk away from the basin to get to them, which leads to people dripping on the floor where others are walking. The set-up just mentioned with a towel dispenser or hand dryer above every basin has the advantage of being more likely to put paper towels or dryers within the same reach as the soap and tap, and perhaps above a bin adjacent to the basin, providing equal access to all elements of handwashing. It will also avoid drips.

In the case of hand dryers, by positioning one on the wall at the height that is comfortable for the average adult (or the average hand dryer installer), some adults and many children will be reaching their hands uncomfortably high, or be blown in the face (Figure 9.12).

> Sometimes the hand dryer is on the other side of the room. I have to wash and dry my hands from the toilet. If I can't dry, my hands will be slippery and the transfer back could be dangerous. If I'm using sticks it's important to dry my hands or I will lose grip with the sticks.
> **PARTICIPANT WHO USES A WHEELCHAIR AND WALKING AIDS**

**Figure 9.11** Sign to alert people to a concealed sensor-operated dryer.

Placing a hand dryer or towel dispenser too high can mean some people cannot use it; placing it too low rarely does. A lower hand dryer or towel dispenser can still be used by a taller adult. As with other elements of handwashing, when more than one hand dryer or paper towel dispenser is provided they can be put at different heights (Figure 9.13).

Finally, beware of bins. Whilst a bin is well-positioned underneath a paper towel dispenser, placing one under a hand dryer can blow litter about or warm what is inside, which could be smelly!

**Experience:** The biggest disadvantage of hand dryers is their noise. This has become a more noticeable problem as hand dryers have become more powerful (and more effective, so perhaps more likely to be in use). The ceramic surfaces within a toilet facility amplify sound. Consequently, hand dryers turn the public toilet into a hectic environment, fracturing the possibility of respite from public life. These can be distressing for children and many groups hypersensitive to sound. The research of John Levack Drever identified problems for '[people with] visual impairment, hearing aid users, Alzheimer's disease, Ménière's disease and, most significantly, hyperacusis sufferers, and hyperacute hearing in autism'.[8] PAS 6463:2022 Design for the Mind recommends either paper towels or low noise hand dryers.[9] If hand dryers are considered necessary, a means to

**Figure 9.12** Child (three) about to be blown in the face by a hand dryer.

dampen sounds in the public toilet could also be designed in. This would also help mask toileting sounds that people do not want to share or hear.

> I also like [hand dryers] as they prevent other people from hearing you when in the loo. I'll sometimes wait until the hand dryer goes off to 'go' as the noise will shield me from the noises I make.
> 
> **YOUNGER ADULT**

**Figure 9.13** Hand dryers at two heights, for different height people. The back wall is tiled to withstand any water blown onto it.

Rather than rely on the hand dryer, a less obtrusive way to mask toileting sounds that is occasionally heard is soft background music or sounds such as birdsong. There could also be a way to turn the dryer off for certain times or audiences, or a switch that users are invited to use to protect themselves and their family from other people using the dryer in their presence, or from the accidental trigger of a sensor.[10]

## One or the other or both …

The question of towels vs dryers does not have to be seen as one or the other. Both have advantages for different people and circumstances. Providing both paper towels and low noise hand dryers would be a sensible solution in the **universal ambulant** or **standard toilet cubicle** as it gives the individual the choice based on their preference and levels of comfort (Figure 8.12 in Chapter 8). After the initial outlay, providing paper towels and a hand dryer would not necessarily be more resource heavy as individuals will use one or the other, rarely both.

## ... or neither

Could people be responsible for their own hand drying? Just as I used to carry a pack of my grandmother's soap leaves (credit card-sized slithers of paper that foamed up with water) for times when there was no soap provided, the same could be adopted for drying hands. In Japanese culture, a *Tenugui* is a small towel that people might carry with them for different uses including hand drying: effective, sustainable and hygienic, but a big cultural shift to implement.

## Sensing the space

Public toilets can be a sensory overload: from their echoey interiors made even louder by a hand dryer to the strong smells of excretion, cleaning products or the air fresheners that attempt to mask them. We want our facilities to be inclusive of people with sensory sensitivities, supportive of people with sensory loss and, more than that, a pleasant, restorative experience that supports our wider wellbeing.

So far, this chapter has looked at some of the acoustic challenges of public toilets. For a public that also includes different abilities and sensitivities with regard to light, touch and smell, what else do we need to consider when designing the facility for the most inclusive sensory experience?

**Smell:** We saw during the pandemic how air circulation slows down the transmission of some viruses in confined spaces. Ventilation will also disperse strong negative smells. Air fresheners can be too strong for people highly sensitive to scent or chemicals[11] or for people with asthma. Ventilation in toilets with floor-to-ceiling walls and doors is particularly important.

In some settings, plants are included. These purify the air and show that the environment provides the conditions in which to thrive. They also show a commitment to creating a pleasant environment for the public, where we might wish to pass time. Finally, it shows that the facility is cared about; someone has chosen to put the plants there and is now taking the time to keep them alive (Figure 9.14).

**Light:** People with sight loss can find public toilets challenging with their overwhelmingly bright 'white equals clean' aesthetic. Sight loss can mean difficulties in perceiving depth or colour, very blurred vision of what is near or far, or a lack of sight of what is in front or in our peripheral vision. Lighting and how it changes can change how people read a space. Spot lighting can be reflected in the glazed surfaces of toilets and tiles, create glare or even reflection.

**Figure 9.14** Indoor greenhouse at London Victoria station. This is underground at the entrance to the women's toilets, along with a bench to wait for others.

Strong shadows can be mistaken for objects or changes in depth. Sensor lighting which only comes on if someone is in the facility or cubicle should not be used,[12] especially in the accessible toilet. Suddenly being plunged into darkness can be not only disorientating but frightening for those who are neurodiverse or have neurodegenerative conditions, as well as young children. Diffused lighting will create a simpler, calmer space to read, as will natural light from windows or overhead skylights during daylight hours (Figure 9.15). If windows can be opened, this will provide natural ventilation, too.

**Contrast:** Strong colour contrast between objects in the facility and the walls and floor around them is important for people with sight loss and neurodiversity. Toilets, basins and many of the other items in the public toilet are often white or stainless steel, so the wall colour or tiles behind should be an alternative colour to make them stand out. The walls and floor should be distinguishable at their junctions, and the door from the cubicle walls.[13] Colour can also add warmth to a space and make items like grab rails less medical in appearance (Figure 9.16). An inclusive colour scheme can be used throughout all toilet facilities, giving the same thought and quality to standard, ambulant, accessible and Changing Places

**Figure 9.15** Natural light through high-level windows above the cubicles. This is at a visitor centre, Shropshire.

**Figure 9.16** Colour choices within a set of toilets (ambulant facility shown here). There is strong contrast between the fixtures and side walls (both white), floor (grey) and tiles (orange). The grab rails (black) contrast with the walls, and the back wall (dark blue) makes the toilet stand out.

toilets. This can be seen by comparing Figure 9.16 with Figure 6.10 in Chapter 6, which show standard and Changing Places toilets at the same venue.

**Pattern:** Bold graphic patterns on floors and walls add visual noise and can make environments confusing (Figure 9.17) or overwhelming.[14] On flooring,

**Figure 9.17** Decorative wallpaper in the cubicle. Elements like this can make toilets more homely, though consultation can help make a suitable choice. Whilst some features stand out, others can be lost in the noise.

**Figure 9.18** Graphical floor pattern, creating the optical illusion of changes in level. This has also masked the join between floor and wall.

strong lines or changes in tone can appear as a change in level (Figure 9.18). Meanwhile, actual changes such as steps can disappear if there is no contrasting edge strip to show that it is there.[15] Keeping a floor in a single colour where variations only exist to mark out a feature will help people to move around safely.

**Touch:** The standard cubicle might be a more comfortable environment than the accessible toilet for someone interpreting the space through touch: everything is within reach, helping navigation. Thought needs to be given to keeping all surfaces clean, and to the material chosen. If an unfamiliar material is used, is it still recognizable to someone seeking to understand the feature without seeing it clearly or at all?

# Designing loo-topia

What more can we provide to create a cleansing, restorative experience within the public toilet? How can we design 'loo-topia'?

## Designing wellness

Using the public toilet can be seen as a ritual.[16] Whilst we may have visited the toilet with the simple need to 'use the facilities', we also gain in other ways. The public toilet offers shelter from the rain and shade from the sun. We can attend to the needs of our bodies by expelling, cleaning, adjusting our dress and fixing our appearance. We can attend to the needs of our minds too: we might stay a moment longer, enjoy the chance to sit, rest our legs or close our eyes, not knowing when we might next be able to switch off (see Chapter 4).

What of the people we are with? Do our babies need changing or feeding? Does anyone need a rest, or somewhere safe to wait while others visit the loo?

To create a space for wellness we can think about all these situations. As well as handwashing there can be a drinking water tap for people to refill water bottles for themselves or their family (Figure 9.19). There can be shelves and mirrors away from the basins for people to check and fix their appearance or to set down loose items whilst using the facilities (Figure 9.20). Mirrors in cubicles as well as communal areas are helpful especially when the cubicle also features a basin. A full-length mirror is a requirement of the accessible toilet to help people who are managing medical conditions to clean themselves and help them redress before

**Figure 9.19** Drinking water tap at a publicly accessible toilet.

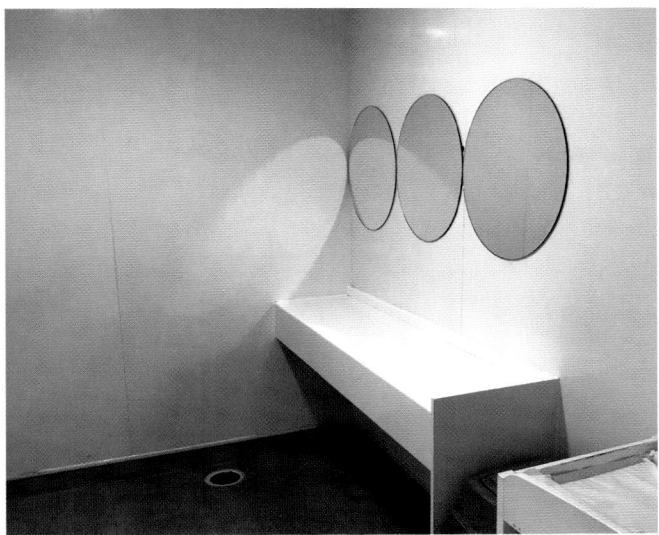

**Figure 9.20** Vanity unit with shelving and mirrors at a family resort. This also doubled as additional space to change a baby. When positioning mirrors at 'head-height', remember this is not the same for everyone.

leaving. A mirror also helps women adjust their head scarves, particularly if there is no women-only space in which to do so outside. Sometimes we misinterpret what we are seeing: mirrors in unexpected places or without frames or covering a wall from edge to edge can be seen not as a reflection but as an extra space, causing at best a double-take or at worst an injury if someone were to walk into it. Some people such as those with dementia may have stopped recognizing themselves: who is this person staring at me in the toilet? One way around this is to have a screen or curtain for a carer to cover the mirror, particularly full-length ones within the cubicle. Figure 6.10 (Chapter 6) shows a screen in a Changing Places toilet that can repositioned, whether to cover the mirror or to give those using the toilet more privacy.

For 'loo-topia' there might be additional rooms or an ante-room for other uses, depending on the needs of the intended users: a quiet space with comfortable chairs and tables for infant feeding, whether by breast or bottle (Figure 9.21); a wudu facility for people to perform ablution (Figure 9.22), a public shower, a seating area for anyone who might need a rest before leaving; a waiting area for those whose friends or family are in the toilet where they will be safe, protected from the weather, and easy to find. Spaces like this can also be used as welfare spaces for public health campaigns, for pop-up clinics or for town centre teams helping people at night-time.

**Figure 9.21** Seating area for bottle feeding at a department store. This location also provided spaces for breastfeeding, for baby-changing and for sitting, alongside a family toilet and drinking water.

**Figure 9.22** Wudu facility for ritual washing before prayer. This example is within the women's toilets of a venue available for public hire.

> I certainly believe that if you treat people well and make it like your own home then they behave much better.
> 
> **WOMAN WITH CONTINENCE CONDITION**

> I was quite amazed with one department store. They have sofa areas where you can feed with your bottle, almost like a café but for people with babies. It's like a whole other world. People come in and go 'so how old is yours?'
> 
> **PARENT**

> I was invited to a hotel this weekend and that was lovely, they even had cologne and big mirrors so you can do your make-up and a very nice lady who you could tip. I was happy to put a pound in the dish.
> 
> **ADULT PARTICIPANT**

The image of the public toilet is not of a utopian space that sustains public life. It is too often a stinky, loud and germ-ridden space with a gloomy exterior and glaringly white within. It is a shift for the senses from whatever lies outside, but not often a pleasant one.

By engaging with people to understand their experiences, designers can create public toilet interiors that meet the needs of body and mind, supporting wellness. It could be an escape rather than a source of sensory overload, offering an antidote to the experience of the world beyond the door. The toilet can give us the privacy to feel and process emotions away from others' eyes and a safe space in which to hide or seek help should we feel threatened by others in the wider environment. The public toilet can be what we need it to be, a restroom within our wider public life.

## Social interactions

The privacy offered by the public toilet only exists within the cubicle. Here we have a space to let go of our emotions away from others' eyes. Once the door opens, we are in an intimate space shared with strangers with its own community of visitors and staff, newcomers and locals. Each has a different level of familiarity and sense of ownership with the space, and whilst we occupy the same room, we must interact to some degree whether we wish to or not.

Imagine you are in an empty public toilet, exiting the cubicle and heading to the basins. Someone else walks in. The vibe has shifted. You tighten a little. Even if we wish to minimize our interactions with strangers as much as possible, we must still make decisions – whether to look at the next person waiting as we come out of the cubicle or let them know if there is a problem with the lock, flush or paper. If we choose a toilet only to be put off by the sights or smells left behind, do we reject it, knowing the person who left it like this is a few feet away? Do we *say* something? Avoiding interaction still requires a sequence of decisions as we navigate social norms and hoping they match with others. Aware of this shifting and permeable boundary between public and private, performative and intimate, can public toilet design go further to ease awkward interactions and build a supportive environment instead?

This becomes a matter for inclusive design when we behave, look or react outside the norm. Someone who has spent a long time in a cubicle may receive disapproving looks or accusations. Someone distressed or struggling with sensory overload could be viewed as behaving strangely. Someone walking out of the accessible toilet may be chastised as not needing to use it. Someone upset or emotional may seem suspicious. Someone who does not look like others may be treated as a threat. Who is permitted within the boundaries of this intimate, protected space?

On the other hand, by being obliged to be together, it can be a space for human connection. Is it wise to keep designing out reasons to talk to each other? A public toilet is a place where we could promote acceptance and tolerance. We all look different, act differently, react differently and have different needs, but in this environment we all share one thing in common: a need for the loo! We want to go alone, in a private space that meets our basic requirements, free from judgement and barriers. We are prepared to wait our turn (if we can) because we understand that everyone else needs the toilet too.

Questioning others' behaviour or right to be in the shared space of a public toilet is not inclusive. Creating confusion or arbitrary rules as to who can or cannot come in has a negative effect on those excluded.

Are there challenges, exceptions and grey areas? Yes. The first time I read an online discussion on a parenting board asking whether a man could go into a women's toilet to change his baby's nappy if that was the location of the baby-changing (a discussion that has reoccurred many times since), 'Of course!' came a flood of responses.

However, one woman who had IBS said she would not be comfortable with that. Her episodes of IBS could mean loud, unpleasant and unexpected bowel movements. This was embarrassing for her in the cubicle of the ladies knowing other women were waiting outside. She would feel much more embarrassed, she said, if she then saw a man had come in. The other women told her she was wrong. They forgot that he had asked if anyone would mind, and she had given her opinion, 'yes'.

No one is right or wrong. We have different, conflicting needs for the same space at the same time. Note that with this discussion – as with most online debates including those in government consultations, social research surveys and in parliament – the setting is a theoretical, poorly defined toilet where the features, walls and layout will change in each person's mind depending on which point someone is trying to make. We have each assumed what the room looks like, how enclosed it is, how the cubicles let sound in or out. We cannot answer a question of who is included and who is excluded when the parameters shift. However, as designers we can consider and weigh-up competing needs and preferences, seek inclusive solutions and create a facility that designs out conflict in the first place.

# Notes

1    Hanson, Bichard and Greed, *The Accessible Toilet Design Resource*.
     T. Slater and C. Jones (2018), M *Around the Toilet: A research project report about what makes a safe and accessible toilet space* [pdf]. Available online: https://aroundthetoilet.wordpress.com/wp-content/uploads/2018/05/around-the-toilet-report-final-1.pdf (accessed 24 June 2024).

2. Building Regulations, *Approved Document T: Toilet Accommodation*.
3. British Standards Institute, *PAS 6463: Design for the mind – Neurodiversity and the Built Environment – guide*.
4. Health and Safety Executive (2024), 'Hot and cold water systems'. Available online: https://www.hse.gov.uk/legionnaires/hot-and-cold.htm (accessed 15 January 2024).
5. Ibid.
6. London Legacy Development Corporation, *Inclusive Design Standards*.
7. Arup (2023), *Part M Research Extension: Toilets* [pdf]. Available online: https://assets.publishing.service.gov.uk/media/64d63baedd15ff0014277fd4/Part_M_Research_extension_toilets_research_report.pdf (accessed 10 January 2024).
8. J. L. Drever, 'Impact on vulnerable sub-groups from ultra-rapid hand dryers', *Acoustics Bulletin* 38(6) (2013): 4.
9. British Standards Institute, *PAS 6463: Design for the mind – Neurodiversity and the Built Environment – guide*.
10. G. Ramster and K. Gaudion, 'Design with many, with some, with one: Designing inclusive spaces with Helen Hamlyn Centre for Design researchers', Royal College of Art, 22 April 2024. Available online: https://www.rca.ac.uk/news-and-events/news/design-with-many-with-some-with-one-designing-inclusive-spaces-with-helen-hamlyn-centre-for-design-researchers/ (accessed 6 June 2024).
11. British Standards Institute, *PAS 6463: Design for the mind – Neurodiversity and the Built Environment – guide*.
12. London Legacy Development Corporation, *Inclusive Design Standards*.
13. Building Regulations, *Approved Document T: Toilet Accommodation*.
14. British Standards Institute, *PAS 6463: Design for the mind – Neurodiversity and the Built Environment – guide*.
15. Building Regulations, *Approved Document M: Access to and use of buildings. Vol. 2: Buildings other than dwellings*.
16. J. Bichard, J. Hanson and C. Greed, 'Please wash your hands', *Senses and Society* 3(1) (2008): 79–84, https://doi.org/10.2752/174589308X266489.

# 10 Rethinking public toilet provision

We have explored the physical design of the toilet: where it should be located, its situation, architecture and the best mix of facilities. We have made it accessible and inclusive of many physical needs. We have also considered our emotional needs, social interactions and designed an inclusive experience.

Yet alongside all this, a public toilet is also a public service. It needs to be financed, built, maintained and sustained, in a way that balances the needs of the service user and those of the service provider.

First, a public toilet must be created. There must be the demand for it and someone willing or required to respond to this demand who has the inclination and finance to do so effectively.

Once provided, the public toilet needs to continue to exist with someone to pay for the rent, rates, utilities, supplies, cleaning and maintenance. We also need people to *do* the cleaning and maintenance, and people to keep it going: to open and close the facility, and to respond to problems. These problems could be with the public toilet's (mal)function, with how people use (or abuse) it, or (anti-)social behaviour between people when inside. A system emerges around it of interactions between one person and another or one person with the space, which might support or threaten the toilet's continued existence.

This chapter shares what we have learnt about the design of publicly accessible toilets as a service. Who is involved in how toilets are provided, paid for, cleaned or managed, and how is this changing? We also share findings from the Engaged[1] project into alternative ways to create and maintain toilet provision that designers of systems and services could explore.

## Who provides it?

### Public toilets

Let's start with our council facilities. Public toilets are the responsibility of the local council alongside things like libraries and rubbish collection. In multi-tiered authorities this falls at district rather than county council level. The service is paid for by council tax and there is a lot to pay for: cleaning, maintenance of the building and facilities, supplies like toilet paper, utilities like water and electricity, and sometimes business rates. Following the Non-Domestic Rating (Public Lavatories) Act 2021,[2] local authorities can exempt themselves and other tiers of local authority from the rates due on public toilet buildings. Complex exceptions still exist, such as toilets run by a public body but located with the units of a private organization (such as a transport hub), or publicly accessible toilets within non-exempt publicly owned buildings like a library.

The challenge is that councils do not have to provide toilets, and with local government finances so stretched, money must be prioritized for the services that they are legally required to provide. Alternative ways of keeping toilets open are being explored. Some look to lower-tier councils such as parish, town and community councils or community organizations, emphasizing that if they do not take on the running of the toilets, the facility will most likely shut down (Figure 10.1). The benefit of the 2021 legislation is that the district council does not then land the parish council with a business rates bill for their troubles.

> As it happens for us, there was no choice – we either did it ourselves or have no toilets. And once you go down that lane of having these facilities close, the village will deteriorate.
>
> **COMMUNITY COUNCIL MEMBER**

**Figure 10.1** Public toilet in a South Staffordshire village. This was formerly run by the district council and is now maintained by the parish council.

## *Publicly accessible toilets*

Other public or third-sector buildings such as libraries, leisure centres, town hall, hospitals, or museums and galleries might become part of a network of toilets within public spaces that we can use without fearing exclusion or needing to buy something to access. This sense of having a right to access facilities within public spaces and buildings is critical for many, especially those who are marginalized or stigmatized.

Other organizations also provide toilets as part of the country's infrastructure. National parks, service stations, train stations and bus stations provide considerable numbers of **publicly accessible toilets** to support movements around the country. For private companies, publicly accessible toilets will attract visitors to their premises and extend the time that they stay there. In the Victorian era, the first department stores provided toilets or 'powder rooms' as part of their offer to women to give them a home away from home in the male-dominated public sphere.[3] Whilst many department stores have been lost in the past decade, some that remain maintain this positive approach; a head office employee told us in 2011 as part of our TACT3 project that they recognized the importance of toilets as part of their customer experience. Consequently, they used the same quality of interior design within the toilets as within the rest of the store. This created a seamless transition from the shopfloor to the toilets rather than treating the loos as an unmentionable. Like department stores, shopping centres are also increasingly providing publicly accessible toilets that welcome people (Figure 10.2), helping them to stay for longer.

Toilets tend to occupy a part of the building with lower retail value. This will be far from the entrance with less footfall or visibility, so not always convenient for a shopper in urgent need. For the retailer this can be an opportunity to create promotions and displays along a known route from store entrance to loo. Drawing people into the shop by providing toilets is a chance to turn them into a customer.

> Because toilets don't make money, they put them in the place where the shops don't want to go, which means they are hard to find.
> **SHOPPING CENTRE ARCHITECT**

Shopping centres continue to recognize the need for publicly accessible toilets within their covered arcades. The MK Centre in Milton Keynes was one of the first to include a Changing Places facility (see Chapter 6). Larger developments or regeneration projects might also include publicly accessible toilets as part of a new neighbourhood. This can take a more traditional form of a separate building within the 'public' space: public in appearance but privately owned and managed. It is difficult to tell who can use the toilets or feels comfortable doing so under these various forms of ownership.

**Figure 10.2** Infant feeding area at a shopping centre. This suburban shopping centre also provides a baby-changing area and Changing Places toilet, alongside standard, ambulant and accessible toilets.

Many charities for conditions that impact continence will provide 'Just can't wait' cards. These can be shown to a business employee to explain that the card holder has a medical condition that means toilet access is needed urgently. The intention is that the employee will be more likely to give someone in need access to the toilet even if it is meant to be just for customers or possibly in a back-of-house space. This is still at the business's discretion and will depend on their own policies and training. For some people, simply having the card makes them feel more confident about going out, even if they have never used it. One thing that undermines this system is a lack of awareness and recognition by owners and employees that it exists, not helped by each charity having a different design for their cards. A national design would be easier to recognize and easier to promote, giving more confidence to the cardholders and increasing the number of businesses willing to help.

People who are marginalized, stigmatized or excluded by society can be especially disadvantaged by toilets in privately owned spaces,[4] due to 'gatekeepers with social power': those whose permission must be sought to access toilets such as a shopkeeper, receptionist or security guard. These gatekeepers can deny access whether by barring entry to a building, or by saying toilets are customer or staff only. Sometimes individuals are denied access just by being part of 'stigmatized communities', or not looking like the imagined customer.

The proliferation of doors controlled by security passes means that receptions and waiting areas may not have toilets for visitors who could be there for some hours. Instead, they must ask permission, or even be escorted to the toilet, if they are allowed in at all. In many ways this infantilizes us: adults still asking permission to use the loo. At one city gallery we spoke with, security staff are briefed to welcome rough sleepers into the building in recognition of the need amongst local homeless people for toilet access. The gallery management were keen that their toilets were truly publicly accessible.

## Community toilet schemes

Publicly accessible toilets have been further expanded by **community toilet schemes**. A scheme is usually initiated by the local council who consider how many participants are needed in which areas to stop too many visitors falling on one business. They also check how accessible the toilets are. This ensures everyone can use the community toilet scheme, including families and people who use wheelchairs, even if not every venue meets all accessibility criteria. A mix of venue types is also needed, as not everyone can or will go into places that sell alcohol, and some venues have age restrictions. As with other privately provided toilets, we are likely to feel uncomfortable or unwelcome entering a space we would not otherwise visit, whether that is a church, a nail salon or a betting shop, reiterating the need for genuine public toilets. Community toilet schemes were initially intended to enhance the toilet provision of a high street, town centre or more broadly by ensuring access 'to a greater range of toilets that are clean and safe, located within managed buildings, and available when people need them'.[5] However, in some places they have replaced public toilets, in particular as a cheaper alternative to the unpopular on-street automatic public toilets.

> Lots of people don't like using [automatic public conveniences]. I've never used one and I'm not sure I ever would! And they're very expensive. Very, very expensive
> **COUNCIL OFFICER**

It is easy to see why community toilet schemes appeal from the council's perspective. Rather than paying £15,000 and £60,000 per public toilet in annual running costs,[6] a council will pay a community toilet scheme participant a nominal fee: around £500 to £1,000 per year, though some do not pay at all. After closing six public toilets, the London Borough of Hounslow began a scheme in 2018 of 127 participants with no financial incentive which continues to operate.[7] By contrast, in 2008 the London Borough of Wandsworth began a scheme which initially paid participants and by 2011 it had 74 participating businesses[8] each receiving £900/year. In 2013, Wandsworth Council sought to make further financial savings by withdrawing the payment, believing participation would continue 'in the spirit of the "Big Society"'.[9] The participants left and the scheme disappeared. Businesses can recognize alternative benefits of a community toilet scheme such as adding community value, additional promotion and welcoming people into a business outside the existing customer base; however, once established, the value proposition agreed between council and business needs to be upheld and realized.

In a few parts of the country a community toilet scheme has been initiated or maintained by someone other than the council. In Kendal in the Lake District, local businesses initiated their scheme as part of their Business Improvement District (BID) activities, and in Lewisham, South London, the council authorized a scheme but it is managed (including an annual awards ceremony!) by the community group, Lewisham Local.

## Who pays for it?

Public toilets are expensive to run, and whilst they add economic value, such as increasing the dwell time in shopping centres or supporting tourism, this value is not captured or in the public domain. So, who will cover the costs of having public toilets? Is it the public purse, or should we as individuals be spending a pound to spend a penny?

There are a few challenges when considering charging people to use a public toilet, where making the wrong choice increases the risk of further exclusion.

### *Who do you charge?*

You could charge everyone, but exceptions start to become obvious quite quickly. Adults may be cared-for or care for another adult. Many more need to accompany young children to the toilet and will be paying for two people for every one wee. This also works the other way around when the adult needs the toilet but cannot leave their kids alone on the street. Quickly you have a situation where whenever one family member needs the loo, every member whether adult or additional children must pay for entry. This is brought into focus every time I visit toilets in a part of Central London popular with tour groups. A4 signs are positioned at each turnstile entrance from the 'Department of the Built Environment' with a picture of a 50p and the words, in capitals, 'all children must pay to use these toilets'. It is not an inclusive welcome, particularly on the global stage. At what age should a child start paying? Will you charge babies? If baby-changing is free, what about a three-year-old who is toilet trained? Does a toddler pay more to access a toilet than if they were still in nappies? Charging per person quickly becomes impractical and can appear miserly.

Some councils have identified other groups to whom they wish or need to give free access. One London borough did not charge those on low incomes, those who work for the council (for some of whom, like street cleaners, the toilets provide necessary infrastructure to carry out their work) or those who are residents. This was monitored through different ID cards, but only works with a full-time attendant to override the payment barrier.

## *Do they have the money to pay?*

> You can't say to someone you can't use the toilet because you can't afford to pay. You can't switch nature on and off.
> 
> **OLDER PERSON WITH IMPAIRED MOBILITY AND REDUCED CONTINENCE**

A 50p charge per person can become a significant expense for a family who visit the toilets several times on a trip, or for a worker on a low income who needs to access public toilets daily, such as a delivery driver/cyclist, taxi driver or maintenance crew. Many systems require coins and in certain denominations, which people may not have to hand, particularly in remote locations where it is more difficult to 'make change'. Many people no longer carry cash since the pandemic and with the growth of contactless payment.

> It is utterly ridiculous that you have to pay 20p. I mean hands up if you have even got a 20p coin on you, so for me if it is not free then it is not a public toilet.
> 
> **PARENT OF YOUNG CHILD**

Contactless payment systems are beginning to appear in public toilets. This could be extended to give free access for certain groups, such as residents, the homeless and those on low income, through an alternative card that opens

**Figure 10.3** 2theLoo publicly accessible toilet in a retail unit at Covent Garden, London.

the gates without payment. Other benefits can also be offered. We visited a facility in Paris operated by 2theLoo, a private company who run many toilets in north-west Europe within places like shopping centres and train stations (and one in the UK, in a retail unit at Covent Garden, London; see Figure 10.3). The entrance barriers issued a receipt that doubled as a coupon redeemable against any vending machine purchases from within the facility, for the value of the entry fee.

## What system is used to collect it?

To enforce payment, a physical barrier accompanies the economic one. This might be at the entrance to the facility, such as the turnstile or paddle gate (Figure 10.4), or at the cubicle, paid into a mechanism that unlocks the door.

In terms of inclusion, there are pros and cons to each. As mentioned in Chapter 6, turnstiles are a physical barrier to the extent of being banned from council-maintained toilets,[10] but an effective way of collecting payment. When the London Local Authorities Act 2012[11] established an exemption for London councils, MPs argued that this was to allow councils to use the more accessible paddle gate design rather than a traditional turnstile.[12] In practice, this was not what happened. At several of the City of Westminster's busiest toilets, contracted out to a private company to manage, old fashioned turnstiles were installed with

**Figure 10.4** Payment via paddle gate that accepts coins and card payment.

a 50p charge. Nearly a decade later, with the toilets returned to local authority control, we are seeing a gradual replacement with paddle gates and contactless payment at some facilities. The reintroduction of turnstiles has not been limited to London boroughs, even though the original act still applies elsewhere.

Payment mechanisms on the cubicle door mean payment is taken per cubicle rather than per person, giving some leeway for families and people with carers to not be charged for every individual. These mechanisms need maintaining. Coins can get jammed, rendering the toilet out of use. They also take choice away from the user over which toilet to use; paying for a cubicle only to open the door and find that the toilet is unhygienic, out of toilet paper or simply out of order is dispiriting and sometimes distressing for a person in need of a loo.

> The vast majority of calls are for the locks. People put money in and it doesn't work, or it's already jammed.
> **MAINTENANCE CONTRACTOR**

We can make more inclusive choices about the method of payment available to the public and the barrier to access that we install. However, we must do so with the awareness any payment mechanism will exclude – by design – some people from accessing the toilet, whether physically or economically.

## Why introduce payments?

At busy facilities, there may be an opportunity for income generation. The public toilet company Healthmatic suggests that a busy facility could attract 50,000 users per annum, or £10,000 for a 20p entry fee, covering two-thirds of their estimated running costs for this size of facility (£15,000). An attended facility could cost £60,000, needing 300,000 users a year to break even.[13] A 50p charge would still require a daily average of 300+ visitors, equivalent to one person every two minutes for a twelve-hour period. It is easy to see how some locations might exceed this on busy weekends or sunny days, but less so on a midweek morning in January.

When calculating potential income, we need to factor in the reduction in visitor numbers both due to exclusion and to some people's objections to paying for a service they believe should be free. Healthmatic estimated a 40 per cent reduction in the number of locals using a toilet when charging is introduced, though visitors would be more willing than locals to pay, making charging a more realistic option in busy, tourist areas.[14]

Even if the operating costs are not covered, the income might meet a shortfall in the budget that allows the toilet to stay open. It could be the difference between a toilet that is well maintained compared to one that is run into the ground. This also becomes a necessity, as people have higher expectations for a toilet that they have paid for.

> Whenever you put money in then it is clean; anywhere there is no money, it's not.
> **OLDER PERSON WITH CHRONIC HEALTH CONDITION**

There is also the possibility that charging could reduce some types of antisocial behaviour: why pay to enter a toilet just to vandalize it?[15] On the other hand, it also provides another opportunity for rebellion (jumping the turnstile), another element to damage (jamming the locks) and requires the safe handling of money. It is concerning that Network Rail acknowledge that the removal of turnstiles from their managed stations 'is leading to increased antisocial and drug-related behaviours',[16] despite full-time cleaners at many of their facilities.

> Just a small amount, 5 or 10p, and you would know you were safe in there. Because then you wouldn't get anyone and everyone drinking, smoking and doing naughty things which does happen sometimes.
> **OLDER PERSON WITH IMPAIRED MOBILITY**

## Voluntary donations

Not all toilets have the visitor numbers and ensuing chaos of a train station terminal in an international city. Some toilets, particularly community-run loos, could do well with an honesty box or charity box, for voluntary contributions (see Figure 10.5). This is a good way to get some income to cover supplies or for a local cause, particularly in places where users extend beyond local residents to grateful visitors, groups or tourists.

## Why remove payments?

Network Rail manage twenty of the UK's train stations, with the rest run by different train operating companies. These twenty include many of the busiest in the country, such as Glasgow Central, Manchester Piccadilly, Birmingham New Street and eleven in London. Ten years ago, Network Rail were charging passengers to access the toilets (50p in most cases), which, due to the very high visitor numbers, generated a huge income: £12.8 million in three years prior to 2015, £2.3 million of which was from London Victoria. In 2014, London Victoria's toilets brought in £600,000.[17]

> You've paid to get on this train the ridiculous amount of money that it costs, and then the station charge you 20p to go to the toilet. And they're the ones that also provide the concessions so you can buy food and drink. That really bugs me actually.
> 
> **PARENT**

Shortly after these figures came to light, Network Rail made London Victoria's toilets free, and began renovating them. The redesign and renovation cost £8.5 million[18] and included several significant design decisions. The men's and women's swapped spaces, giving the women's facility the larger footprint.[19] The designers used a very high-quality yet durable design aesthetic with a bronze, brass, rose gold and white colour scheme (Figure 10.6), and added a Changing Places toilet. Since then, Network Rail have revised their approach to public toilets as part of their 'Putting Passengers First' policy, which also includes free Wi-Fi, more seating, lift access and drinking water fountains.[20] Toilet charges have been removed from all Network Rail's toilets, and many more of their station loos have been renovated. Their new approach to toilet design is well documented as part of their station design standards, in *NR/GN/CIV/200/04, Public Toilets in Managed Stations*, 2021.[21] Toilet design is also referred to many times in their 2020 inclusive design standard.[22]

**Figure 10.5** Donation box for Heart of Hathersage community-designed and built toilets. The new toilet block also included a public and community space. Hathersage, Derbyshire. Credit: Rosanna Traina.

Why the U-turn in charging for toilets? We can see a few possible arguments for this new approach. Passengers have already paid for train tickets, making them customers who might be frustrated to be charged for toilet access, particularly when toilets on the train are free (and if they are stuck at the station for longer because trains are delayed or cancelled). More hospitality and retail has been

**Figure 10.6** Standard toilets at Victoria Station, London.

introduced to many stations making them a destination in themselves, which also means the station needs the infrastructure, such as benches and toilets, to support people spending time there. The design standards also show commitment to accessibility and inclusion as a motivating factor, so it could also be that this was seen as the right thing to do.

## Haven't we already paid for this?

Whilst some people are happy to pay for a decent loo, others see it as an essential public service paid for through tax and should not be treated as a commercial exercise: councils 'should' provide public toilets, and these toilets 'should' be free. However, as councils do not have to provide them, no budget is protected for the purpose of maintaining public toilets. Where can money come from within a council to create toilet facilities? Perhaps from other budgets that are earmarked for things that could be improved by public toilet provision, or that address the consequences of a lack of loos: street cleaning, parks management, libraries and leisure centres, high street regeneration, public health, social isolation and active travel.

> We would never charge for toilets in the [city entertainment district], as charging would encourage people to revert to street urination.
>
> **CITY COUNCIL OFFICER**

In all these spaces, public toilets indirectly play a role, and one or more facilities could be initiated through a connected project. Through interviews with a council officer, urban designer and police officer as part of our Engaged research project, we identified specific funds that councils could consider, to get toilets built or redeveloped, such as Safer Streets Funds, Neighbourhood Committee Funds, Community Ward funding or Additional Restrictions Grant Funds for economic recovery.

> The high street is the perfect place for [public toilets]. There is a drive for regeneration and to recover high streets, and that means making the high street a pleasant experience – but people don't factor in toilets [and what they provide] as part of this.
>
> **ENGAGED EXPERT INTERVIEW**

Councils and community groups can also apply for grants, though a representative for a community-run toilet shared that they had found it difficult to secure funding for a toilet due to misunderstandings and confusion around who provides toilets. The sentiment from funders was that someone else (such as the local authority) should be paying for the capital costs. In the end they found it easier to be awarded money for another purpose, such as a café or information centre that happened to include a toilet, rather than the toilet itself, even though this was the impetus behind the project. Redevelopments and regeneration projects could cover the costs of a build through section 106 or community infrastructure levies.[23]

Once a toilet is built, covering the ongoing costs is more of a challenge. Are there alternative models or financial incentives that could help with the ongoing cleaning and maintenance of council-managed public toilets? A debate in the House of Commons as part of the Levelling Up and Regeneration Bill[24] floated the idea of a reduction in business rates based on the square footage of the toilet, if that toilet was made 'publicly accessible'. No calculations were made as to how significant a saving this would be, but it could be a more significant offer for community toilets than the financial incentives offered by community toilet schemes. It could even establish non-customer access as the norm for toilets in businesses rather than the exception. There would need to be more political will to explore the option. It also would not address the quality of the toilets provided or how inclusive they are in their design.

The Royal Society for Public Health asked councils for their views on other ways of raising funds for public toilets as part of their 2020 investigation into the country's public toilets. Popular ideas including advertising (78 per cent), sponsorship (62 per cent) and even benefactors (67 per cent), floating the idea of tax breaks or gift aid as a way of incentivizing individuals or companies to support public toilets. Tax-based ideas included taking a penny from the cost of public transport tickets (45 per cent), or a tax on cafés and bars (51 per cent).[25]

## Who cleans and maintains it?

### Who cleans toilets?

Automatic public conveniences were called so because of their automatic cleaning cycle between uses, but these are in decline. The rest are cleaned by people, and there are a few different models for how this works. It could be someone who spends their whole working day cleaning the same facility. Toilet attendants will have a room to take breaks in, and their constant presence is valued; they take ownership of the toilets.

> She gets paid, she has a white net curtain which she has hung up in her office, nice bright and clean, you should have a look! And the toilet is clean and if it's raining they put down cardboard so it doesn't get all muddy. Nice toilet.
> **OLDER PERSON WITH REDUCED CONTINENCE**

Other toilets may also have a constant presence, where the cleaner is kept in constant activity by a very high volume of visitors. If visitor numbers are not so high, or a permanent presence is not necessary, a cleaner or team of cleaners will visit a few toilets on their rounds. This might be the council's own cleaning team, a cleaning contractor or a toilet management company who provide cleaning as part of the contract with the council.

> There is a suggestion to stop having full-time attendants. This is driven by budget cuts, but there is a legitimate argument. In the middle of winter there may not be any visitors around at all.
> **PARKS MANAGER**

A recent suggestion by Kilburn Older Voices Exchange (KOVE), a campaign group in North West London was for a similar model to be used within a community toilet scheme. If participating businesses found that a higher frequency of cleaning was needed to serve the wider community, could they share a mobile cleaner between them or have it funded in part or fully by the council as a condition of the scheme?

When the toilet is part of a larger building or development, the toilets are cleaned as part of the general cleaning of the building. In smaller buildings, the staff, such as hospitality staff in cafés and restaurants, might clean the toilets as part of their role. Whilst cleaning toilets is not a glamorous job, it is a very important one that needs to be given more respect – and pay – than it currently receives. If toilets are not kept clean, we cannot use them. Regular cleaning also keeps things well maintained and is a chance to spot anything that needs fixing. Even though we all clean the toilets in our homes, cleaning toilets is another area – like designing toilets, promoting toilets or simply needing toilets – where our toilet taboo and cultural attitude towards excretion makes it difficult to discuss, recognize or reward as we should. It is testament to the Loo of the Year awards,[26] an annual award scheme since 1987 where winning facilities will proudly display their certificates for years, that they have a special award for 'Attendant of the Year'.

> Elsewhere in the station if you want to ask about a train you're unlikely to ask a cleaner, you'd find someone else, but in the toilets you've got no choice. So language is important. It should be a priority job.
> **LONDON STATION MANAGER**

The cleaning staff, as with the attendant, perform another important role. They provide a presence in this unusual environment where we retreat from public space but are still close to other strangers visiting the loo. The cleaner is more trusted than the anonymous user, through their professional capacity, identification or uniform. Their eyes reduce antisocial activity between people, or misuse of the facility. Cleaners and attendants can spot people who might need assistance too.

> That's part of the beauty of having someone cleaning every toilet at every visit, he has to wait for each toilet to be empty, and therefore notices if someone's hiding in one.
> **CLEANING CONTRACTOR**

> At the time there was a lot of concern from council members about drug abuse. We certainly didn't want to provide an opportunity for that, so we felt quite strongly that it was attended.
> **CITY COUNCIL OFFICER**

Full-time cleaners or attendants could be encouraged to have more of a dialogue with the public, where appropriate. Signage can tell people where the attendant can be found or reached. They could have name badges or an enhanced role by providing hygiene supplies or supporting access needs. Training to understand and support different users, with empathy, could enhance their role.

When designing inclusive public toilets, toilet cleaners and maintenance workers are an important and perhaps overlooked user group. Their involvement helps us to understand physical design challenges: where dirt or flooding occurs or is difficult to address; where their time is spent (and could be saved); what equipment is available and effective; and also to get a unique insight into the dynamics and interactions they experience or observe when working in the facilities.

## Designing feedback

Many people may be involved in the cleaning, maintenance and management of a publicly accessible toilet. One person might unlock the facility, another cleans it, another performs general maintenance or perhaps specific trades need to be called. Someone else pays the bills, and another entity own it. These people all want the toilet to be looked after, but many toilets have no one on-site to oversee it. How do we show that a toilet is cared for if the staff are not there? If, as a visitor, we find there is a problem, who do we tell and how?

When cleaners are not on-site, we can show their presence in other ways. Many public and workplace toilets have a notice sheet that is updated to show how long it has been since the last check, and that regular checks are made. These uninspiring A4 sheets are very much record-keeping and not presented as something for the user to take an interest in. More could be made of this, perhaps as a poster directed at users that celebrates the commitment to regular cleaning. This could also be a way of encouraging users to report problems, by showing who to report them to and that the provider really does want to know if something needs attention between checks.

There are other ways to show hygiene and cleaning are taken seriously. Some facilities had a digital countdown to the next toilet check. A few have 'How clean is this toilet?' touchscreens or buttons (which puts in mind two further questions: 'what is done with the results?' and 'how clean is this button?') (Figure 10.7). A request for feedback, whether through contact details, a screen or a QR code, all indicate that cleanliness is important and that there is someone around to take

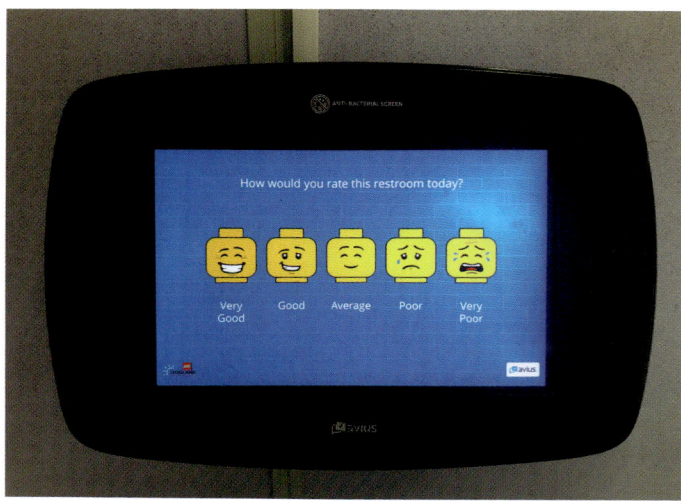

**Figure 10.7** 'How would you rate this restroom today?' survey. Legoland, Windsor.

action if negative reports are made. Going a step further would be to find a way to inform people when their suggestions are acted on.

For a lot of issues it is confusing for a user to know whether to speak to a cleaner, phone a helpline or write to the council. How do we address immediate problems (there's no toilet paper; I'm locked inside and cannot get out) as opposed to longer-term issues (the third toilet on the right is missing a hook; the light sensor is not on for long enough; the toilets are not open when I need them)? For immediate problems, people need the information located in the real world – in this case the public toilet, rather than on the website, although a QR code in-situ could be one means of accessing contact details.

It helps to be clear that communication streams such as phone, text or email will go to the right person, who that is and what they are responsible for. In most cases, a single point of contact should be responsible for taking and directing feedback from the public, rather than telling them it is not within their remit or to contact a different company instead. If giving feedback becomes a hassle for the user, they will not bother. Anyone working in the facility also needs some customer relations training to take in the information and see that it is passed on. A joined-up system will mean that whoever the user speaks to, the message will reach the person who can address it, even if that communication needs to pass between different companies.

## Guardians of the toilet

A different model of guardianship is being introduced in parks. In different parts of the country, cafés have been built in parks with public toilets in the same building or directly adjacent. Whilst the public toilet serves the whole park, it also provides toilets for the café customers to use. Depending on the contract, the management, maintenance and/or cleaning of the toilets is then carried out by the café operator, just as if they were the café's toilets, but with a higher footfall.

These toilets can be built to a better standard to meet the needs of all park users rather than the minimum required by a café. By being linked to the café, both physically and in who the toilets serve, there is more natural surveillance. This comes about in a few ways: through the official guardianship of the café (we know who is managing the toilets); regular cleaning (someone is nearby to keep the toilets in service); and other users (there are more people in that part of the park, due to the café). This addresses a lot of the problems of park toilets, where toilets had been located out of the way, behind bushes, and where there may be extremely low numbers of people in winter or after dark. When the Queen Elizabeth Olympic Park was created after the 2012 London Olympics, two pavilions at either end were included in the design. Both had large public toilet facilities and a public café under the same roof and each café manages the toilets. This model could be an effective and more widely adopted way of ensuring publicly accessible toilets are provided as part of a council or publicly owned building, rather than a business only creating customer-only loos. Back in 2006, the government's strategic guide *Improving Public Access to Better Quality Toilets* proposed that 'in appropriate circumstances – such as leasing a Council building for use as a community café – a clause might be included allowing non-paying customers to use toilet facilities';[27] an approach also suggested in 2019 in Welsh Government guidance on toilet strategies.[28]

# Engaged: How to change things for the better

The challenges of managing, financing and maintaining a public toilet will not go away, but that does not mean we need to stick with the current way of doing things. Perhaps we are missing something – an alternative model, an innovation, a cultural shift – that would help us respond to these challenges differently. What is new in the world of toilet provision?

## A toilet on every high street

Let us start where we left off, looking at businesses and public toilets operating in symbiosis, already seen in the context of public parks. Could more public toilets be designed with this relationship to a business?

Our project, 'Engaged: A toilet on every high street' (see Chapter 1), investigated whether a similar model would work for the high street, where we proposed reusing empty commercial properties in part as a public toilet alongside a business that occupied the remaining commercial space. The business would then manage, supervise or clean it (Figure 10.8).

There are a few examples of models like this being applied in urban settings. In Westbourne Grove, West London, residents requested that a retail space was designed into the proposal for a new public toilet building. The result, built in 1994, was an award-winning building designed by architects CZWG where the rental income from the unit – a flower shop – offsets the running of the attended facility (Figure 10.9). In Wolverhampton, the city council rent an empty unit from the shopping centre, which the council converted into a public toilet. Opened in 2006, *WCityStop.info* includes a reception desk with council information and a digital kiosk to access council services, alongside standard and accessible toilets, a feeding room and shower, all without charge. It was also trialled as a base for health services to support people and the night-time economy on busy nights like New Year's Eve (Figure 10.10).

**Figure 10.8** Early graphic for the Engaged model, showing a retail unit as both public toilet and bookshop. Design: PiM.studio Architects. Credit: PiM.studio Architects/Engaged.

**Figure 10.9** Award-winning public toilet with flower shop. Westbourne Grove, London.

**Figure 10.10** WCityStop.info, providing public toilets and council information from a repurposed retail unit. Wolverhampton.

## What are the challenges?

For the Engaged model, we interviewed experts across local and national government, urban design, crime prevention, retail and toilet management,[29] who recognized several potential benefits. Firstly, the toilet could be specified to meet whichever needs were currently not being met by the existing local infrastructure. It could respond to local culture and demographics and be of a scale required for a public toilet rather than a customer-only loo. The property could be configured to suit the business and toilet needs (which might result in separate or shared entrances), and to meet accessibility standards. Also, the business through their role as a guardian could provide the natural surveillance to discourage misuse compared to an unattended public toilet. This might encourage users to treat the toilet better too, when they can put a face to the person responsible for it, and it will also help people to know who and how to report problems to keep the toilets better maintained.

> If it's community-owned and community-managed it won't get damaged.
> **COMMUNITY CAMPAIGNER FOR PUBLIC TOILETS**

The challenges would be developing an appealing contract and incentive for the business, such as rent reduction on a council-owned property compared to another location, so they are not overwhelmed or disadvantaged by also maintaining the toilets, particularly if it takes time away from their primary occupation. If the setting was busy, it might work better for toilets to remain within the council's portfolio for cleaning and maintenance with the business only providing a presence to oversee things day to day.

Employees may also be anxious about how to speak with a wider range of visitors than their own business attracts, and how to keep the environment inclusive or respond to problems or conflict outside their normal customer relations. This could be addressed through training such as inclusion or disability awareness, or guidance from local charities or community support officers. The commercial or community activity itself may need to be appropriate to reflect the people coming in to use the toilet, recognizing that people may still feel inhibited by whether they 'fit in' with others in the facility, particularly if the two purposes share an entrance or entry space.

> Could the [presence of a knitting group] discourage young people from using the public toilet?
> **ENGAGED EXPERT INTERVIEW**

It is also a challenge to identify appropriate units that meet multiple requirements. There needs to be sufficient space in the unit to provide enough toilets with enough remaining space for the adjacent business, as well as routes to each where the two activities oversee but do not inhibit each other. The location needs to have good external natural surveillance and footfall if it is to work as essential infrastructure for the high street, whilst not attracting such high rents that it becomes unfeasible. The cost of bringing the building up to standard, particularly for accessibility and inclusion, may also be significant if a property is old or been empty for a long time.

> For every year a unit in an older building lays empty … it becomes more expensive to bring it back into use
> **ENGAGED EXPERT INTERVIEW**

## Alternative models for Engaged

There is a lot to consider in terms of setting up, managing and financing this model, but as we have seen with park toilets, it is a model that can work and work well and it feels as if there is scope to explore it in more contexts. New models based on Engaged emerged during our expert interviews and through ongoing engagement with council regeneration officers. Ideas include:

1. Using the whole floorplan of a vacant unit to create an inclusive public toilet and creating a network of local businesses that share responsibility for managing, cleaning and maintaining it.
2. Funding the installation of an inclusive toilet for public use within a successful, occupied unit or community space.
3. Converting some cubicles within existing public toilet buildings or extending the building for commercial use (Figure 10.11).
4. Use of council- or community-owned buildings rather than those owned by private landlords.
5. Designing inclusive public toilets into new developments where appropriate access and entrances can be created, and architecture can support how the toilet is positioned in relation to other activity spaces whether commercial, community or cultural (museums, theatres, galleries).
6. Creating toilets within land earmarked for future development alongside other 'meanwhile' use, such as box parks, incubator spaces, food growing and outdoor markets.

**Figure 10.11** Concept design for an extension to a public toilet unit, as a coffee shop. Designer: Madelaine Dowd. Credit: Madelaine Dowd.

This last proposition was one that we developed further into detailed designs for public toilets within shipping containers. This is a trend particularly in cities where land that falls within a long-term local development plan can house temporary commercial developments, often for ten to fifteen years, until permanent development (e.g. for housing) is required and secured. As shipping containers are a common construction for these pop-up developments, sometimes branded 'box parks', our partners on Engaged, PiM.studio Architects, developed drawings for how inclusive toilets would fit in these units (Figure 10.12). A container could either be fitted entirely with toilets with other activities taking place in other units, or divided to be part-toilet, part-activity space.

**Figure 10.12** Two shipping containers, where one is a toy library and the other is a public toilet, with public play space in between. Design: PiM.studio Architects. Credit: PiM.studio Architects/Engaged.

An important driver of creating inclusive toilets in containers is that they not only provide facilities for the wider neighbourhood but for the other occupants of the temporary development whatever its purpose, including those employed there. Community gardeners, market traders and food delivery drivers need toilets to be able to work yet are some of the occupations most likely to find they do not have facilities they can use.

## The night-time neighbourhood

The night-time neighbourhood would benefit from new models of toilet provision. The current response to late-night toilet demand consists mostly of plastic urinals dropped around a city from the back of a truck on a Friday and Saturday night, or occasionally, a permanent urinal that is unlocked at night-time. Female urinals, or devices like the *shee-wee* that help women use standard urinals, have been trialled at festivals. This continues the low cost, temporary solution to street urination: pre-formed indestructible plastic that requires no plumbing or electrics. Whilst some people may feel comfortable using outdoor urinals, particularly with the benefits of darkness and alcohol, they do not suit everyone, do not meet many physical needs and do not serve uses for toilets beyond urination.

People who work in the evening, early morning or night-time need the same quality of inclusive public toilet provision as anyone else, including a space to withdraw and revitalize themselves. The wellbeing of delivery drivers is a key consideration within night-time infrastructure.[30] Welfare space for food delivery drivers was a recurring topic during Engaged. This is needed to keep workers safe and warm with vehicle parking and access to water and toilets (Figure 10.13). By providing new facilities for new audiences in our ever changing cities we are enabling growth for night-time economies and supporting a community that can look out for more traditional occupants of the city at night-time, such as people leaving bars and clubs who may be vulnerable or in need of help.

Exploring temporary solutions for public toilets, whether temporary means fifteen years or three hours on a Saturday night, creates an opportunity to innovate in how toilets function. Building new and imaginative public toilets also presents an opportunity to explore more sustainable materials and options. Toilets can be fitted with solar panels, grey water for flushing and rainwater filtering. The exterior walls and roof can be used for urban cultivation or planting. The arrangement of units creates new public spaces between them, for resting, gathering or physical activity (Figure 10.14). Waterless or composting toilets can be trialled enabling toilets to be located where they are needed, even if this is without connections

**Figure 10.13** Concept design for a new public amenity: part-public toilet, part welfare space for delivery drivers. Design: PiM.studio Architects. Credit: PiM.studio Architects/Engaged.

**Figure 10.14** Concept design for public toilet and co-working space, with public seating and planting. Design: PiM.studio Architects. Credit: PiM.studio Architects/Engaged.

to mains water or sewerage. The infrastructure around waterless or composting toilets, to find alternative means of washing and of processing, reusing or disposing of waste would need to be explored, but the opportunity to test them with the public to find how people respond to such a cultural shift could be an interesting next step.

Regeneration officers mentioned to us how frequently toilets are raised by the public during the initial community engagement for a development project but how difficult it is to maintain a high profile for these facilities all the way through to realization. Competing demands from urban design, developers and construction can diminish the need for toilets and drown out the community's voice. Providing temporary toilets on development land is a way to demonstrate that there is a real need from the community, test different designs and create reliance on the toilets in the location. This ensures that when a site is developed, the toilets are recognized as part of the local area and a critical element of neighbourhood regeneration.

# Notes

1. Ramster, Bichard, Dowd, Knight and Traina, 'Engaged: A toilet on every high street'.
2. Non-Domestic Rating (Public Lavatories) Act 2021.
3. B. Lancaster, *The Department Store: A Social History* (London: Leicester University Press, 1995).
4. A. Smoyer, A. Pittman and P. Borzillo, 'Humans peeing: Justice-involved women's access to toilets in public spaces', *PLoS ONE* 18(3) (2023): e0282917, https://doi.org/10.1371/journal.pone.0282917.
5. Department of Communities and Local Government, *Improving Public Access to Toilets: A Strategic Guide*.
6. Royal Society for Public Health, *Taking the P\*\*\**.
7. S. Bhandari, 'Hounslow Council promotes public toilet locations across the borough', *The Chiswick Herald*, 7 February 2018. Available online: https://chiswickherald.co.uk/hounslow-council-promotes-public-toilet-locations-across-the-borough-p7685-95.htm (accessed 8 January 2024).
8. Bichard and Knight, 'Improving public services through open data: public toilets'.
9. Wandsworth Borough Council, 'Environment Culture and Community Safety Overview and Scrutiny Committee – 17 April 2013'. Available online: https://www.wandsworth.gov.uk/media/3400/community_toilets_change_of_policy_appendix_2_to_paper_no_13-284_april_2013.pdf. (accessed 8 January 2024).
10. Department of Communities and Local Government, *Improving Public Access to Toilets: A Strategic Guide*.
11. *London Local Authorities Act 2012* Part 3 Section 6.
12. Hansard, *London Local Authorities Bill*. H.L. Vol. 516 col. 384 (13 October 2010). Available online: https://hansard.parliament.uk/commons/2010-10-13/debates/10101328000003/LondonLocalAuthoritiesBill(Lords)(ByOrder) col. 384 (accessed 8 January 2024).

13  Healthmatic (2017), *Smarter Public Conveniences*. Available online: https://www.healthmatic.com/wp-content/uploads/2019/04/Healthmatic_Smarter_Public_Toilets_2018.pdf (accessed 28 October 2024).
14  Ibid.
15  British Toilet Association and Hertfordshire Constabulary Crime Prevention Design Service, *Publicly Available Toilets: Problem Reduction Guide*.
16  Network Rail, *Design Manual NR/GN/CIV/200/04: Public Toilets in Managed Stations*.
17  I. Aron, 'Victoria station is making millions from people using the toilets', *TimeOut*, 7 September 2015. Available online: https://www.timeout.com/london/blog/victoria-station-is-making-millions-from-people-using-the-toilets-090715 (accessed 8 January 2024).
    Press Association, 'Relief at last: Toilet charges suspended at two London train stations', *The Guardian*, 10 December 2016. Available online: https://www.theguardian.com/uk-news/2016/dec/10/toilet-charges-suspended-at-two-london-train-stations-victoria-charing-cross (accessed 8 January 2024).
18  C. Kerr and D. Hammond, 'Off the rails: Rail bosses splash out £8 million doing up old toilets at Victoria station', *The Sun*, 21 August 2019. Available online: https://www.thesun.co.uk/news/9764364/rail-bosses-splash-out-8million-doing-up-old-toilets-at-station/ (accessed 8 January 2024).
19  Network Rail, 'London's busiest toilets close for £4m revamp – but you still won't need to spend a penny when they reopen', 20 December 2018. Available online: https://www.networkrailmediacentre.co.uk/news/londons-busiest-toilets-close-for-gbp-4m-revamp-but-you-still-wont-need-to-spend-a-penny-when-they-reopen (accessed 28 January 2024).
20  Network Rail, 'Passengers first – from free toilets to Access for All', 19 March 2019. Available online: https://www.networkrail.co.uk/stories/passengers-first-from-free-toilets-to-access-for-all/ (accessed 8 January 2024).
21  Network Rail, *Design Manual NR/GN/CIV/200/04: Public Toilets in Managed Stations*.
22  Network Rail (2020) *Design Manual NR/GN/CIV/300/04: Inclusive Design*. Available online: https://www.networkrail.co.uk/wp-content/uploads/2021/06/NR_GN_CIV_300_04_Inclusive-Design.pdf (accessed 8 January 2024).
23  R. Traina, I. Knight, G. Ramster, J. Bichard and M. Dowd, *Engaged: First Findings Report on the National Need for Public Toilets, and 'Engaged' as an Alternative Model for High Street Provision* (London: Royal College of Art, 2022).
24  Hansard, *Levelling-up and Regeneration Bill*. H.C. Vol. 720. col. 875 (20 October 2022). Available online: https://hansard.parliament.uk/Commons/2022-10-20/debates/d14be0c1-bf42-4216-bcf1-5d44a90261e9/Levelling-UpAndRegenerationBill(TwentySixthSitting)?highlight=toilet%202018# (accessed 8 January 2024).

25. Royal Society for Public Health, *Taking the P\*\*\**.
26. Wikipedia, 'Loo of the Year Awards'. Available online: https://en.wikipedia.org/wiki/Loo_of_the_Year_Awards (accessed 15 October 2024).
27. Department of Communities and Local Government, *Improving Public Access to Toilets: A Strategic Guide*.
28. Welsh Government, *The Provision of Toilets in Wales: Statuary Guidance*.
29. Traina, Knight, Ramster, Bichard and Dowd, *Engaged*: First Findings Report on the National Need for Public Toilets, and 'Engaged' as an Alternative Model for High Street Provision.
30. Mayor of London, *Developing a night time strategy, Part 1: Guidance on process* [pdf]. Greater London Authority. Available online: https://www.london.gov.uk/sites/default/files/210317_gla_1_night-time_strategies_part_1.pdf (accessed 15 July 2024).

# 11 Conclusion

After a successful visit to an inclusive public toilet, what's next? Before too long, we will need to go through the whole process again: another toilet in a new context with a different set of user requirements and design responses. A day out to the seaside features a toilet with an inclusive design that is built to withstand the sea air and sand. On the way back, the toilet at the train station has an attendant to support different needs and who checks cubicles for criminal activity. Approaching home, we pass the village loo that serves toddlers suddenly desperate for a wee, older people keeping up their daily routine and bus drivers passing through. It's now managed and cleaned by local people. Toilets are designed to meet the needs not only of the users but also the wider context and environment in which they are located.

The context of use is a consideration of design that the public understands, and which influences expectations. It gives designers the opportunity for creative responses to standards. The inclusive toilet is not a one-size-fits-all fixed design, but a set of parameters in which we work when making design choices. If our choices meet people's needs, we have our inclusive toilet, and we can then go further to design something fitting, beautiful and restorative.

We hope that *Designing Inclusive Public Toilets: Wee the people* has helped you to understand the complexity of using a toilet when away from home and how this is impacted by the design of the environment, products and service that make up the public toilet. People's needs do not exist in isolation, so it is not enough to design for just one, whether that need might be wheelchair access, sight loss or the needs of children. Accessibility and inclusion are constantly widening to include multi-generational neighbourhoods, neurodiversity, gender identity and wider cultural preferences. We have overlapping identities within each of us and multiple dis/abilities that impact our use of public toilets. If one aspect of identity or ability is not designed for, it can knock out someone's use of the toilets no matter how well we have designed for others.

How do we prioritize competing needs and abilities within the public, or even within ourselves? Who is still underrepresented? Our own research has not yet gone far enough to include those stigmatized through poverty, ethnicity or mental health. Who we include and how we engage them in the research is as creative a challenge as the design of the toilet itself. Community-led design can empower marginalized people whose experience of poor toilet provision is overlooked.

An inclusive design approach will serve us beyond the design of the toilet. Public toilets are the petri dish of accessibility where every challenge of the built environment comes together in one facility. If designers get this right, they can get anything right, which is just as well as the toilet is no use on its own. An inclusive toilet on the high street serves no one if the shops themselves are not accessible. No one is coming to the neighbourhood just to use the loo; it is the infrastructure, not the destination. But the lessons learnt from designing inclusive toilets can be extended to our wider built environment and the products and services that support it. Maybe we could take a leaf out of New Zealand's and Japan's approaches and design amazing public toilets that will make people come to the neighbourhood just to visit the toilets!

Heralding public toilets as the ultimate design challenge could be their saviour, just as their downfall up to now has been from being disparaged, even vilified, and consequently overlooked. We cannot stress enough the importance of *talking* about toilets. The toilet taboo that affects us in day-to-day conversations continues in professional and policy-making circles. During our research we consistently find that guidance for the high street, urban design, active travel and public health does not mention toilets. It is so rare that it is easier to highlight a few that do: the inclusive design standards for the 2012 London Olympic and Paralympic Games, which continue in a new guise through the London Legacy Development Corporation;[1] Network Rail's Toilets in Managed Stations design standard;[2] and the Mayor of London's Night-time Strategy.[3] These three documents were initially developed for three distinct contexts – sporting venues, transport hubs and out-of-hours infrastructure – yet their impact can reach further, by recognizing inclusive public toilets as fundamental to the success of the built environment.

Where is the equivalent guidance for high street regeneration, for cycling and walking, or tourism? Passing references to 'amenities', 'facilities' or 'necessities' is not enough. Toilets need to be added as a key section of their own for them to be considered seriously and adopted into the wider urban design and regeneration of our towns and cities. The design and provision of publicly accessible toilets falls through the cracks between policy interests. Whilst privately we know how important good toilets are to us, it is not easy to be the one in the room to say 'what are we going to do about loos?', yet that is what it will take, in multiple departments across multiple organizations. Whether civil servant or minister, council officer or council member, it is no one's jurisdiction to focus on the toilets. Consequently, they are forgotten rather than being a central part of the infrastructure that underpins our public realm. Is this the effect of the toilet taboo at policy level? We need to get over this! Toilets, as we have shown, are vital for public health, for culture and leisure, and for getting people from A to B.

**We, the people**, want public toilets to be both accessible and sustainable, and environmental sustainability can be both a driver and beneficiary of radical design. The twentieth-century responses to water management in toilet design have been disappointing – push-down taps and twin flushes can render the toilet unusable. Is the public toilet an opportunity to educate and fascinate in how we use water for expelling our waste and restoring cleanliness? Do we need to use water at all? Flushing with water is not an essential component of waste management. Composting toilets whether composting is on-site or as part of a system could have a much greater role to play and give designers a real challenge to incorporate inclusion, behaviour change and sustainability in a public facility. Is our resistance to alternative models of managing waste part of our cultural disgust at what our bodies expel, or is it because we do not know how to use the produce? What can we learn from other countries regarding water use and sustainable models of waste management? Many are exploring these issues despite poor infrastructure and struggling economies.

Inclusive design must stand its ground, especially when balancing design-out-crime and defensible space initiatives. We encourage designers of public toilets to work closely with police architectural advisers, recognizing what is a robust necessity and what is an unfriendly and unwelcoming barrier to use. Whilst closing a toilet stops it being a scene of crime, the eradication of public toilets cannot be the solution.

Perhaps we should take the toilet out of the crime wave and replace it as an essential component of public health? What if the public toilet is shared with a wider wellbeing one-stop shop? Might the future feature the faecal transplant collection point or how about using our waste for energy? How much are we flushing away that can be reused in our quest for 'planet before people'? How can we embrace exciting new technologies as designers, planners or policymakers? Augmented and virtual reality can highlight pressure points in proposed toilet designs to find what works, especially for mobility and ease of use. It can observe human behaviour, to understand how we make choices and how design can influence or challenge these norms. What we consider normal in toilet design does not need to be set in stone. Cultural and societal norms evolve and people adjust. What would the inclusive toilet of the future look like if designers were not bound by what is currently acceptable, but could (sensitively and compassionately) experiment, innovate and explore new norms that support acceptance and inclusion in this public-private space? Designing for planet, for experience, for public health might require wider cultural and behaviour changes – the next challenge for inclusive design.

**Figure 11.1** 'This way to your new public toilets' promotional and directional sign, for Lloyd Street, Manchester. This announced Manchester's first Changing Places facility in a public toilet, 2013.

## Notes

1 London Legacy Development Corporation, *Inclusive Design Standards*.
2 Network Rail, *Design Manual NR/GN/CIV/200/04: Public Toilets in Managed Stations*.
3 Mayor of London (2020), *Developing a night time strategy, part 1: guidance on process*.

# Glossary

**Accessible lock/flush/tap** A hand-operated feature that is operable by people with reduced hand strength or dexterity, such as people with arthritis or children. One way to assess if a feature is accessible is whether it can be operated with a fist.

**Accessible toilet** The toilet indicated with a symbol of a person in a wheelchair. It is termed the 'unisex accessible toilet' by British Standards or 'wheelchair-accessible unisex toilet' by Building Regulations. This toilet is intended for disabled people in general, not only those who use wheelchairs. People self-define as needing this toilet.

**Ambulant toilet/cubicle** This is designed for people with impaired or limited mobility, not including those using a wheelchair. It features grab rails and a larger activity space, preferably with an outwards-opening door. Building Regulations and British Standards advise that an ambulant toilet is provided alongside standard cubicles.

**Community toilet scheme** Also called a comfort scheme, this is a local network of businesses providing **publicly accessible toilets**, often managed and promoted by the council. Many councils offer the business an annual financial incentive (normally less than £1,000) in exchange for letting non-customers use their toilets. Participating businesses display signage saying they are part of the scheme. Participating businesses include cafés, pubs and community centres. Councils may also include toilets in public buildings such as libraries.

**Fully enclosed cubicle** A toilet cubicle where the walls and door extend from the floor to the ceiling, as a lockable room. These are laid out in one of two ways: as separate rooms that include handwashing accessed off a corridor or the street (**universal toilet**); or as rooms within a larger room that contains handwashing facilities. The **accessible toilet** is always a fully enclosed cubicle design with its own handwashing facilities.

**Gender-neutral/unisex toilets** Toilets where gender or sex is not a factor in determining the right of access. Other terms are *all-gender* or *non-gendered*. The opposite scenario is a **separate-gender toilet**. Approved Document T of the Building Regulations (2024) uses **universal** for gender-neutral **fully enclosed** cubicles (with individual handwashing facilities), but *unisex* for **accessible toilets**. In this book we use *gender neutral* except when referring to a historic context or to guidance that uses *unisex*. Our definition of gender-neutral toilets encompasses **fully enclosed** or **partitioned** cubicles, and those with individual or shared handwashing facilities, unless specified.

**Partitioned cubicle** A toilet cubicle where the walls and door provide visual privacy within a certain height range, where gaps are permitted at the top of the cubicle and the ceiling, and the bottom of the cubicle and the floor. These are often part of a row of cubicles and are set within a larger room containing handwashing facilities.

**Public toilet** A council-maintained toilet block, or, more generally, a toilet we use as a member of the public. In this book, we use public toilet as shorthand for all **publicly accessible toilets**, whilst being clear to distinguish between council-maintained public toilets and publicly accessible toilets when relevant.

**Publicly accessible toilet** Any toilet that the public can access away from home, except for customer-only toilets and exceptions such as workplaces and educational settings. These are a mix of publicly and privately maintained toilets, including **public toilets**, toilets in the transport network, toilets in large retail facilities, toilets in public buildings (e.g. town halls, libraries, hospitals), community toilet scheme participants and any other toilets where the provider permits non-customer use.

**Separate-gender toilet** Standard toilet facilities that are designated *men's* and *women's*, with corresponding signage and separate entrances. These also have separate-gender handwashing. Building Regulations and British Standards use the term *separate-sex* or *single-sex*, reflecting sex not gender as the recognized characteristic under the Equality Act. We prefer to use gender, as day-to-day access relates more to how we identify and present rather than to our biology or legal documents. Transpeople have access to the separate-gender toilet for the gender that they identify as unless a specific case is made.

**Standard cubicle/toilet** The minimum design of toilet provision, for non-disabled people.

**Universal toilet** In the past, we have used this to mean an **accessible toilet** that is also available to everyone due to being the only toilet provided, for example a single accessible toilet in a café. The new Part T of the Building Regulation (2024) uses this term differently, to mean unisex/gender neutral (as opposed to their term 'single-sex') for a fully enclosed toilet with handwashing within the cubicle of either ambulant or standard design. This design can also be designated as separate-gender provision.

# Recommended Reading

All the texts cited in *Designing Inclusive Public Toilets: Wee the people* and listed in the notes at the end of each chapter are recommended. However, for readers who may want to know more and dive in a little deeper we recommended the following academic collections, popular publications and design guides.

Anthony, K. H. (2017) *Defined by Design: The Surprising Power of Hidden Gender, Age and Body Bias in Everyday Products and Places*. New York: Prometheus Books.
(This work looks at fashion, products and buildings and highlights how the design of many everyday products neglects to consider that 'one size does not fit all'.)

Cavanagh, S. and V. Ware (1990) *At Women's Convenience: A Handbook on the Design of Women's Public Toilets*. London: Women's Design Service.
(The original design guide that placed women at the heart of design. Sadly out of print, but contains a good overview of the history of London's provision inequalities and design recommendations that included children's provision.)

Cavanagh, S. (2022) 'Public in-conveniences: A practical guide to improving standards'. Available online: https://www.publicinconveniences.org.uk (accessed 28 June 2024).
(A guide from Susan Cavanagh, author of *At Women's Convenience* (see above) and the founder of All Mod Cons which became the British Toilet Association.)

Community Ownership Support Service (2018) *Public Toilets – How Communities are Responding to the Closure of Public Toilets*. Available online: https://dtascommunityownership.org.uk/sites/default/files/Public%20Toilets%202022.pdf (accessed 28 June 2024).
(A guide focusing on how Scottish communities have responded to a lack of public toilets. A good launching point to find out more about community-led and -run public toilets.)

George, R. (2008) *The Big Necessity: Adventures in the World of Human Waste*. London: Portabello Books.
('Lets talk about poo and why we won't talk about it and how we get rid of it from a global perspective.)

Gershenson, O. and B. Penner (2009) *Ladies and Gents: Public Toilets and Gender*. Philadelphia: Temple University Press.
(A collection of essays that cover the politics and art of the toilet.)

International Transport Workers Federation (2019) *Toilet Rights are Human Rights! Transport Workers Sanitation Charter*. Available online: https://www.itfglobal.org/sites/default/files/node/resources/files/ITF_SanitationCharter_EN_0.pdf (accessed 28 June 2024).

(A global perspective on the issue of access to toilets for transport workers.)

Lowe, L. (2018) *No Place to Go: How Public Toilets Fail our Private Needs*. London: Coach House.

(An excellent overview of why the lack of public toilets causes so many problems for so many people.)

Marshall, M. (2017) *Toilet Talk. Accessible Design for People with Dementia*, 2nd edn. Available online: https://www.hammond.com.au/hubfs/HammondCare/HC%20Resource%20Library/eBooks/Toilet-Talk-Accessible-Design-for-People-with-Dementia-Mary-Marshall.pdf (accessed 28 June 2024).

(A design guide from Australian organization Hammond Care focusing on the needs of people with dementia.)

Molotch, H. and L. Noren (2010) *Toilet: Public Restrooms and the Politics of Sharing*. New York: New York University Press.

(Another collection of essays, with a slightly more United States focus.)

Zeldovich, L (2021) *The Other Dark Matter: The Science and Business of Turning Waste into Wealth and Health*. Chicago: University of Chicago Press.

(An overview of how we can reimagine the outputs of 7 billion people and help save the planet.)

# Bibliography

AgeUK London. *Public toilets in London: The views of older Londoners* [pdf], 2022. Available online: https://www.ageuk.org.uk/bp-assets/globalassets/london/campaigns/out-and-about/ageuk_london_loos_final.pdf (accessed 10 January 2024).

Alzheimer's Society. *Dementia-friendly retail guide* [pdf], 2018. Available online: https://www.alzheimers.org.uk/sites/default/files/2019-07/AS_NEW_DF_Retail_Guide_Online_09_07_19.pdf (accessed 30 January 2024).

American Restroom Association. 'Potty parity', n.d. Available online: https://americanrestroom.org/potty-parity/ (accessed 12 December 2023).

Aron, I. 'Victoria station is making millions from people using the toilets', *TimeOut*, 7 September 2015. Available online: https://www.timeout.com/london/blog/victoria-station-is-making-millions-from-people-using-the-toilets-090715 (accessed 8 January 2024).

Arup. *Part M Research extension: Toilets* [pdf], 2023. Available online: https://assets.publishing.service.gov.uk/media/64d63baedd15ff0014277fd4/Part_M_Research_extension_toilets_research_report.pdf (accessed 10 January 2024).

BBC News. 'Greggs loses takeaway battle in Hull', 18 May 2016. Available online: https://www.bbc.co.uk/news/uk-england-humber-36320384 (accessed 20 January 2024).

BBC News. 'Greggs withdraws loo legal challenge', 13 June 2017. Available online: https://www.bbc.co.uk/news/uk-england-humber-40262371 accessed 24 January 2024).

BBC News. 'The power of the purple pound explained', 21 February 2017. Available online: https://www.bbc.co.uk/news/av/business-39040760 (accessed 21 December 2023).

BBC News. 'Squat toilets in Rochdale shopping centre', 15 July 2010. Available online: https://www.bbc.co.uk/news/uk-england-manchester-10644118 (accessed 3 January 2024).

Beanland, C. 'Coronavirus: Lack of public toilets in lockdown and social distancing will change the way we use loos', *The i*, 19 May 2020. Available online: https://inews.co.uk/news/coronavirus-lockdown-public-toilets-429370 (accessed 8 June 2024).

Bech Hansen, R. 'The West should be on war footing for the next pandemic', *The Telegraph*, 22 May 2024. Available online: https://www.telegraph.co.uk/global-health/science-and-disease/defence-against-next-pandemic-needs-more-than-global-treaty/ (accessed 8 June 2024).

Bellmann, F., Ypma, L. and Polack, D. 'Women move differently – what everyone working in mobility should know', 9 January 2020. Available online: https://www.weforum.org/agenda/2020/01/mobility-in-2020-a-female-perspective/ (accessed 19 June 2024).

Bhandari, S. 'Hounslow Council promotes public toilet locations across the borough', *The Chiswick Herald*, 7 February 2018. Available online: https://chiswickherald.co.uk/hounslow-council-promotes-public-toilet-locations-across-the-borough-p7685-95.htm (accessed 8 January 2024).

Bichard, J. *Extending architectural affordance: The case of the publicly accessible toilet*, PhD thesis, Bartlett School of Graduate Studies, University College London. 2015. Available online: https://discovery.ucl.ac.uk/id/eprint/1467131/ (accessed 2 January 2024).

Bichard, J. and Hanson, J. 'Inclusive design of "away from home" toilets'. In R. Cooper, G. Evans and C. Boyko (eds), *Designing Sustainable Cities*. Chichester: Wiley-Blackwell, 2009.

Bichard, J., Hanson, J. and Greed, C. 'Please wash your hands', *Senses and Society* 3(1) (2008): 79–84. https://doi.org/10.2752/174589308X266489.

Bichard, J., Hanson, J. and Greed, C. 'Who put the P in policy? The reality of guidelines and legislation in the design of the accessible toilet', *Proceedings of INCLUDE 2007 conference*. London: Royal College of Art. Available online: https://discovery.ucl.ac.uk/id/eprint/2999/ (accessed 18 January 2024).

Bichard, J. and Knight, G. 'Improving public services through open data: Public toilets'. *Proceedings of the Institution of Civil Engineers – Municipal Engineer* 165(3) (2012): 157–65. https://doi.org/10.1680/muen.12.00017.

Bichard, J. and Ramster, G. 'A mighty inconvenience: How Covid-19 tested a nation's continence'. *Built Environment*, 47(3) (2021): 402–16. https://doi.org/10.2148/benv.47.3.402.

Bladder & Bowel Community. 'Stoma care', 2024. Available online: https://www.bladderandbowel.org/bowel/stoma/ (accessed 10 January 2024).

Bladder & Bowel Community. 'Stress urinary incontinence (SUI)', 2024. Available online: https://www.bladderandbowel.org/bladder/bladder-conditions-and-symptoms/stress-urinary-incontinence/ (accessed 10 January 2024).

Bladder & Bowel Community. 'Urinary frequency - How often should you pee?', 2024. Available online: https://www.bladderandbowel.org/bladder/bladder-conditions-and-symptoms/frequency/ (accessed 10 January 2024).

Bladder & Bowel UK. 'Why squatting for toilet function is good for health', 2021. Available online: https://www.bbuk.org.uk/squatting-for-toileting-health/ (accessed 3 January 2024).

Boast, H. 'Public toilets and public luxury', *New Socialist*, 30 September 2023. Available online: https://newsocialist.org.uk/public-toilets-and-public-luxury/ (accessed 24 November 2023).

Bobinger, S. 'Women: Don't hover over the toilet seat', The Ohio State University Wexner Medical Centre, 24 July 2020. Available online: https://wexnermedical.osu.edu/blog/dont-hover-over-the-toilet-seat (accessed 12 July 2024).

Bovens, L. and Marcoci, A. 'The gender-neutral bathroom: A new frame and some nudges'. *Behavioural Public Policy* 7(1) (2020): 1–24. DOI:10.1017/bpp2020.23.

British Standards Institute. *BS6465: Part 1 Sanitary installations. Code of practice for scale of provision, selection and installation of sanitary appliances*. London: British Standards Institution, 2006.

British Standards Institute. *BS6465: Part 2 Sanitary installations. Code of practice for space requirements for sanitary appliances*. London: British Standards Institution, 2017.

British Standards Institute. *BS6465: Part 3 Sanitary installations. Code of practice for the selection, installation and maintenance of sanitary and associated appliances*. London: British Standards Institution, 2006.

British Standards Institute. *BS6465: Part 4 Sanitary installations. Code of practice for the provision of public toilets*. London: British Standards Institution, 2010.

British Standards Institute. *BS8300-2 Design of an accessible and inclusive built environment*. London: British Standards Institution, 2018.

British Standards Institute. *Guidance on safe working during the COVID-19 pandemic* [pdf], 2020. Available online: https://www.bsigroup.com/en-AU/topics/novel-coronavirus-covid-19/covid-19-guidelines/ (accessed 2 January 2022).

British Standards Institute. *PAS 6463: Design for the mind – Neurodiversity and the Built Environment – guide* [pdf], 2022. Available online: https://www.bsigroup.com/en-GB/insights-and-media/insights/brochures/pas-6463-design-for-the-mind-neurodiversity-and-the-built-environment/ (accessed 27 June 2024).

British Toilet Association and Hertfordshire Constabulary. *Publicly Available Toilets Problem Reduction Guide* [pdf], 2014. Available online: http://www.btaloos.co.uk/wp-content/uploads/2014/01/PubliclyAvailableToiletsProblemReductionGuide.pdf (accessed 2 January 2024).

British Toilet Association. Activities. Available online: http://www.btaloos.co.uk/?page_id=305 (accessed 8 January 2024).

Brixton Business Improvement District. 'Brixton BID launches new Go Before You Go campaign', 20 December 2017. Available online: https://brixtonbid.co.uk/go-before-you-go/ (accessed 20 December 2023).

Building Regulations. *Approved Document G: Sanitation, hot water safety and water efficiency*, 2015. Available online: https://www.gov.uk/government/publications/sanitation-hot-water-safety-and-water-efficiency-approved-document-g (accessed 21 December 2023).

Building Regulations. *Approved Document M: Access to and use of buildings. Vol. 2: Buildings other than dwellings* (amended 2020) [pdf], 2015. Available online: https://assets.publishing.service.gov.uk/media/60b0ea89d3bf7f43560e324a/Approved_Document_M_vol_2.pdf (accessed 21 December 2023).

Building Regulations. *Approved Document T: Toilet Accommodation* [pdf], 2024. Available online: https://assets.publishing.service.gov.uk/media/664329a0ae748c43d3793a28/ADT_2024pdf (accessed 3 June 2024).

Building Regulations. *Fire Safety Approved Document B: Building regulation in England covering fire safety matters within and around buildings*, 2010 (updated 2024). Available online: https://www.gov.uk/government/publications/fire-safety-approved-document-b (accessed 12 December 2023).

Bupa. 'Crohn's disease', 2021. Available online: https://www.bupa.co.uk/health-information/digestive-gut-health/crohns-disease (accessed 10 January 2024).

Bupa. 'Irritable Bowel Syndrome (IBS)', 2023. Available online: https://www.bupa.co.uk/health-information/digestive-gut-health/irritable-bowel-syndrome (accessed 10 January 2024).

Bupa. 'Ulcerative colitis', 2021. Available online: https://www.bupa.co.uk/health-information/digestive-gut-health/ulcerative-colitis (accessed 10 January 2024).

Cavanagh, S. *Queering Bathrooms: Gender, Sexuality and the Hygienic Imagination*. Toronto: University of Toronto Press, 2010.

Centre for Accessible Environments. *Good Loo Design Guide*. London: Centre for Accessible Environments, 2004.

Changing Places. '2,000 Changing Places Toilets milestone reached in UK', 15 November 2023. Available online: https://www.changing-places.org/news/view/2-000-changing-places-toilets-milestone-reached-in-uk (accessed 19 December 2023).

Changing Places Consortium. *Changing Places: The practical guide* [pdf], 2021. Available online: https://toiletmap.s3.eu-west-1.amazonaws.com/content/Changing%20Places%20a%20Practical%20Guide.pdf (accessed 28 June 2024).

Chavez-MacGregor, M., van Gils, C. H., van der Schouw, Y. T., Monninkhof, E., van Noord, P. A. and Peeters, P. H. 'Lifetime cumulative number of menstrual cycles and serum sex hormone levels in postmenopausal women', *Breast Cancer Research and Treatment*, 108(1) (2008): 101–12.

Coleman, R. 'The case for inclusive design – An overview', *Proceedings of the12 Triennial Congress, The International Ergonomics Association and The Human Factors Association of Canada, Toronto*, 1994. Available online: https://www.yumpu.com/en/document/view/47045819/the-case-for-inclusive-design-a-an-design-for-all#google_vignette (accessed 20 January 2024).

Colostomy UK. 'Guide to stoma-friendly accessible toilets', 2023. Available online: https://www.colostomyuk.org/campaigns/toilets/ (accessed 4 June 2024).

Cook, J. 'UK's first consumption room for illegal drugs given go-ahead', *BBC News*, 27 September 2023. Available online: https://www.bbc.co.uk/news/uk-scotland-66929385 (accessed 9 January 2024).

Cooper, R., Evans, G. and Boyko, C. (eds). *Designing Sustainable Cities*. Chichester: Wiley-Blackwell, 2009.

Crabbe, E. 'Bexhill: Public toilets closed in cost-cutting trial reopen', *The Argus*, 13 December 2023. Available online: https://www.theargus.co.uk/news/23984007.bexhill-public-toilets-closed-cost-cutting-trial-reopen/ (accessed 19 December 2023).

Crabtree, A., Mercer, G., Horan, R., Grant, S., Tan, T. and Buxton, J. A. 'A qualitative study of the perceived effects of blue lights in washrooms on people who use injection drugs', *Harm Reduction Journal* 10(22) (2013). Available online: https://harmreductionjournal.biomedcentral.com/articles/10.1186/1477-7517-10-22 (accessed 8 January 2024).

Crimaldi, J. 'Toilets spew invisible aerosol plumes with every flush – here's the proof, captured by high-powered lasers', *The Conversation*, 8 December 2022. Available online: https://theconversation.com/toilets-spew-invisible-aerosol-plumes-with-every-flush-heres-the-proof-captured-by-high-powered-lasers-195717 (accessed 1 January 2024).

Crisis. Everybody In. How to end homelessness in Great Britain. Available online: https://www.crisis.org.uk/media/239951/everybody_in_how_to_end_homelessness_in_great_britain_2018.pdf (accessed 30 October 2024).

Crohn's and Colitis UK. 'Not every disability Is visible', 2024. Available online: https://crohnsandcolitis.org.uk/our-work/campaigns/not-every-disability-is-visible (accessed 18 January 2024).

Crowley, J. *The Invention of Comfort: Sensibility and Design in Early Modern Britain and Early America*. Baltimore: Johns Hopkins University Press, 2001.

Czajkowski, K., Broś-Konopielko, M. and Teliga-Czajkowska, J. 'Urinary tract infection in women', *Menopause Review* 20(1) (2021): 40–47. https://doi.org/10.5114/pm.2021.105382.

Data Map Wales. 'National Toilet Map'. Available online: https://datamap.gov.wales/layers/geonode:national_toilet_map (accessed 6 December 2023).

Dawson, M. 'Home is the most dangerous place for women, but private and public violence are connected', *The Conversation*, 24 November 2021. Available online: https://theconversation.com/home-is-the-most-dangerous-place-for-women-but-private-and-public-violence-are-connected-171348 (accessed 9 January 2024).

Department of Communities and Local Government. *Improving Public Access to Better Quality Toilets: A Strategic Guide* [pdf], 2008. Available online: https://webarchive.nationalarchives.gov.uk/ukgwa/20120920031546mp_/http://www.communities.gov.uk/documents/localgovernment/pdf/713772.pdf (accessed 30 January 2024).

Department of Communities and Local Government. *Improving Public Access to Toilets Guidance on Community Toilet Schemes and SatLav* [pdf], 2008. Available online: https://webarchive.nationalarchives.gov.uk/ukgwa/20120920031420mp_/http://www.communities.gov.uk/documents/localgovernment/pdf/1064520.pdf (accessed 2 January 2024).

Department of Health and Ageing. 'Minister puts public toilets on the map', 19 September 2001. Available online: https://archive.ph/20121126224046/http://www.health.gov.au/internet/main/publishing.nsf/Content/health-mediarel-yr2001-bb-bb01080.htm (accessed 18 January 2024).

Department of Levelling Up, Housing and Communities. 'Rough sleeping snapshot in England: Autumn 2022', 2023. Available online: https://www.gov.uk/government/statistics/rough-sleeping-snapshot-in-england-autumn-2022 (accessed 8 January 2024).

Department of Levelling Up, Housing and Communities and Ministry of Housing, Communities and Local Government. *Building Regulations Fire Safety Approved Document B. Building regulation in England covering fire safety matters within and around buildings* [pdf], updated 2022. Available online: https://www.gov.uk/government/publications/fire-safety-approved-document-b (accessed 12 December 2023).

*Disability Discrimination Act 1995 Part III*. Available online: https://www.legislation.gov.uk/ukpga/1995/50/part/III (accessed 21 December 2023).

Drever, John L. 'Impact on vulnerable sub-groups from ultra-rapid hand dryers', *Acoustics Bulletin* 38(6) (2013): 4.

Easton, M. and Data Journalism Team. 'Postcode checker: How has your high street changed since 2020?' *BBC News*, 6 December 2022. Available online: https://www.bbc.co.uk/news/uk-63799670 (accessed 6 December 2023).

Elmsworthy, E. 'High street shops are inaccessible to nearly half of disabled people', *The Mirror*, 3 December 2018. Available online: https://www.mirror.co.uk/news/uk-news/high-street-shops-inaccessible-nearly-13682141 (accessed 2 May 2024).

Endpoint. 'Exploring the design implications of gender-neutral wayfinding signage,' 10 February 2022. Available online: https://www.weareendpoint.com/wayfinding-news-and-views/exploring-the-design-implications-of-gender-neutral-wayfinding-signage (accessed 18 January 2024).

*Equality Act 2010*. London: HMSO. Available online: https://www.legislation.gov.uk/ukpga/2010/15/contents (accessed 20 June 2024).

Fleck, J. *Are You an Inclusive Designer?* London: RIBA Publishing, 2019.

Foottit, L. 'Greggs ducks toilet provision following council dispute', *British Baker*, 25 February 2015. Available online: https://bakeryinfo.co.uk/news/greggs-ducks-toilet-provision-following-council-dispute/619849.article (accessed 24 January 2024).

Fuller, C. 'Council to close public toilets in cost cutting trial', *BBC News*, 18 October 2023). Available online: https://www.bbc.co.uk/news/articles/crg171rv1d0o (accessed 19 December 2023).

Goldsmith, S. *Designing for the Disabled: The New Paradigm*. London: RIBA Publications, [1963, 1967] 1976. Reprinted London: Routledge, 1997.

Gouk, A. 'The true cost of litter and fly tipping in England', *In Your Area*, 27 August 2020. Available online: https://www.inyourarea.co.uk/news/the-true-cost-of-litter-and-fly-tipping-in-england (accessed 7 January 2024).

Greater London Authority. 'Designing London's recovery', 2023. Available online: https://www.london.gov.uk/programmes-strategies/business-and-economy/support-your-business/challenge-ldn/past-challenges/designing-londons-recovery (accessed 2 January 2022).

Greater London Authority. 'Designing London's recovery: Improving public toilets', *Talk London*, 2023. Available online: https://www.london.gov.uk/talk-london/topics/recovery-covid-19/designing-londons-recovery/surveys/938# (accessed 10 January 2024).

Greater London Authority, *London at night: An evidence base for a 24-hour city* [pdf], 2018. Available online: https://www.london.gov.uk/sites/default/files/london-at-night-full-final.pdf (accessed 12 December 2023).

Greater London Authority. 'Talk London', 2024. Available online: https://www.london.gov.uk/talk-london/ (accessed 2 January 2024).

Greater London Authority. 'The London Plan: The spatial development strategy for Greater London', 2021. Available online: https://www.london.gov.uk/programmes-strategies/planning/london-plan/the-london-plan-2021-table-contents (accessed 23 May 2024).

Greed, C. *Inclusive Urban Design: Public Toilets*. Oxford: Architectural Press/Elsevier, 2003.

Gregory, A. 'More than 42m adults will be overweight by 2040', *The Guardian*, 19 May 2022. Available online: https://www.theguardian.com/society/2022/may/19/more-than-42m-uk-adults-will-be-overweight-by-2040 (accessed 20 January 2024).

Guild of Architectural Ironmongers. 'Replacing the accessibility symbol' Health and Safety Executive. *Workplace health, safety and welfare. Workplace (Health, Safety and Welfare) Regulations 1992*, n.d. Available online: https://www.gai.org.uk/GAI/News/News-Items/2023/Replacing-the-accessibility-symbol-a-GAI-survey.aspx (accessed 29 January 2024).

Hansard. *Levelling-up and Regeneration Bill (20 October, 2022)*. H.C. Vol. 720. col. 875. Available online: https://hansard.parliament.uk/Commons/2022-10-20/debates/d14be0c1-bf42-4216-bcf1-5d44a90261e9/Levelling-UpAndRegenerationBill (TwentySixthSitting)?highlight=toilet%202018# (accessed 8 January 2024).

Hansard. *London Local Authorities Bill (13 October 2010)*. H.L. Vol. 516 col. 376. Available online: https://hansard.parliament.uk/commons/2010-10-13/debates/10101328000003/LondonLocalAuthoritiesBill(Lords)(ByOrder) (accessed 11 January 2024).

Hansard. *London Local Authorities Bill (13 October 2010)* H.L. Vol. 516 col. 384. Available online: https://hansard.parliament.uk/commons/2010-10-13/debates/10101328000003/LondonLocalAuthoritiesBill(Lords)(ByOrder) col. 384 (accessed 8 January 2024).

Hansard. *Non-Domestic Rating (Public Lavatories) Bill (17 March 2021)*. H.L. Vol. 811, col. 432. Available online: https://hansard.parliament.uk/lords/2021-03-17/debates/90B02AA3-684B-4374-A2D1-22520CBFE582/Non-DomesticRating(PublicLavatories)Bill# (accessed 11 January 2024).

Hansard. *Written Answers to Questions (8 Jun 2005)*. H.C. Vol. 434, Part 83, col. 563W. Available online: https://publications.parliament.uk/pa/cm200506/cmhansrd/vo050608/text/50608w03.htm#50608w03.html_wqn0. (accessed 11 January 2024).

Hansard. *Written Answers (13 Mar 2008)*. H.C. Vol. 473, Part 66, col. 584W. Available online: http://www.publications.parliament.uk/pa/cm200708/cmhansrd/cm080313/text/80313w0012.htm (accessed 11 January 2024).

Hanson, J., Bichard, J. and Greed, C. *The Accessible Toilet Design Resource* [pdf]. London: University College London, 2007. Available online: https://discovery.ucl.ac.uk/id/eprint/4847/1/4847.pdf (accessed 2 January 2024).

Health and Safety Executive. *Workplace health, safety and welfare. Workplace (Health, Safety and Welfare) Regulations 1992. Approved Code of Practice and Guidance.* Available online: https://www.hse.gov.uk/pubns/books/l24.htm (accessed 28 December 2023).

Health and Safety Executive. 'Hot and cold water systems', 2024. Available online: https://www.hse.gov.uk/legionnaires/hot-and-cold.htm (accessed 15 January 2024).

Healthmatic. *Smarter Public Conveniences* [pdf], 2017. Available online: https://www.healthmatic.com/wp-content/uploads/2019/04/Healthmatic_Smarter_Public_Toilets_2018.pdf (accessed 28 October 2024).

Help the Aged. 'Memorandum by Help the Aged' *to The Communities and Local Government Provision of Public Toilets Inquiry*, 2008. Available online: https://publications.parliament.uk/pa/cm200708/cmselect/cmcomloc/memo/public/ucm1302.htm (accessed 10 January 2024).

Hillier, B. and Hanson, J. *The Social Logic of Space*. Cambridge: Cambridge University Press, 1989.

HM Government. *COVID-19 Secure: Safer Public Places – Urban Centres and Green Spaces* [pdf]. Available online: https://assets.publishing.service.gov.uk/media/5fa31272d3bf7f03acd139fc/201102_PDF_ready_CO_updates_Guidance_Safer_Public_Places_During_Covid_v7.7.pdf (accessed 12 December 2023).

Hoskin, D. 'Toilet Talk: Looking for non-gender-specific toilets?' *The V&A Blog*, 9 March 2017. Available online: https://www.vam.ac.uk/blog/news/toilet-talk-looking-for-non-gender-specific-toilets (accessed 18 January 2024).

Johnson, A. 'Brits left raging at 50p public toilets – but there's a cheeky plan to get it free', *The Mirror*, 1 June 2024. Available online: https://www.mirror.co.uk/news/weird-news/brits-left-raging-50p-public-32937741%20Accessed%208%20June%202024 (accessed 8 June 2024).

Johnson, H. '"Squat" toilets to be abandoned after public outrage', *Manchester Evening News*, 9 August 2010. Available online: https://www.manchestereveningnews.co.uk/news/local-news/squat-toilets-to-be-abandoned-after-public-895943 (accessed 3 January 2024).

Jones, L. and Schraer, R. 'Reality check: Public toilets mapped', *BBC News*, 15 August 2018. Available online: https://www.bbc.co.uk/news/uk-45009337 (accessed 7 January 2024).

Kale, S. 'The ride of period pants: Are they the answer to menstrual landfill – and women's prayers?' *The Guardian*,1 September 2021. Available online: https://www.theguardian.com/society/2021/sep/01/the-rise-of-period-pants-are-they-the-answer-to-menstrual-landfill-and-womens-prayers (accessed 10 January 2024).

Kerr, C. and Hammond, D. 'Off the rails: Rail bosses splash out £8 million doing up old toilets at Victoria station', *The Sun*, 21 August 2019. Available online: https://www.thesun.co.uk/news/9764364/rail-bosses-splash-out-8million-doing-up-old-toilets-at-station/ (accessed 8 January 2024).

Killermann, S. 'All gender restroom sign: AKA my doodle of a toilet that became A Thing', 2014. Available online: https://www.samkillermann.com/work/all-gender-restroom-sign/ (accessed 20 June 2024).

Kira, A. *The Bathroom: Criteria for Design*. New York: Ithaca, [1966] 1976.

Knight, G. and Bichard, J. *Publicly Accessible Toilets: An Inclusive Design Guide* [pdf], 2011. Available online: https://rca-media2.rca.ac.uk/documents/Publicly-accessible-toilets-2.pdf (accessed 28 May 2024).

Knox, J. *Kiwi-As Toilets: Where to Go When You Need to Go New Zealand*. New Zealand: BookPrint Ltd., 2018.

'Lady's Guide to the 9 best loos in London', *A Lady in London*. Available online: https://www.aladyinlondon.com/2016/01/best-loos-london.html (accessed 21 December 2023).

Lambton, L. *Temples of Convenience & Chambers of Delight*. Stroud: Tempus Publishing Ltd, 2007.

Lancaster, B. *The Department Store: A Social History*. London: Leicester University Press, 1995.

London Assembly Health Committee. *Transcript of Agenda Item 7 – Access to Public Toilets in London* [pdf], 14 September 2021. Available online: https://www.london.gov.uk/about-us/londonassembly/meetings/documents/s92736/Minutes%20Appendix%201%20Transcript%20Health%20Committee%20September%202021.pdf (accessed 17 January 2024).

London Legacy Development Corporation. *Inclusive Design Standards* [pdf], 2019. Available online: https://cdn.disabilityinnovation.com/uploads/documents/Inclusive-Design-Standards.pdf?v=1572970889 (accessed 24 June 2024).

*London Local Authorities Act 2012 Part 3 Section 6*. Available online: https://www.legislation.gov.uk/ukla/2012/2/section/6/enacted (accessed 24 November 2023).

*Loo of the Year Awards*. Available online: https://www.loo.co.uk (accessed 2 January 2024).

Mackett, R. L. 'Mental health and travel behaviour', *Journal of Transport & Health* 22(2021).

Mayor of London. *Developing a night time strategy, part 1: Guidance on process* [pdf]. Greater London Authority, 2020. Available online: https://www.london.gov.uk/sites/default/files/210317_gla_1_night-time_strategies_part_1.pdf (accessed 22 January 2024).

Ministry of Housing, Communities and Local Government. '£30 million investment to provide Changing Places toilets', 4 March 2021. Available online: https://www.gov.uk/government/news/30-million-investment-to-provide-changing-places-toilets (accessed 21 December 2023).

Ministry of Housing, Communities and Local Government. 'Further businesses and premises to close: Guidance', 2020. Available online: https://web.archive.org/web/20200325165536/https://www.gov.uk/government/publications/further-businesses-and-premises-to-close/further-businesses-and-premises-to-close-guidance (accessed 23 January 2024).

Ministry of Housing, Communities and Local Government. *Open doors pilot programme: Evaluation report* [pdf], 2020. Available online: https://assets.publishing.service.gov.uk/media/5fb65741e90e0720929a03ce/Open_Doors_Evaluation_Report.pdf (accessed 10 January 2024).

Ministry of Housing, Communities and Local Government, Simon Clarke MP and Department of Environment and Rural Affairs, Rebecca Pow MP. *Public Access to Tips and Toilets* [pdf], 28 June 2020. Available online: https://assets.publishing.service.gov.uk/media/5f803d5e8fa8f51e81ae0084/Joint_letter_Simon_Clarke_MP_and_Rebecca_Pow_MP.pdf (accessed 12 December 2023).

Moore, S. E. H. and Breeze, S. 'Spaces of male fear: The sexual politics of being watched', *The British Journal of Criminology* 52(6) (2012): 1172–91. https://doi.org/10.1093/bjc/azs033.

MSIC Evaluation Committee. *Final report on the evaluation of the Sydney medically supervised injecting centre. Sydney: 2003* cited in *Safer Drug Consumption Facilities – Evidence Paper* [pdf]. Scottish Government, October 2021. Available online: https://www.gov.scot/binaries/content/documents/govscot/publications/research-and-analysis/2021/10/safer-drug-consumption-facilites-evidence-paper/documents/safer-drug-consumption-facilities-evidence-paper/safer-drug-consumption-facilities-evidence-paper/govscot:document/safer-drug-consumption-facilities-evidence-paper.pdf (accessed 8 January 2024).

*National Rail Access Map*, 2024. Available online: http://accessmap.nationalrail.co.uk/ (accessed 18 January 2024).

Nazerali, I., Ramster, G. and Bichard, J. *Publicly Accessible Toilets after COVID-19* [pdf]. Royal College of Art Helen Hamlyn centre for Design, 2021. Available online: https://rca-media2.rca.ac.uk/documents/PAT_COVID19.pdf (accessed 2 January 2024).

Network Rail. *Design Manual NR/GN/CIV/200/04: Public Toilets in Managed Stations* [pdf], 2020. Available online: https://www.networkrail.co.uk/wp-content/uploads/2021/06/NR_GN_CIV_200_04-Public-Toilets.pdf (accessed 8 January 2024).

Network Rail. *Design Manual NR/GN/CIV/300/04: Inclusive Design*[pdf], 2020. Available online: https://www.networkrail.co.uk/wp-content/uploads/2021/06/NR_GN_CIV_300_04_Inclusive-Design.pdf (accessed 8 January 2024).

Network Rail. 'London's busiest toilets close for £4m revamp – but you still won't need to spend a penny when they reopen', 20 December 2018. Available online: https://www.networkrailmediacentre.co.uk/news/londons-busiest-toilets-close-for-gbp-4m-revamp-but-you-still-wont-need-to-spend-a-penny-when-they-reopen (accessed 28 January 2024).

Network Rail. 'Passengers first – from free toilets to Access for All', 19 March 2019. Available online: https://www.networkrail.co.uk/stories/passengers-first-from-free-toilets-to-access-for-all/ (accessed 8 January 2024).

Newman, T. 'The 7 wonders of poop', *Medical News Today*, 1 February 2019. Available online: https://www.medicalnewstoday.com/articles/324254 (accessed 7 January 2024).

Newton, F. 'Let the people piss', *Tribune*, 26 April 2021. Available online: https://tribunemag.co.uk/2021/04/let-the-people-piss (accessed 20 December 2023).

NHS. 'Overview: Bowel incontinence', 4 March 2021. Available online: https://www.nhs.uk/conditions/bowel-incontinence/ (accessed 10 January 2024).

NHS. 'Clostridium difficile (C. diff) Infection', 8 February 2022. Available online: https://www.nhs.uk/conditions/c-difficile/ (accessed 7 January 2024).

NHS. 'About furosemide', 21 February 2022. Available online: https://www.nhs.uk/medicines/furosemide/about-furosemide/ (accessed 10 January 2024).

NHS. 'Urinary incontinence', 15 June 2023. Available online: https://www.nhs.uk/conditions/urinary-incontinence/ (accessed 10 January 2024).

NHS. 'Recovery. Hip Replacement'. 6 March 2024. Available online: https://www.nhs.uk/conditions/hip-replacement/recovery/ (accessed 12 July 2024).

*Non-Domestic Rating (Public Lavatories) Act 2021*. Available online: https://www.legislation.gov.uk/ukpga/2021/13/contents (accessed 9 January 2024).

Norman, D. *The Design of Everyday Things*. New York: Basic Books, 1988.

O'Dwyer, L. 'Why queues for women's toilets are longer than men's', *The Conversation*, 23 August 2018. Available online: https://theconversation.com/why-queues-for-womens-toilets-are-longer-than-mens-99763 (accessed 21 December 2023).

Office of National Statistics. 'Nature of sexual assault by rape or penetration, England and Wales: Year ending March 2020', 18 March 2021. Available online: https://www.ons.gov.uk/peoplepopulationandcommunity/crimeandjustice/articles/natureofsexualassaultbyrapeorpenetrationenglandandwales/yearendingmarch2020 (accessed 8 January 2024).

Office for National Statistics. 'Deaths related to drug poisoning in England and Wales: 2022 registrations', 19 December 2023. Available online: https://www.ons.gov.uk/peoplepopulationandcommunity/birthsdeathsandmarriages/deaths/bulletins/deathsrelatedtodrugpoisoninginenglandandwales/2022registrations (accessed 8 January 2024).

Office for National Statistics. 'Deaths of homeless people in England and Wales: 2021 registrations', 23 November 2022. Available online: https://www.ons.gov.uk/peoplepopulationandcommunity/birthsdeathsandmarriages/deaths/bulletins/deathsofhomelesspeopleinenglandandwales/2021registrations (accessed 8 January 2024).

Office for National Statistics. 'Conceptions in England and Wales', 30 March 2023. Available online: https://www.ons.gov.uk/peoplepopulationandcommunity/birthsdeathsandmarriages/conceptionandfertilityrates/bulletins/conceptionstatistics/2021 (accessed 20 January 2024).

Parkin, S. and Coomber, R. 'Fluorescent blue lights, injecting drug use and related health risk in public conveniences: Findings from a qualitative study of micro-injecting environments', *Health and Place* 16(2010): 629–37. Available online: https://ora.ox.ac.uk/objects/uuid:d9f9b17b-b4a4-47e1-a6b5-890e57235c90/download_file?file_format=application%2Fpdf&safe_filename=Parkin%2BBBlue%2BLights%2BHealth%2BPlace%2B2010.pdf&type_of_work=Journal+article (accessed 8 January 2024).

Penner, B. 'A world of unmentionable suffering: Women's public conveniences in Victorian London', *Journal of Design History* 14(1) (2001): 35–52.

Penner, B. 'Designed-in safety', *Places Journal* October 2013. https://doi.org/10.22269/131015.

Penner, B. *Bathroom*. London: Reaktion Books, 2013.

PiM.studio Architects. https://www.pim.studio.

*PointX*. https://www.pointx.co.uk/suppliers.

Press Association. 'Relief at last: Toilet charges suspended at two London train stations', *The Guardian*, 10 December 2016. Available online: https://www.theguardian.com/uk-news/2016/dec/10/toilet-charges-suspended-at-two-london-train-stations-victoria-charing-cross (accessed 8 January 2024).

Prostate Cancer UK. *Urinary problems after prostate cancer treatment* [pdf], 2022. Available online: https://shop.prostatecanceruk.org/pdf/publication/urinary_problems-ifm.pdf (accessed 10 January 2024).

Prostate Cancer UK. *Lifting the lid on male incontinence* [pdf], 2023. Available online: https://prostatecanceruk.org/media/r25l0esd/6999_boys_need_bins_brochure_digital_final-3.pdf (accessed 24 January 2024).

*Public Health Act 1936 c.49 Part II 'Public sanitary conveniences'*. Available online: https://www.legislation.gov.uk/ukpga/Geo5and1Edw8/26/49/part/II/crossheading/public-sanitary-conveniences/enacted (accessed 17 January 2024).

*Public Health Act 1936 s. 87(3)(c) (revised)*. Available online: https://www.legislation.gov.uk/ukpga/Geo5and1Edw8/26/49/part/II/crossheading/public-sanitary-conveniences (accessed 11 January 2024).

*Public Health (Wales) Act 2017 Part 8*. Available online: https://www.legislation.gov.uk/anaw/2017/2/part/8/enacted (accessed 18 January 2024).

*Public Lavatories (Turnstiles) Act 1963 c.32*. Available online: https://www.legislation.gov.uk/ukpga/1963/32 (accessed 29 January 2024).

Ramster, G., Bichard, J., Dowd, M., Knight, I. and Traina, R. '*Engaged: A toilet on every high street*', no date. Available online: https://www.rca.ac.uk/research-innovation/research-centres/helen-hamlyn-centre/engaged-a-toilet-on-every-high-street/ (accessed 2 January 2022).

Ramster, G. and Gaudion, K. 'Design with many, with some, with one: Designing inclusive spaces with Helen Hamlyn Centre for Design researchers'. Royal College of Art, 2024. Available online: https://www.rca.ac.uk/news-and-events/news/design-with-many-with-some-with-one-designing-inclusive-spaces-with-helen-hamlyn-centre-for-design-researchers/ (accessed 6 June 2024).

Ramster, G., Greed, C. and Bichard, J. 'How inclusion can exclude: The case of public toilet provision for women', *Built Environment* 44(1) (2018): 91–115.

Reynolds, W. S., Kowalik, C., Kaufman, M. R., Dmochowski, R. R. and Fowke, J. H. 'Women's perceptions of public restrooms and the relationship with toileting behaviours and bladder symptoms: A cross sectional study', *The Journal of Urology* 204(2) (2020): 310–15. https://doi.org/10.1097/JU.0000000000000812.

Ribas Goody, A. 'Living archives'. In *Matrix Open: Feminist Architecture Archive*, 2021. Available online: https://web.archive.org/web/2023.1210235140/ http://www.matrixfeministarchitecturearchive.co.uk/explore/living-archives/ (accessed 20 June 2024).

Riley-Smith, B. and Gutteridge, N. 'One in four chance of a "catastrophic" pandemic in five years', *The Telegraph*, 3 August 2023. Available online: https://www.telegraph.co.uk/politics/2023/08/03/national-risk-register-danger-of-pandemic-in-five-years/ (accessed 12 December 2023).

Royal Society for Public Health. *Taking the P\*\*\*: The Decline of the Great British Public Toilet* [pdf]. Royal Society for Public Health, 2019. Available online: https://www.rsph.org.uk/static/uploaded/459f4802-ae43-40b8-b5a006f6ead373e6.pdf (accessed 7 January 2024).

Sanders, J. and Stryker, S. 'Stalled: Gender-neutral public bathrooms', *The South Atlantic Quarterly* 115(4) (2016): 779–88. DOI: 10.1215/00382876-3656191.

Saner, E. 'The war against wild toileting: Is there any way to stop people weeing – and worse – in the street?' *The Guardian*, 5 April 2023. Available online: https://www.theguardian.com/society/2023/apr/05/the-war-against-wild-toileting-stop-weeing-street-urinating (accessed 7 January 2024).

Schum, T. R., Kolb, T. M., McAuliffe, T. L., Simms, M. D., Underhill, R. L. and Lewis, M. 'Sequential acquisition of toilet-training skills: A descriptive study of gender and age differences in normal children', *Pediatrics* (109) (2002): 48–54.

*Sexual Offences Act 2003*. 'Sexual activity in a public lavatory'. Available online: https://www.legislation.gov.uk/ukpga/2003/42/section/71 (accessed 8 January 2024).

Shove, E. *Comfort, Cleanliness and Convenience: The Social Organisation of Normality*. Oxford/New York: Berg, 2003.

Slater, T. and Jones, C. *Around the Toilet: A research project report about what makes a safe and accessible toilet space* [pdf], 2018. Available online: https://aroundthetoilet.wordpress.com/wp-content/uploads/2018/05/around-the-toilet-report-final-1.pdf (accessed 24 June 2024).

Smoyer, A. B., Pittman, A. and Borzillo, P. 'Humans peeing: Justice-involved women's access to toilets in public spaces', *PLoS ONE* 18(3) (2023). https://doi.org/10.1371/journal.pone.0282917.

Stanwell-Smith, R. *Taking the P\*\*\*: The Decline of the Great British Public Toilet* [pdf]. Royal Society for Public Health, 2019. Available online: https://www.rsph.org.uk/static/uploaded/459f4802-ae43-40b8-b5a006f6ead373e6.pdf (accessed 7 January 2024).

Stead, N. 'Avoidance. On some euphemisms for the "smallest room"'. In O. Gershenson and B. Penner (eds), *Ladies and Gents Public Toilets and Gender*. Philadelphia: Temple University Press, 2009.

Stromberg, J. 'Everybody poops. But here are 9 surprising facts about feces you may not know', *Vox*, 22 January 2015. Available online: https://www.vox.com/2015/1/22/7871579/poop-feces (accessed 28 December 2023).

Taylor, A. 'Why public toilets need to be more dementia friendly', Alzheimer's Society, 2017. Available online: https://www.alzheimers.org.uk/blog/why-public-toilets-be-more-dementia-friendly (accessed 22 January 2024).

The Toilet Map. Available online: https://www.toiletmap.org.uk (accessed 2 January 2024).

The Toilet Map. Toilet explorer. Available online: https://www.toiletmap.org.uk/explorer (accessed 2 January 2024).

The National Public Toilet Map. 'About the toilet map'. Available online: https://toiletmap.gov.au/about (accessed 18 January 2024).

The Old Vic. 'What to expect at the Old Vic: Loos'. Available online: https://www.oldvictheatre.com/visit/when-you-visit/ (accessed 18 January 2024).

The Old Vic. 'Our loos now offer 'self-selection' …', Twitter, 2 October 2019. Available online: https://twitter.com/oldvictheatre/status/1179336786537005057?s=20 (accessed 18 January 2024).

Thomson, S., Smith, M. and Hulley, S. *CivicWatch Good Practice Guide: Street Urination. London*. Jill Dando Institute of Crime Science, University College London. 2004.

Toilets Innovation and New Knowledge Exchange (TINKLE). Available online: https://tinkle.rca.ac.uk (accessed 2 January 2024).

Traina, R., Knight, I., Ramster, G., Bichard, J. and Dowd, M. *Engaged: First Findings Report on the National Need for Public Toilets, and 'Engaged' as an Alternative Model for High Street Provision* London: Royal College of Art, 2022.

UK Parliament. 'Public Lavatories: Coronavirus', 2020. Available online: https://questions-statements.parliament.uk/written-questions/detail/2020-07-07/70519 (accessed 12 December 2023).

UK Parliament. 'Written Evidence Submitted by the Urology Trade Association', 2021. Available online: https://committees.parliament.uk/writtenevidence/41388/pdf/#:~:text=In%202017%2F18%20alone%2C%20treating,diagnosis%2C%20and%20increased%20patient%20expectation (accessed 28 December 2023).

UK Paruresis Trust. *Paruresis Symptoms & Problems*, 2023. Available online: https://www.ukpt.org.uk/what-is-paruresis/spectrum-of-severity (accessed 15 December 2023).

UNICEF. *Child Friendly Cities and Communities*, 2023. Available online: https://www.unicef.org.uk/child-friendly-cities/about-child-friendly-cities-communities/ (accessed 20 January 2024).

Van Hautegem, K. and Rogiest, W. 'No more queueing at the ladies' room', *People Queue Magazine*, 2017. Available online: http://peopleqm.blogspot.com/2017/07/no-more-queueing-at-ladies-room.html (accessed 21 December 2023).

VivaCity 2020. 'Urban sustainability for the twenty-four hour city'. Available online: http://www.vivacity2020.co.uk/ (accessed 27 January 2024).

VivaCity Publications. *The Toilet Paper Newsletters*. Available online: http://www.vivacity2020.co.uk/publications/index.html (accessed 2 January 2024).

Wandsworth Borough Council. *Environment Culture and Community Safety Overview and Scrutiny Committee – 17 April 2013* [pdf]. Available online: https://www.wandsworth.gov.uk/media/3400/community_toilets_change_of_policy_appendix_2_to_paper_no_13-284_april_2013.pdf (accessed 8 January 2024).

Wang, K. and Palmer, M. H. 'Women's toileting behaviour related to urinary elimination: Concept analysis', *Journal of Advanced Nursing* 66(8) (2010): 1874–84. https://doi.org/10.1111/j.1365-2648.2010.05341.x.

Waste Industry Safety and Health Forum. *Managing Offensive/Hygiene Waste Safely. Formal Guidance Document* [pdf], 2015. Available online: https://www.wishforum.org.uk/wp-content/uploads/2019/06/WASTE-22-.pdf (accessed 28 December 2023).

Watkins, I. 'London's most beautiful (and bizarre) toilets', *Design My Night*, 2023. Available online: https://www.designmynight.com/london/blog/london-beautiful-bizarre-toilets-instagram (accessed 21 December 2023).

Welsh Government. *The Provision of Toilets in Wales. Statuary Guidance* [pdf], 2018. Available online: https://www.gov.wales/sites/default/files/publications/2022-02/the-provision-of-toilets-in-wales-local-toilets-strategies.pdf (accessed 9 January 2024).

Wikipedia. 'Loo of the Year Awards'. Available online: https://en.wikipedia.org/wiki/Loo_of_the_Year_Awards (accessed 17 October 2024).

Wilson, C. 'Grace Warnock – A sign to change attitudes', The V&A Blog, 8 August 2018. Available online: https://www.vam.ac.uk/blog/projects/grace-warnock-a-sign-to-change-attitudes (accessed 18 January 2024).

World Design Organisation. 'SquatEase', 2021. Available online: https://wdo.org/programmes/wdip/shortlist-gallery/squatease/ (accessed 3 January 2024).

World Health Organization. *Global age-friendly cities: A guide* [pdf], 2007. Available online: https://iris.who.int/bitstream/handle/10665/43755/9789241547307_eng.pdf?sequence=1 (accessed 10 January 2024).

World Health Organization. 'Antimicrobial resistance', 2023. Available online: https://www.who.int/news-room/fact-sheets/detail/antimicrobial-resistance (accessed 28 December 2023).

Wynn-Davis, S. 'Hastings key worker asks for publicly accessible toilets to be reopened', *Hastings Observer*, 28 April 2020. Available online: https://www.sussexexpress.co.uk/news/politics/hastings-key-worker-asks-for-publicly-accessible-toilets-to-be-reopened-2552845 (accessed 23 January 2024).

# Index

2theLoo publicly accessible toilet 232

abuse, gender-based 52
access
    choosing and placing products 45
    for cleaning 45–6
    for disabled people 23–4
    and limits on employment 69–70
accessibility regulations and guidance 46–9
    *see also under names*
accessible flush 180, 259
accessible lock 144, 147, 259
accessible tap 200, 201, 259
accessible toilet 6, 52, 97, 121–3, 139, 259
    baby-changing facilities in 128
    basin in 197, 204
    bins in 184
    design 43
    flush 178, 180–2
    grab rails in 186
    lighting 214
    lock 147, 152
    mirror 218
    paper towels in 206
    shelves 158
    size 44, 139
    symbol for 97–8, 103
    toilet lids on 170, 171
    toilet paper dispenser 174, 175
activity spaces in front of the toilet 139
additional rooms 219, 220
age-friendly communities 68
AgeUK 67
    London Loos 67
    Out and About 67
air freshener 117, 191, 213
air/water flush system, combined 172
alarms 148, 188–90

All Gender Restroom sign 101
all-gender toilets *see* gender-neutral/unisex toilets
alternative toilet sign 102, 103
ambulant toilet/cubicle 44, 46, 47, 124–7, 142, 143, 259
    location 126
    basin 197
    colour choice 214, 215
    grab rails 44, 101, 187, 188
    outwards opening door 142–3
    symbol 101
    towels and hand dryers 212
ambulant urinals 128
American Restroom Association 120
ante-room 219, 220
antibiotics 25, 60, 144, 167
anti-crime measures 35
anxiety 67–9
architecture 43–5
augmented reality in proposed toilet design 257
automatic public conveniences (APCs) 149, 239

baby-changing facilities 44, 50, 128
    for disabled adults 128
    hook 155
    space within the cubicle 129
    table 60, 157
basins 197–200
    at child-height 45, 50
    in cubicles 52, 53, 62, 197
    height of 51
    location 197
    position of 199
    wheelchair-user accessible 198, 199
bicycle parking 110–11
blue ultraviolet lights 6, 27–8, 50

Boast, Hannah: 'Public Toilets and Public Luxury' 24
body size, large, access and 44, 45
Bodyform 61
Bovens, Luc 120
bowel incontinence 59
box parks 249
Boys need Bins campaign (Prostate Cancer UK) 184
Bristol's Legible City 91
British Standards
    BS5810 *see* BS8300
    BS6465 47, 125, 126
    BS8300 6, 23, 47, 115, 122, 123
    PAS 6463 41, 47–8, 210
British Toilet Association 7, 27
Brixton Business Improvement District (BID), South London: 'Go before you go', 113
Building Regulations
    *Approved Document M: Access to and Use of Buildings. Volume 2: Buildings other than Dwellings* ('Part M') 6, 23, 46, 115, 122, 123, 124, 139
    *Approved Document T: Toilet Accommodation* ('Part T') 44, 46, 99, 124, 126

café toilets 79–80
Campaigns promoted in toilets 65
catheters, catheter use 59, 158
Centre for Accessible Environments: *Good Loo Design Guide* 165
Changing Places consortium 90
Changing Places toilet 123–4
    changing table 60
    design 52
    destination 77, 78
    flush systems 183
    map of 90
    regulations 46, 47
    screen to cover mirror 219
    symbol 93, 98, 99
*Changing Places: The practical guide* 123

charities 65, 228
child step stool 199
child toilet seats 129, 154, 155, 156, 168, 169
child toilets 45, 50, 129, 168, 169
child-height wash basin 45, 50, 199–200
children 120, 128–9
    access of products 45
    and locks 148–9
    *see also* baby-changing facilities
city park toilets 79
cleaning 239–42
    access for 35
    cleaning staff 239–41
    feedback 241–2
cleanliness 117–18
close-coupled cistern 170
*Clostridium difficile* 25
clothing, checking 63
Cockfield, Colin 25
Coleman, Roger 41, 45
colostomy 45, 60
Colostomy UK 158
colour contrast 214–16
    on doors 116
colour-coded lighting for toilet availability 145
column of clearance 44
comfort, sense of 118–19
commercial space, toilet access in 68
community connections 67–8
community-led design 256
community notices 65
community toilet schemes 93, 229–30, 259
community toilet signs 93–5
composite (resin) toilets 166, 167
composting toilets 257
contactless payment 231, 233
continence pads or pants 60
conversations in 66
Cornwall Council 33
corridor width 142–3
cottaging 26
council facilities 225–6

council tax 226
Covid-19 pandemic 34, 50
   national incontinence and 70–3
   sign pointing to toilets and handwashing during 196
Creative Commons Attribution licence 34
criminal activity 25, 50, 255
Crisis 27
Crohn's and Colitis UK: 'Not Every Disability Is Visible' 97
Crohn's disease 47, 60
Crowley, John: *Invention of Comfort, The* 118
cubicle, selection of 121–7
customer-only toilets 20, 72, 79, 82, 150, 243, 246
CZWG 244

defecation 57, 59–61
degree of impairment 21
dehydration, deliberate 67
dementia 47, 101, 150, 203, 219
Department for Transport 90
Design Out Crime 7
Designing London's Recovery programme 10
destinations
   large 77
   smaller 78
directional signs 91–3
Disability Discrimination Act (DDA) (1995) 6, 51, 121
disabled people
   access 23–4
   access to goods and services 48
   design requirements for 21
disposal bins 183–6
   in men's toilets 53, 184
diuretics ('water tablets') 58
door locks *see* locks
door signs 95–8
doors 140–3
   at entrance 111–12
   floor-to-ceiling 143
   self-closing 141
   unmarked 116
Dowd, Madelaine 10
Drever, John Levack 210
drinking water tap 218
drips 140
Drug Consumption Facilities 35
drug misuse 25, 27–8
drying hands 206–13
Dyson Airblades 207

electronic locks 148, 149–50
Elizabeth Line 82
emergency pull cord 188
emergency release mechanism 148
Engaged: A toilet on every high street' project 9–10, 243–51
Engineering and Physical Sciences Research Council (EPSRC) 6
environmental sustainability 50, 61, 257
Equality Act (2010) 48, 121
Euan's Guide card 190
euphemisms 25

faecal incontinence 59–61
faecal transplants 25
feedback 241–2
fingerpost signs 91, 93, 94
fire doors 143
fire exit 98
fire regulations 111
fire risk 207
Fleck, Julie 41, 45, 46
floor-to-ceiling walls 52
flooring 140
floors, wet 140
flush 45
   design 177–80
   hand-operated 181
   plume 170
   position 181–3
   system 171–2
foam plugs 60
Four Seasons restaurant, Manhattan 20

Freedom of Information requests 32, 33, 34
frequency incontinence 58
full enclosed toilet/cubicle 111, 120, 121, 124–7, 134–7, 148, 259
future, designing for 53

gate lines at stations 81–2
gatekeepers 150
gender-neutral/unisex toilets 23–4, 52, 62, 99–100, 120–1
Goldsmith, Selwyn: *Designing for the Disabled* 22–4, 35
grab rail 52, 186–8
Grace's Sign 97, 98
graffiti 28, 29, 65–6
gravity hinges 140
Great British Public Toilet Map, The *see* Toilet Map, The
Great Exhibition, London (1851) 15
Greed, Clara: *Inclusive Urban Design: Public Toilets* 6
Greene, Catherine 7
Greggs, Kingston-upon-Hull 79
guardianship 243
*Guidance on safe working during the COVID-19 pandemic* 8

halting stations 15
hand dryers 207–8, 209–12
    dexterity 209
    experience 210
    height for a wheelchair user 45
    noise of 6, 45, 210
    position (height) 209–10, 211, 212
    visibility 209
hand-operated flushes 181
handrails 115–16
hands, drying 206–13
handwashing 63, 73, 120, 195–206
    basins 197–9
    communal, outside cubicle 197–9
    soap 205–6
    spout 203–4

taps 200–3
    water temperature 204–5
Hanson, Julienne 6
Hatagaya Toilet 108, 109
Health Services Advisory Committee 25
Healthmatic 23
Help the Aged 67
hereditaments 32
Hertfordshire Constabulary 7
hinges 140–3
hooks 154–7
    on back of door 63
    bag hook 154
    choice of 156
    for coats and bags 45
    design 157
    height to place it 154
    opposite urinals 161
hovering 62, 167–8
Hundertwasser, Friedensreich 109
Hundertwasser public toilets, Kawakawa, New Zealand 109, 110
hygiene 50

ileostomy 60
illegal substance use *see* drug misuse
    impairment, types of 21
*Improving Public Access to Better Quality Toilets* 243
Inclusive Design of Public Toilets in City Centres (2003–2006) 6
inclusive design of public toilets 49–53
    best practice 51
    can one design fit all? 52–3
    research phase of the design process 49–51
inclusive service 42
incontinence 47, 58–61, 70–71, 120
infant feeding area at shopping centre 228
information poster 66
invisible disabilities 53
irritable bowel syndrome (IBS) 47, 59–60, 71

Japan
    squat toilet 173
    *Tenugui* 213
    see also Tokyo Toilet Project (The)
Jennings, George 15

Kendal, Lake District: Business Improvement District (BID) activities 230
Kentaro Honma laboratory, University of Tokyo 108
Kilburn Older Voices Exchange (KOVE) 239–40
Killermann, Sam 101
Kira, Alexander 21, 25, 35, 167
    *Bathroom, The* 18–22, 133
Knight, Indira 10
Kotaro Imai laboratory, Japan 108

Landmark Solutions 34
laxatives 60
leaving the cubicle 190–1
Legible London 91
Lenin, V.I 24
Levelling Up and Regeneration Bill 238
lever-arm tap 200, 201
lever flush 45, 180
lever taps 45, 200, 203
Lewisham Local 230
lighting 114, 213–14
    blue ultraviolet 6, 27–8, 50
    diffused 214
    natural 214
    sensor 214
    spot 213
Living Streets UK 68
local area information boards 93
location 77–87
    challenges relating to 25–31
    footfall 247
    natural surveillance 247
    of urinals 127
    site 43, 48–50
    temporary 247

lock indicators 141, 142, 144–6
locks 45, 143–50
    accessible lock 144, 147
    children and 148–9
    electronic 148, 149–50
    thumbnail 144
    keys 152
    opening and closing 146–7
    outside 150–4
    passcode 150, 151–2
    penny-in-door locking system 17, 18
    RADAR keys 152–4
London Borough of Hounslow 230
London Borough of Richmond-upon-Thames 72
London Borough of Wandsworth 230
London Legacy Development Corporation (LLDC) 256
    Inclusive Design Standard (2019) 125, 128, 139
London Local Authorities Act (2012) 18, 232
London Olympic and Paralympic Games (2012) 125, 164, 256, 243
London Plan 77
Loo of the Year awards 240
looking for toilets 90
loo-topia 217–22

Mackett, Roger 68
maintenance 241–2
Maps of toilets
    online 8, 33–4, 88–90
    physical 91–3
Marcoci, Alexandru 120
Mayor of London
    Designing London's Recovery programme 10
    Night-time Strategy 256
menstrual cups 53, 61, 62
menstruation 57, 61–3, 120
men's toilets
    bins in 164, 184
    time spent in 120

*see also* urinals, separate-gender toilets
mirrors 26, 60, 97, 158, 218–19
    in cubicles 218
    full-length 51, 60, 218
    reflections in 137
MK Centre, Milton Keynes 227
mobile workforce 69–70
mobility scooters 53
Muslims 63, 197

nappy bins 184
National Public Toilet Map of Australia 89, 90
National Rail Access Map 90
National Rail Enquiries 34
national toilet logo 94
natural lighting 214
Nazerali, Imran 8
Neontribe 34
Network Rail 17, 90, 234
    removal of toilet charge 235–7
    Toilets in Managed Stations design standard 256
neurodiverse people
    built environment and 47–8
    colour and 112
    designing for 6, 41
    door signs and 95, 100
    flushing 172
    handwashing 204
    lighting 214
    product 45
    variety of 47
New Dynamics of Ageing programme 7
Newton, Frances 72
night-time neighbourhood 249–51
Night-time Strategy, Mayor of London 256
night-time toilet infrastructure 113–14
noise of hand dryers 6, 45, 210
Non-Domestic Rating (Public Lavatories) Act (2021) 33, 51, 226
non-gendered toilets *see* gender-neutral/unisex toilets

Norman, Dom: *Design of Everyday Things, The* 178
number of public toilets 32–4

Old Vic Theatre, London 98
older people 41, 43, 67–8, 126, 129, 255
online information 88–90
on-street automatic public toilets 52
Open Doors pilot programme 68
Open Street Map project 34
opening hours 102, 103, 112–14
Ordnance Survey 32, 33–4
    Points of Interest dataset 33–4, 90
Orkney Council 72
outwards-opening doors 124, 143
    grab rails 44
    self-closing hinges 142
overflow incontinence 59
overhead skylights 214

paddle gates 18, 232, 233
paddle-lever flush 181, 182, 183
paper towel dispenser 46
paper towels 45, 206–7, 209–12
    dexterity 209
    experience 210
    position (height) 209–10, 211, 212
    visibility 209
parking 109–10
Parkinson's disease 47
parks 26, 68, 79, 243, 244
partitions
    between cubicles 134–6, 259
    between urinals 136–8
paruresis 127, 136
passcode lock 150, 151–2
pattern 216–17
payment 226
    access 115
    collecting system 232–3
    money for 231–2
    public service and 237–9
    reason for 234
    removing 235–7

responsibility for 230–9
   voluntary donations 235
   who is charged 230–1
payment systems or card-activated doors 153
Penner, Barbara 15
Pennington, Miles 108
penny-in-door locking system 17, 18
*Perfect Days* (film) 108
period pants 61
physical needs 63–4
pictograms 96, 97, 100
PiM.studio Architects 10, 249
plants 213, 214
platform-side toilet 82
PointX 34
popular perspectives of public toilets 24–5
potty parity 120
pregnancy 17, 44, 57, 59, 139, 165
press taps 200–1, 257
privacy 26, 35, 63–4
   designing 133
   drug use and 27
   effects of loss of 21–2
   violations 20
   walls 112, 113, 134–6
products, accessible 45
provision, responsibility for 225–9
   public toilets 225–7
   publicly accessible toilets 227–9
psychological effects of loss of continence 21–2
Public Health Act (1848) 15
Public Health Act (1936) 16–17
Public Health Act (Wales) (2017) 51, 95
Public Lavatories (Turnstiles) Act (1963) 17, 18
Public Lavatories (Turnstiles) Act (1967) 51
Public Lavatories (Turnstiles) Act (2008) 18
Public Sector Geospatial Agreement 34
public toilets for pandemic and post-pandemic environments 8–9

publicly accessible toilets 6–8, 32, 34, 77–104, 152, 153, 225–9, 243, 256, 260
   finding 87–95
   number of 32, 34
   where needed 77–87
*Publicly Accessible Toilets: An Inclusive Design Guide* 7
*Publicly Available Toilets Problem Reduction Guide* 7, 28
publicness, notion of 19, 20
push-button tap 202
push-button flush 179–80
pushchairs, space for 50, 129, 156

Queen Elizabeth Olympic Park 243
queuing 119–20

RADAR keys (National Key Scheme) 150, 152–4
railway stations 17, 78, 81–3
   access for wheelchair users 81
   charging for toilets at 235–7
   gate line at 81–2
   queueing at 119
   ticket office toilets 83
reputation of public toilets 25, 35
retail space, toilet access in 68
reusable sanitary products 53, 61
   *see also* menstrual cups
Ribas Goody, Ailo 65
ritual washing before prayer 63
Robust Accessible Toilets (RATs) 7
Rothesay public toilets, Isle of Bute, Scotland 15, 16
rough sleeping 27
Royal Society for Public Health (RSPH) 26, 30, 67, 239
   *Taking the P\*\*\*: The Decline of the Great British Public Toilet* 24, 68

safety 24, 107–9
Sainsbury's exit signage 116, 117
sanitary bins 63, 183–6

sanitary pads 61
Scotland: Drug Consumption Facilities 35
security passes 229
self-closing doors 142
sensor flush 177–9, 181
sensor-flush sign 179
sensor lighting 214
sensor taps 202–3
sensory overload 47
sensory shutdown 47
separate-gender toilets 52, 121, 124–6, 128, 139, 260
services, access for 45–6
sex 25, 26–7
Sex Discrimination Act (2008) 17
sexual assault 26
Sexual Offences Act 2003 26
sharps bin 28
sharps chutes 28
shelves 158–60, 218
   above the cistern 158
   within reach of the toilet 63
   by urinal 160
shipping containers 248–9
shopping centres 7, 77, 78, 90, 107, 123, 174, 199, 227, 228, 232, 244
Shove, Elizabeth 118
shy bladder syndrome *see* Paruresis
signage 116
signs
   behaviour 30–1
   feedback 241–2
   location 81–2, 103
   symbols 78, 85, 95–103
   destination 90–1
   directional 91–4
   community toilet 93, 95
   door 95–103
   opening times 102–4
   exit 102, 117
single-sex toilet cubicle *see* separate-gender toilets
single-sheet dispensers 175, 176
size of toilet cubicle 44, 139–40, 156

skylights 214
smells 24, 117, 118, 134, 191, 213
soap 29, 43, 45–6, 65, 195, 197, 199–200, 205–6
soap dispensers 45–6, 205–6
social interactions 66, 222–3
sounds 47, 122, 124, 141, 210–12, 223
spatula lever flush handle. 181–3
spending a penny 15
spot lighting 213
spout 203–4
squat toilets 172–4
squatting 172–4
stainless-steel toilet pan 166
stairs 115–16
standard cubicle/toilet 7, 125–6, 260
stomas/stoma care 28, 53, 60–1, 154, 158, 197
stoma-friendly cubicle 158, 159
stranger danger 19, 167
street urination and defecation ('wild toileting') 30, 31
stress incontinence 58–9
symbols *see* signs; symbols

taboo 25, 133, 256
*TACT3: Tackling ageing continence through theory, tools and technology* 7, 90
TalkLondon (GLA) 10
tampons 61, 62
taps 45
   accessible 200, 201
   designs 200
   drinking water 218
   lever 45, 200, 203
   lever-arm 200, 201
   operating 200
   press 200–1, 257
   push-button 202
   sensor 202–3
   twist 200
thumbnail locks 144
toilet attendants 118, 231, 239–41, 255

toilet brush 191
toilet lid 170–2, 173
toilet backrest 170–1
Toilet Map, The (Great British Public Toilet Map) 7, 8, 32, 34, 70, 89–90
toilet material 165–7
    ceramic 165
    composite resin 165
    stainless steel 165
toilet pan 164
    height 164–5
    orientation of 164
toilet paper 45
    lack of 24
toilet paper dispensers 174–6
toilet paper drum roll 174, 175
*Toilet Paper, The* 6
toilet queue 119–21
toilet roll holder 46
toilet seat 167–70
    child 168
    sign 163
toilet strategy 34, 35, 85–7, 243
Toilets Innovation and New Knowledge Exchange (TINKLE) 8, 9
Tokyo Toilet project, The 108
train travel 68–9
    electronic locks 150
    overhead display 81
    services 52
    toilets 81–3, 149
Traina, Dr Rosanna 10
Transport for London (TfL) 82
travelling, finding toilets 68–9, 87–95
trip-chaining 80
trough urinals 137
    with partitions 138
turnstiles 17, 232–3
twin flushes 257
twist tap 200

ulcerative colitis 47, 60
ultraviolet lights 6, 27–8, 50
UNICEF Child Friendly Cities initiative 129

unisex accessible toilet *see* gender-neutral/unisex toilets
universal keys 150
Universal toilet 99, 124–7, 197, 212, 260
UriLift 16, 17
urinal 16, 136–8
    choice of 127–8
    fees for 17
    height 129
    individual, lockable 138
    with partitions 137
    privacy screens 26
    Victorian 15–16
urinary incontinence 58, 59, 70, 71
urinary tract infections (UTIs) 120, 167
urination (having a wee) 57, 58–9
urostomy 60
urostomy bags 45

V&A Dundee 97, 98
Valuation Office Agency (VOA) 32–3
vandalism 25, 28–9, 234
ventilation 118, 134, 213
Victoria Station, London 99, 235, 237
Victorian public conveniences 15–16, 137
violence, gender-based 26
virtual reality 257
visual 'noise' 47
*VivaCity 2020: Urban Sustainability for the Twenty-four Hour City* 6, 24, 90, 165, 181
vomiting 57, 63
voyeurism 26

Wales
    data 32, 34
    national toilet logo 95, 101
    toilet strategies 34, 35, 85–7, 243
walls 134–6
    at entrance 112, 113
    cubicle 134–6
water
    cleansing 176–7
    temperature 204–5

*WCityStop.info* 244, 245
wellness, designing 218–22
Welsh Toilet Map 34
Wenders, Wim 108
Westbourne Grove, West London 244
Westminster City Council 72
wheelchair-accessible unisex toilet *see* accessible toilet
wheelchair use
   access for 22, 43
   accessible baby-changing 128
   basin access 198, 199
   dimensions 53
   height of the toilet pan 165
   power chair 43
wild toileting 30, 31
women's toilets
   history of 15, 17
   queue 119–20
   safety 121
   symbol 96
   time spent in 120
   *see also* separate-gender toilets
World Health Organization guide to age-friendly cities 68
Wudu facility 221